CARLTON

Carlton Leach

With Jason Allday

Copyright © 2021 CARLTON LEACH LTD

All rights reserved. Independently published.

ISBN: 9798479518287

As they say, ours is not to reason why, but living on the edge many inevitably fall and die, but I made it to the end with my head held high.

DEDICATION

It was at completion of writing this book, that I was to hear of the passing of a trusted and once close friend.

The message I received was that Shawn Birch had died from an illness, which was very saddening news that couldn't have been prepared for and was far from expected.

A good friend of mine for almost two decades, whose departure has left a big hole in both my life and the lives of many others. I hope you've now been able to find peace, Shawn, and I dedicate this book to you and to all the good times we had.

ACKNOWLEDGMENTS

I am, of course, grateful to all those that have remained by my side, that is to say my close friends and family who have supported me in my 'endevours', but there are a couple of people who I want to specifically thank for their involvement in this book: Nicky Hamilton, award winning photographer - You understood exactly what I wanted to achieve and went above and beyond for me.

Jay - Most will never understand Jay's involvement fully, especially as he declines to be given any public recognition for his work, but if it wasn't for him, I wouldn't have embarked upon this book at all; a person who I consider as my confident, my lead and above all, a person trusted in all aspects of my life…he helped me to pinpoint both the need and timing for this book's very existence, not to mention the effort and work that he tirelessly invested in helping to put it all together.

CONTENTS

	Forward	Pg 1
1	Dad	Pg 8
2	School Days	Pg 38
3	Some Have No Shame	Pg 53
4	Football Days	Pg 69
5	Over The Years	Pg 91
6	The New Game	Pg 108
7	The White Isle	Pg 128
8	Worth A Mention	Pg 153
9	Family Life	Pg 172
10	Rise	Pg 219
11	Ultras	Pg 233
12	España	Pg 267
13	The Missing Man	Pg 275
14	Magaluf	Pg 290
15	Stark Raving Mad	Pg 299
16	There For Your Own	Pg 318
17	Friends	Pg 329

FOREWORD
Jason Allday

Carlton, his associates, villains, money getters and scoundrels who are involved in crime, whether it be directly or by association, will give testament that the hand they've been dealt, the path trodden and the direction they have taken has been an unforgiving one; as quick as those that they cared for celebrated the welcoming of a life, often found that one was being taken from them, but in retrospect, they accept it's a life and choice they made and one largely of their own making.

As of writing this, my friendship with Carlton is one of almost 15 years and my knowing some of the same villains, scoundrels and those of the (collective) old school on a personal level from a young adult life, at one point or another and much like Carlton, have told me of the few benefits of their life-style choices and that's them now reaching a stage of their lives, where they can stop lying about their age and start (jokingly) bragging about it – as eventually, (some) people will reach a point in their lives and try to turn back their "odometers," - essentially falsifying and hiding their past. I've found this with neither Carlton nor them! All wear their scars, bumps, and bruises as a badge of honor, and many will humbly give further statement that all were gained over the years - none were easy, but all were necessary. If what they said was questioned, I'd have to say it's justifiable; as there'd be less truth in their words if anything said was without the benefit of knowledge or experience, as what mattered most from all of what was said and done, was how well a man has "walked through the fire."

A common element that remains in society today, is we are all imperfect people living in an imperfect world. It's within this same tarnished populace, that a small collection of people loyally remain and identify with what was once a standard amongst men – integrity. There was once an orthodox common code seen and respected across the board with the old school and it was one that was sworn to, lived by, and followed to the letter and it's that same group of men who practiced it without question; I'd phrase it "from the cradle to the grave." It was also a time when the wisemen and teachers of the old school paved a way, not only for those that practiced what was preached, but who were also willing to die for … and it was this same code and these men of old that were respected, as all were raised by the same rules and gods. It's this standard that remains to be a common currency and established doctrine within a respected community of men that Carlton proudly aligns himself with and allows them to be leaders of both the old and new school ways…and gives justification of who Carlton is, what he does and how he conducts business.

Often refuted are the "old school ways" and one thing I want to clear up here and now is, (being that I'm someone of principles and having a level of integrity that's even seen in crime), it isn't people just claiming to be "old school," it's as much a daily practice, as it is a common fucking courtesy in a life-long commitment, in what and how proper people, live, work and operate. People's failing or refusal to accept the established ground rules has (quite rightfully) cost quite a few liberty takers a necessary hard learned lesson. Part of the problem is a belief that some people think they can play both sides of the fence.

The hypocrisy in villainy – a question I've heard on numerous occasions is, "How can you give support or have friends that are criminals?" Very easily, as those of a certain "standard," have the privilege of being called a villain and in my view, hold weight when they give advice and say what's deemed right or wrong! Plus, all be it a valued question, is one that I'll always see whose asking, as I've often found that those with the dirtiest of hands, will often point their own grubby fingers at those they feel are beneath them; comically enough, it's a level of criticism or questioning by failed, low-life criminals who were unable to get ahead, as they either failed to understand or bypass the game and its "rules" or who themselves got a taste of good old karma. Firstly, know that what I'd call "proper villains" NEVER target or go after straight-goers; women and kids are of the same equation. Secondly, it's largely only like-minded villains who ever get caught up in conflicts and the situation ends up with either loss of limb or life. From experience, the ones who say they are a victim, have more often than not, caused conflict themselves and none more than the plastic gangsters of this world; people who will try to live, profit and emulate a villain's way and existence, but as soon as they're either questioned or find they can't stomach a bit of resistance, go running to the police, giving evidence and make an attempt at distancing themselves from the crime or the incident that they got themselves into – they're also more commonly known as **grasses**!

The true hypocrisy is with those that claim a moral high ground over a collective or level of society, they themselves failed at (being part of) … a sort of bitter resentment against a group of men, who they failed at becoming. Lastly, I'll say that those that have committed any level of crime, aren't always of the collective known as villains. Snatching a woman's handbag, stealing a kid's bike or breaking into an everyday person's car or home doesn't make you of their ilk – by your own omission and (petty) efforts it's shown you to be nothing more than a low life scumbag and someone who needs to change direction…… proper people don't take from their own, nor do they shit on their own doorstep; a villain's advice would be to change course and find success in life by grafting, as you've proved to be nothing more than a soulless petty thief. I'd add that who better to learn from and listen to than those that know the true cost of crime – my own attempts, involvement and criminal convictions warned me that there's less chance of failure and more success in grafting and it was the same "criminals" that ensured that by their guidance I'd work and live a more fruitful life in different parts of the world and without the threat of a serious stretch as many of them have experienced.

The moral fabric once seen in everyday life, has been poorly substituted for a practice employed by certain (fascistic) elements of society, that has been seen multiple times in history. It was this same ignorant and self-centered, and often unelected body who taught their young and impressionable populace that turning on your elders was an honorable and necessary way for a community or nation to survive. There for your own, has been a doctrine and standard that Carlton has committed to, as by my interpretation, the strength in any group of people is one of "more pawns than kings." Without politicising a shared belief, when the people fear the government, you have a tyranny, when the government fear the populace, you have a democracy and a voice. Many would agree, the sooner people realise there's strength in numbers, the working class will gain a better and stronger self-representation and will be something any working-class community can be both in control and proud of.

"You can be anything you want to be," is a phrase Carlton tells both his children and grandchildren often. "I do what I know best," is one that he's commented to both myself and a few others, as this philosophy has allowed him to provide via opportunities that have presented themselves to Carlton, yet ironically, the same legitimate opportunities were, in most cases there as much for Carlton as those he aligns with closely, but as a good few have said, they simply didn't identify or see them (as I and many others did). Is this either Carlton's or their excuse? No, that's not their style, as either Carlton or the proper people that I'd called villains, live by a standard, easy to understand set of rules… "Use me as an example and not an excuse in what you should be doing, Jase" was a common line given. As much with Carlton as the people I've been around, many who have gone, I can't think of a single one, who if they were being honest, would want a single day's life of crime for any of their own children or for them to follow in their footsteps.

As much as Carlton never found a steady, successful relationship early on in life, this doesn't translate that he doesn't respect or understand the institution itself. I believe he was simply wired this way and no amount of sitting him down and explaining the rights, wrongs and expectations of a husband was ever going to "set him straight," as truth be known, and if he was going to put his hand on his heart, I would be willing to bet my life he does respect and understand the responsibility and commitment needed, but again, I do believe Carlton is made a certain way and as much as he followed a life in organised crime and an existence that demanded a life style away from a "traditional" family, by falsifying it and living a life that simply wasn't him, would've been hypocritical and only put innocent people's lives in danger! Carlton would rather be disliked or draw a level of criticism against him for being honest and not putting people through misery and loss.

I was raised and educated with a belief that a man's integrity was as much a representation of himself as those he stood with and for… it also identified who you would be willing to fight for and against. I am also someone that is willing to live and die by a moral code that dictates that a man's survival and success is one that will never supersede or go against the rights over any amount of wrong, and none more are deserving of this commitment than those I call family and if I was to apply that same belief and MO to anyone, it would be Carlton.

Some people will say having friends and family that rely on you can be an impediment and a liability, given Carlton's past and history, when I asked him this same question, he answered, "But in another sense it's amazing how you can be forced to grow up when you aren't only thinking of yourself. When someone's best interests as much as their health and wellbeing are dependent on your existence, they ultimately become more important than you. This can be a perfect opportunity to act in a selfless way."

Family is what defines some, and none more than with Carlton, but by reflection, it can be said it has remained one of the biggest tests in his life. A family, for any parent worth their weight, is something that requires an immense level of commitment and an invested selfless amount of a person's life, all the while without any promise of success or return, and by Carlton's standard, if a man can remain humble and committed to that of other's lives, then there has to be a lot said about and for that same man. If I was to quote a saying that holds weight and encapsulates Carlton's selfless belief, it would be, "A society grows great when old men plant trees in whose shade they know they shall never sit in."

Friends, much like the players in a football team, will favour you as much as they did the club they signed to and much like their contracts, their loyalty and willingness to remain on the team is one that will fade quicker than the snide logos on that cheap "designer" jacket you got down the market. It's a fact, that people simply come and go, but the loyalty I've witnessed in some, is something I value over any player that's gone through my beloved West Ham. It could also be suggested by some, that with the "modern age" and social media, that the concept and idea of what a "friend" is, has changed. I disagree and that couldn't be any further from the truth – all that's changed is (some) people's willingness to be honest with not only themselves but the very definition of what a friend is. Carlton has been let down countless times, even to the point when those closest to him have commented, "Why the fuck did you have anything to do with him to begin with, Carl?" The fact remains, he will always try and see the best in a person, always has, always will. To be any less, wouldn't then be who he is, only a reflection of who they are. He'll never expect people to change because of who he is, as I believe friends are there initially because of what they want, need, or have to offer. Loyalty, dependency, and honesty are traits of those closest to me as they are with Carlton, and typically why he has more "acquaintances" than friends…. and of that he has very few (friends)… as even Carlton will say, "People simply come and go, it's not that they're all "bad," as common courtesy and a person's willingness to help doesn't always translate to them wanting or needing "friendship," only that they were being a decent human being, but to have someone that has the willingness and ability in "being there" is what then makes you family." From my own personal experience, having someone call you consistently throughout the week, forgetting that you're not up as early as them on any given day isn't them being selfish, forgetful or a measure of their closeness in terms of them in your life, it's their willingness to call you and checking up and seeing how you're doing is! When reading the opening to this book, Carlton nodded, smiled, and asked me to add just one more statement – "Loyalty is measured by a few things, and a commitment to the wellbeing and health of another are just a few of those commendable measures."

1 DAD

I was born to strict, working-class parents in London's East End, where your up-bringing was usually tough, but morals and traditions still existed. We weren't piss-poor, and my sister and I certainly weren't abused, but being a bit of a little fucker, I was no stranger to a clip round the ear, the belt, or a whack with a slipper, one time I even remember my mum smacking me with a coat hanger! The older of two siblings, I tended to cop the blame when something went wrong while our folks were out.

As a boy, I didn't know many details about my dad's past, he didn't speak about it, and I suppose I didn't think there was that much to know really! Dad was a nice, normal gentleman, who seemed to be liked by anyone who knew him. His father wasn't around when he was growing up and at 14 years old, my dad joined the Merchant Navy. He travelled the world twice over, but all me and my sister knew about his time in the service was that he had a pet monkey on board the ship! He left the Navy to have a life and a family with my mum, so with the money he'd saved up, he bought a café in Brent Cross, which I believe they later sold.

Incidentally, to this day I don't know how I ended up being Christened 'Carlton' in a 1950's London! My mother told me once that it was either that or Eugene, so I'm sorry to all the Eugene's reading this, but that would have cause me an extra 3 fights a week, so Carlton will do fine!

I know it's cliché, but it really isn't until you're a parent yourself that you truly realise what you put your parents through! I was a typical mischievous boy, not a nasty or horrible kid, but somehow, I always seemed to end up in trouble or at the centre of a situation. I think it was my 7th birthday when I got a Batman outfit as my present. I loved Batman, so I was made up with it, I was chasing the other kids around in the street, probably driving them all mad! I wanted to stand up high and look around the city like Batman did, then fly in and have a punch-up with a bad guy. So, I clambered up onto the roof of dad's Austin A40, struck my Batman pose, then proceeded to leap off in my attempt to fly across Newham-Gotham. Needless to say, being Batman didn't end too well for me; several hours and a couple of x-rays later, the hospital explained to my parents that I had some sprains and a broken arm.

I regularly fell out of trees that I'd climbed, but one time in particular, I fell from a tree and landed on some broken glass…how's ya' fucking luck! Another trip to the hospital; this time I had to have several stitches in one arse cheek. I had an argument one day with another kid in the street, fuck knows what about, but I chased him down the road. I was definitely going to catch him. I'm telling ya', if only that van hadn't run me down! Luckily for me it was only going slowly.

My mum used to get so angry at me over shit like this, but my dad was always the calming influence. He'd say his piece to me, don't get me wrong, but he talked to me about the problems I'd caused rather than yelling at me. It was a similar story any time I was sick as a child, I wanted my dad to be with me and my mum just didn't have the patience anyway. Dad would sit up all night with me if I was being sick or in any pain. He'd be the one to put his hand on my shoulder, hold my hand, or stroke my hair to comfort me. When I was a small boy, I went through a phase of headaches and hallucinations at night; I was so grateful for my dad being there for me, I felt so cared for and all I needed in that moment was him. Looking back, I don't know how he stayed up all night with me and still went to work the next day, especially when the hallucinations went on for months! No matter how busy dad was, he regularly found time for me and my sister. We often played football together and he always came to all my matches when I played.

We lived 10 minutes from Upton Park, and I

remember being out in the street one match day in 1964, up on dad's shoulders in my claret 'n' blue scarf giving it some with the wooden rattle. I loved the atmosphere on match days in East London, even then as a small boy, it was a massive buzz! I asked my dad to take me to a game, but that day was the last home fixture of the season, so dad said we'd go next season. True to his word, the 65-66 season came around and the first chance we got it was off to the Boleyn. We set off on foot from the house, I was carrying my crate to stand on so I could see the game; looking back, for a 6-year-old boy it probably weighed a ton, but I didn't notice through excitement! Dad bunged the guy on the turnstiles a few bob, I ducked under and in we went to the West Stand. Us kids would stand on our crates with a packet of nuts or crisps and occasionally shout out something we'd heard an adult shout, while the dads would stand together and have a beer while they watched the game. That day was a proper turning point in my life!

Having been a Navy man, dad was a really strong swimmer, who loved the sea. Whenever we visited a coastal town for a day out, he'd say, "Come on, boy!" and he'd take me into the water on his back and swim for miles. One weekend we went down to Brighton and with me on his back, he swam out so far that when I looked back, the pier looked small! I remember the waves seeming fairly big and strong, but he just kept going through them, we both loved it! As our father was a keen swimmer, me and my sister were quite excited the day dad said he was going to teach us to swim. We went to Romford Road Baths, and I was a bit confused as to why we were following dad to the deep end, given that it was our first ever swimming lesson, but all was revealed when dad threw me in and said, "Go on Son, move your arms n legs, paddle like a dog!" I made it back to the side of the pool where I was hoping for a lift out, but he told me to climb out myself. I didn't realise it at the time, but that day, I learnt more than just to swim! Without consciously realising it, I learnt the very definition of the phrase "Throwing you in at the deep end" and the benefits of doing so. I know that had I gotten into any trouble in that water, my dad would have been in there and got me out safe and sound in seconds, which encompasses my dad well really; he let me make my own mistakes sometimes, he knew there was long term benefit from not having everything come easy, but he was right there if I needed him.

When I became a teenager, the trouble that found me only got worse! One morning I decided to bunk off school, so I climbed over the railings, but I slipped and the spike on top of the fence went straight into my calf muscle! I was holding onto the fence, with the spike in my leg like a fucking kebab. Luckily, some people were nearby to lift me off and call for an ambulance! When I was 14, we went away to a holiday park at Westward Ho, it was one of the ones with the chalets, a little arcade, and a club house. We'd planned to meet with some other families there that my parents knew, and they'd arranged it so that all the boys stayed in one chalet, all the girls in another and then of course the parents would have their own ones. I started hanging about with an 18-year-old girl in the group called Tina, playing pool, smoking, having a sneaky booze. Hanging out with Tina quickly changed to hanging out of Tina! Back home in London, both sets of parents thought that we were just friends. I used to slip round to Tina's over near the Elephant and Castle any chance I got, until one night when her younger brother caught us at it and phoned his parents at their local pub: "Mum, Dad, that Carlton's on top of Tina in her room!" I was banned from seeing Tina, of course, but we later found out that the ban was a bit too late, and she was pregnant.

In my final year at school, I had a girlfriend called Theresa. It was as long-term or serious as school year relationships get and we were in love. It had been less than a year since the news about Tina's pregnancy and I found out that Theresa was pregnant! Inevitably, her parents tried to ban us from seeing each other, one day I had a big row with her old man in their lounge, which almost came to blows. We continued to meet up and more often than not she'd come to our house. In those days, teenage pregnancies were viewed in about the same light as they were in the 1800's! It was a nightmare; she couldn't go to school, she wasn't allowed out until after dark, she wasn't to discuss the situation with friends and her parents hid her from their neighbours the whole time. By the end of the 9 months, I'd inadvertently isolated myself from all my friends, everything had become about me and Theresa. I got a call one day to say that she'd already had the baby, if I'd have been given half a chance, I would've been there with her, but her parents made sure that wasn't going to happen. She spent 7 days in hospital, which was standard back then and as soon as she got home, they were on our case to organise an adoption that neither of us really wanted, but we were kids who had only just turned 16 and both living at home with our parents. I got told after the birth had been registered that my name wasn't put on the certificate, another kick in the teeth that I had been powerless to do anything about. All I got was some of those tiny photos of the baby just after he was born, which I actually went on to carry in my wallets over the next 26 years. The pair of us got sent into London to organise the adoption papers ourselves, which for a couple of kids was pretty daunting. Within weeks of being born, her parents handed the baby off to the adoption agency as quickly and as quietly as they could. In truly defiant teenage style, we continued seeing each other for some months after, probably out of comfort as much as love, but eventually we drifted apart. Theresa had gone back to school to finish her exams and I was working, so it was inevitable.

To add insult to injury, we got a knock at the door one day and it was people from the adoption agency. The baby had been with a new family for a few months and Theresa and I had done our best to move past what had been forced upon us and now suddenly they were in my parent's house saying that we could apply to adopt the baby! My mum said that if I wanted to go for it, she'd give up her career to help, but anyone employing the smallest amount of logic would ask themselves as I did, how could a 16-year-old boy take a baby away from a good home and parents that could give him so much more than I could then?

Through all the hassles and stresses, my dad always stood by me, he was always there for me. That didn't change into adulthood! I bought my first car off of my mate's dad, it was a Vauxhall Viva with the vinyl roof, and I was feeling chuffed to bits with myself as I pulled into the petrol garage to fill it up. I was less pleased a few miles down the road from the petrol station when the car came to a spluttering halt…I'd put diesel in the fucking tank! Of course, I called on my ol' man for help, as I thought there would be some way to solve this problem and he'd know exactly what to do. dad had an Austin A40, which he'd hand painted blue with a brush. Any time he'd ever (kindly) given me a lift in it, I'd prayed no one would see me in this thing! It had the crank handle to start it up. The bonus was whenever the roads were iced up on a cold morning, that car would fire up and dad would be driving off as the neighbours were sitting struggling to start their cars, but nevertheless, I hated being seen in it by my mates. Just as I thought the shame of going down the A13 Newham Way in that hand painted car was over, I found myself at the side of the road waiting for it to come round the corner to tow me home! We drained the fuel out of my car and filled it with petrol, by some miracle it was ok after that, whereas modern cars now would be fucked.

I'd always loved him, but it wasn't until later on in life I realised that even though I'd never treated my dad badly, I probably reached my 40's before truly appreciating what we had. Into his 60's, when I had my own home and kids, my dad would still come and help me out with all sorts of things, electrics, cars, the garden, plumbing, the roof, all sorts. Everything "normal" in life, I learnt from him, from football to swimming, DIY to engines, I have my dad to thank for what I know. Every time I ever saved a few quid on a call out, I had my dad to be grateful to.

Dad was a Freemason and he'd always gone on at me to join, but I really wasn't interested. One time I had a quick look over the books and information he kept, which he knew pretty much inside out, I remember thinking 'fuck all that'! Sometime after my 30th, I decided I would agree to join, which my dad was pleased to hear! The son of a Freemason is called a Lewis and provided you're willing to play ball and jump through a few hoops, your father can get you in and help you become a Mason too. I'd started out driving him to his lodge meetings because otherwise, he wasn't able to go anymore due to a knee replacement he'd had. As an added bonus for him, me driving him meant he could relax and have a drink with his friends! The lodge meetings became my time to spend with my dad and a part of me wishes I'd done it sooner. I realised why he'd wanted me to join for so long and I'm glad that I did, eventually.

The beginning of the end - When we first discovered that our dad had dementia, I felt sick when I started to consider what was ahead for him and for all the thoughts that flooded into my mind, nothing could prepare me for what was in store of us all. Dementia is a fucking horrible and cruel illness; the term dementia actually encompasses different conditions that affect the brain, including Alzheimer's disease. If you're on the wrong end of dementia, you will have the displeasure of facing a variety of symptoms adversely affecting your cognitive function, ranging from memory loss, inability to perform everyday tasks, impaired thought processes and severe confusion. With my past life experiences, both written and unwritten about, to this day there is nothing I fear more than dementia as there's a possibility it could be hereditary and coming for me at any moment; unlike man, it's unstoppable and there's very little you can do about it.

Of course, it all started with forgetfulness that could be forgiven of any person in their 70's, but it gradually worsened and became memory loss, which was joined by falls and strange behaviour. Forgetting the grand-kids names for a few seconds can be laughed off at the dinner table in any household, but when your elderly relative goes to the shops for a paper and forgets who he or she is, where they are and where they live, it's a serious problem and simply heartbreaking for anyone that has a family member that experiences it.

My dad ended up in Queens (hospital) for quite some time towards the end and I'd like to give a mention to the all the staff there who cared for him, they do a great job under increasingly immense pressure; thank you all. One afternoon I arrived on the ward at Queens to visit my dad and to my dismay, he had a cut on his head! I had a right go at the nurses about taking proper care of him, but it turned out that dad had been getting out of bed to try to go to the bathroom on his own when he thought the nurses weren't around, you see, in his mind he was still an able-bodied man and he intended to maintain his dignity. Sadly, he wasn't really able to do either of these things anymore. My hero had become weak and vulnerable and all I wanted to do was help and protect him, as he had done for me and my sister as children.

When I took my son Carl and my daughter Madison to visit him one time, dad forgot Carl's name. I could see that this upset Carl and really frustrated my dad, we all knew how much he loved all of his grandchildren. I remember thinking 'Fuck! I do not want to end up like this'. All the family visited dad in the hospital as often as possible and we coordinated so that someone was there each day. It was a bit of a trek for me up from Essex, but

Gemma and I still went most days, knowing how bad things were, we could lose him any time. Whenever my dad was in pain, he always called out, "Carlton, are you there?" and over the weeks, his voice was becoming gradually quieter and softer. He couldn't stay in the hospital indefinitely, so Tracy worked hard to find and organise dad a decent care home, one that would be able to cope with his condition.

The visits continued at the care home like they had at the hospital, as did dad's physical and mental decline. A few of us arrived to visit dad one morning and headed to his room, we walked in, and he said hello to us all, we all stared back in a bit of shock because he had put his pants on over his trousers without realising! I stepped forward and said, "Who did you come as Dad, Superman?" We had always bantered all of our lives and I wasn't about to stop and treat him differently. In terms of the condition, that was a good day because he'd been able to stand up and dress himself, but that was one of the last times.

On another occasion, I arrived, signed in and went up to dad's room, however, he wasn't there. My initial reaction was to feel a bit annoyed that, knowing who I was visiting, they hadn't told me where my dad was, but I realise I can (possibly…sometimes) be a little bit impatient. I decided not to give it too much thought though as I walked back along the corridor, through the day lounge and back to the reception to enquire with the staff: "I'm looking for my Dad, Norman Leach" I explained. Seeming a little surprised, the young lady replied, "He's sitting just over there." She pointed towards the large communal lounge that I'd had to pass through twice already, so I scanned the room from left to right, thinking that she'd made a mistake. "Norman's just there, sir." Came the receptionist's voice as she pointed more directly towards a man in an armchair. I thanked her and walked closer to him, I thought 'What the fuck! No wonder I missed him sitting there.' Dad was slumped in an armchair; his glasses had fallen off and he was wrestling with his half-untucked shirt and its buttons to smarten himself up. I helped with his shirt and told him not to stress. His teeth were rattling so I took them out, too. He'd lost so much weight in a couple of days that I hadn't recognised him at all. When Tracy arrived shortly after, I said to her, "For fuck sakes, we've got to get him out of here." He needed to be assessed properly by medical professionals, so it was back to the hospital.

Dad's second spell in the hospital was even harder and things just went from bad, to terrible. He didn't have a decent dressing gown, so I took him mine up, so he was comfortable, but where he'd lost so much weight it absolutely swamped him. Even though he'd pretty much lost all sense of anything that was going on in the world, I still used to take him a newspaper. I don't know if he used to stare at it to humour me, or if he actually was reading it, but one time he'd sat there for ages looking through it, so I said, "You enjoying that paper are ya', Dad?" He replied, "Yeah, yeah it's good boy, thanks." "That's interesting Dad, coz it's upside down!" We laughed a little about it as I turned it around for him. He'd always ask me how West Ham were doing and I kept telling him they're doing great and playing really well! One time I convinced him they'd won 3 trophies, the girls told me I shouldn't mess around like that but as I said, we'd always had good banter anyway, plus I figured if he died that day, he'd go out happy as ever, thinking his team had won 3 trophies!

Whenever Gemma and I arrived at the hospital, she'd always go and get dad a cup of tea. So, off she went to the machine one time while I helped dad onto his Zimmer frame to take him for a short walk along the landing. We stopped to look out of the window and have a chat; he told me that I should keep hold of Gemma, she's a good one. Then he got really upset, telling me that he doesn't want to live in this state anymore, how he'd been around the world and lived his life, he'd been able to protect and provide for those he cared for, but now look at him. He cried and I felt like crying too, he was right, it's no way to live at all. That was to be the last proper, two-way conversation I'd ever have with my dad, because from that point on, he'd only ever say an odd word here and there. Someone suggested to me that this could've been him sticking two fingers up at life; if life was going to take away his ability in a coherent conversation, then he wouldn't let it beat him…. he wouldn't let it win and he'd have the last word.

Dad needed to go to a specialist nursing home, so we found him one in Upminster. We got him a ground floor room with a big window and views of the garden; by this point it was only these small things we could do for him to make him as comfortable as possible. A gentleman to the end, dad always managed to say thank you to every nurse or carer who helped him or brought him something. I'll never forget that whenever anyone asked him what he'd like to eat, he always replied "sardine sandwich." I don't know if he was getting us all at it, or if he really did want a sardine sandwich for breakfast! - dad would always have the last laugh. After a matter of weeks in the 24-hour care nursing home, dad was basically existing (not living) in a cot-type bed, in adult nappies, spitting his food out; nothing in my life to date has been so tough as to see him like that, words cannot describe it.

The family were gathered round dad, who lay there helpless. I said "Sorry, but can I have the room please? Everyone out." I sat alone with my dad, held his hand, and ran my fingers through his hair. I said, "Are you ok Dad?" He bravely replied, "Yeah boy." I drew a deep breath and continued; "You're tired ain't you Dad? You know you can go big sleep if you want, don't ya'?" He just squeezed my hand, as though to signal me, he was too weak to say another word. The day after next, my dad died in his sleep.

The man I knew as my dad had gradually shrunk into a shadow of his former self and disappeared; at the end, the man before us wasn't really my dad. Due to this fact and also because I'm sure that being in that state would have been mental torture for him, it was a sense of relief when dad passed away. If you've ever seen a relative suffering towards their end, you will understand me. Our dad deserved a proper fucking send-off and Tracey and I agreed that we wanted to give him the best funeral we could, so we set about planning something personal and special. We worked day and night, ringing around suppliers, discussing options between us, considering what dad would have preferred and of course, dealing with the guest list. Gemma was a massive help with the funeral, my phone rings a lot on a normal day but it was ringing off the hook for weeks after dad died and she would take calls for me, pass on messages and updates to people and help track who we'd invited. On the day of the funeral, there was around 150 people there, we couldn't all fit in the church! Obviously, we had family members and some of mum and dad's old friends there in good numbers, plus members of his lodge looking sharp in suits. The rest of the crowd was made up of villains and West Ham hooligans who all came along to show their respect and to support me; it was quite a sight! Thank you to everyone who turned out on the day and supported me in the run up to it. The coffin was draped with a Bobby Moore shirt, 'I'm Forever Blowing Bubbles' played while a bubble machine filled the air with bubbles, just like they always had at Upton Park when we visited as father and son. At the end we released 83 claret 'n' blue balloons, 1 for every year of dad's life. Loads of people awkwardly found a way to explain that, even though nobody likes funerals, it had been a really good day, which is exactly what we wanted! My speech that day was the most difficult time I've ever had to speak in public, in part because there were so many people there, but more so because these were to be my final words to the man who had tirelessly been there for me throughout my entire life, a staunch man who contributed so much towards the man I became.

Carly, Jamie-lee and Jodie surpassed themselves when it came to helping out and taking care of their grandparents whilst dad was really ill. Throughout the ordeal, they showed the same immense inner strength that dad always had, and I was so proud of them. That's not to detract from anyone else's efforts, it's just that the 3 of them were best placed to help and they really came through. My nephew, Thomas, was also amazing throughout that time and he's a credit to his parents.

Just 9 months after my dad passed away, my mum died too. She hadn't been in the greatest of health for a long time and right up until he physically couldn't, my dad had taken care of her, their home, their personal affairs, everything. Me and the family would check in on them and of course, we'd be there if they needed anything, but my folks were independent, and dad wouldn't call to ask for help unless he really needed it. Frankly, it was probably inevitable that once dad died, mum wouldn't be around for very long after. Many people believe in widows dying of a broken heart and maybe there's something in that, maybe there's a more practical reality that's close to the broken heart theory, I don't know, but what a shitty 18 months the family had had! It was only after dad's funeral that it hit me just how mentally draining it is to have a close relative be struck with dementia. Every time I'd get home from visiting dad in the hospital or the care home, I felt exhausted, like I'd been carrying bricks around a building site all day (in fact, probably worse). When my mum died, I felt terrible for the kids. They'd watched what had happened to their grandad, buried him, barely finished grieving and now their nan had died. Needless to say, everyone pulled together, and we got through.

All his life, my dad was nothing but a gentleman, a simple man who lived for his family and was entirely unmaterialistic. Even though he'd always loved cars and engines, he'd never bought himself a nice car, even though he could have. One time, I was looking after a wealthy client who asked me to leave him at his hotel for the day and said that I could use his Rolls Royce in the meantime! I went straight over to pick my dad up and took him out in this polished-up Roller for his favourite slap-up meal: Pie, mash and liquor! This is what I mean, if he could eat out anywhere in the country, he'd either choose a pie 'n' mash shop, or fish 'n' chips! So, you can imagine my surprise when my sister tells me one day that my dad actually had another child, in Germany! Tracy found out that while he was in the Navy, he'd had a girlfriend in Germany with whom he'd fathered a daughter! I couldn't fucking believe it, I had to laugh when I found out! It was before the wall came down, so maybe he couldn't get them to the other side of the Iron Curtain!

Dad had been into powerlifting in his younger days, but his knee snapped so he'd been forced to give that up. He was also a brown belt in judo, but there was only 1 time in my whole life when I ever really saw any aggression from him and that was sticking up for my mum; her family was a large catholic one and the weddings would usually get out of hand! My mother was often in the centre of things and one particular time when the tables were going up in the air, someone threw a beer in her direction. Dad picked the man up 3 inches from the floor by his braces and threw him away like he was taking out the rubbish! As a kid, I laughed at that sight but forgot all about it until a family friend, Tony, told us a story about dad one day: Tony was a big fella, over 6ft tall. He worked at a power plant with dad and one day he was arriving to work when he saw dad walking in too. He crept up behind dad for a laugh and jumped on his back. Tony explained that before he knew what had happened, dad had thrown him over his shoulder and onto the ground like a sack of potatoes!

I have a vivid memory from childhood of these 2 men that used to come to our house in sharp, tailored suits, smelling of Old Spice. One time I asked my dad, "Who are they Dad?" and one of the men said something like, "I'm your ol' uncle, lad!" Sometimes they used to give me and my sister a pound before they disappeared into the kitchen with dad and the door closed. I found out that the men worked for the Krays and dad used to sell knock-off gear for them, these fellas were the cash collectors!

Dad had a second café for a time. Called Mocha in Ilford, it was fairly famous locally. When I was there, dad always seemed to be one of the lads, liked and respected. I couldn't put my finger on it at the time, but there was just something about the people in there and around dad. Turns out that all the bouncers from the Palais used to go in after work for some food! So why had dad gone to such lengths to ensure that us kids never really saw that inner darker side of him? Why had he never told us any of the cool or interesting stories he had? I can only conclude that he wanted us to love him for who he was as a father and as a man. He didn't want or need to impress us in any other way, and I can't describe the amount of respect I have for him because of this.

Looking back at the relationship I had with him and experiencing things for the first time in my childhood, I couldn't have wished for it to have been with anyone more than my dad. The frustration, sadness and pain I felt in the closing years of his life is overshadowed by the laughs and banter that I'll always keep and value, more than any amount of cruelness that life unfairly gave one of the proudest and strongest men I've ever had the pleasure of knowing. You're in my thoughts daily and there isn't a day that passes I wish I could just have one more chat with my all-time hero.

Rest in Peace Dad, I miss you to this day.

Tracy – "It wasn't all sunshine, roses and Christmas trees growing up with Carlton though, that's for sure!"

There is an eighteen-month age gap between us, Carlton being the older. Carlton was born in Forest Gate, and I was born in Woodgreen North London in mum and dad's café. Mum had a difficult birth and recovery after Carlton was born so when she found out she was pregnant with me the gin bottle came out together with the hot bath; fortunately, it did not work but I do love my gin!

We moved to 3 Westbury Terrace in Forest Gate, as mum and dad decided that living above the café was not the ideal setting to raise a family, especially with the late-night openings. For extra security around the home and cafe, our parents got an ex-police dog called Bruno, who, like most pets, quickly became a part of the family. To ensure Bruno didn't get jealous when I was born, dad taught him lots of things that meant he became involved, even down to fetching the changing bag for mum (those dogs are so intelligent and love to learn)! One day, one of the uncles came over and when he saw me and Carlton, he clapped his hands together and simultaneously said, "Come 'ere you two, give me a hug!" Bruno heard the big clap and loud voice, which was enough for him to think we were in some kind of imminent danger, so he did what he thought was right and lunged for our uncle! Luckily, dad stopped him, and everyone saw the funny side! There was another time, when Carlton's mates where round and the usual wrestling was taking place; Bruno growled and starting tugging at one kid's clothes to pull him off of me, again, I guess he was just doing his job, but shortly after that, dad said that he was giving Bruno to the RAF to be on the safe side…as an adult I'm now a bit dubious of that story, but I'm going to go with dad's version!

We loved growing up in Westbury Terrace, mum and dad got to know all the neighbours well and we spent many holidays and Christmas's with our neighbours and their kids; the three main families being the Holmes, Haimowitz and Gunner's. To this day we still keep in contact with them, especially Martin and Ira Haimowitz and their daughter Mia, all of whom are like extended family.

An influential thing happened in our childhood whilst living in Westbury Terrace and its full credit to our parents that, likely without realising it, Carlton and I were passed down a type of tolerance that, in fact, the world could still use more of, even in 2021! We're considering the 1960's here and the first black family moved into the street, next door to us to be precise, but unlike others, our parents welcomed them like any other family they'd ever met. The family were absolutely wonderful people, who we ended up spending a lot of time with over the years and I even used to watch over their younger children whilst their mum popped to the shop sometimes. We used to exchange Christmas presents between our families and one year, they bought Carlton a camera, but I don't mean a plastic, kids toy camera, this was a real one, which must have cost a pretty penny in those days.

It wasn't all sunshine, roses and Christmas trees growing up with Carlton though, that's for sure! Actually, it was rather difficult at times and as the reader may have established by now, it could be referred to as "unconventional" (to put it mildly), but I can say with absolute surety that I would not change one day of my life with him. It may sound cruel to some, that Carlton would make me have fights with him almost every day when we were children, but it made me tough and unafraid of getting hurt, though I still did try to avoid fighting or confrontation with my peers through school because I didn't feel the need or desire to fight or prove myself in any way. Everyone at my secondary school thought I was the quite studious one, little did they know who my brother was, never mind who he was to become and that I could actually look after myself! Even though I avoided scraps at all costs, and without consciously realising it at the time, Carlton had actually helped to give me self-confidence and inner strength, which is useful in many situations, not just against threat of physical violence.

Our dad was always hard working, having a regular job by day and then doing private work in the evenings for extra cash. Mum went back to work once Carlton and I were both in Junior school and for a while I had a childminder, until one day there was an incident involving my getting lost, then found and taken in by a stranger. That saw the end of the childminder's role, as our parents decided I would be safer on my own with Carlton, thus, he and I ended up being "latch-key kids!"

This is where the fun starts, because Carlton and I were left a lot to our own devices which didn't always end well…windows got broken during some of our fights and I can't remember the number of times we forgot our key. Fortunately, we found other ways to get into the house, which makes me think; it's a good job there weren't many burglars around at that time…or maybe we just didn't have anything worth stealing! One method we used was for one of us to clamber down the old coal shoot to get in, another was to climb over a neighbour's wall, through their garden into ours and between the two of us we would find some way of getting a window open to climb through.

Although Carlton was always taunting, fighting or pestering me as we were growing up, he was also very protective as well. I remember when I was in our Junior School playground and standing against the railings watching the kids play football when the ball came over in my direction, a kid shouted at me to kick it back and not liking the way he spoke to me I refused. He came straight over and kicked me hard in the leg, but unbeknown to me or the nasty kid, Carlton had seen the whole thing unfold and was storming over. Through my eyes as a child, it seemed to me as if my brother lifted this child far off of the ground with ease and threw him halfway across the playground floor, maybe in reality it wasn't so dramatic, but what I do remember accurately is that I was so scared we would be in terrible trouble that I did a runner! Anyway, I was grateful to my bigger brother for being there for me!

Carlton had a very mischievous streak which didn't always end well for me. For example, one day I was lying on the sofa with my eyes shut and Carlton decided to get our cat and drop her onto my face. Even though she would never hurt me her instinct, as she was falling back to solid ground, was to get her claws out and I ended up with a big cut down my face which wouldn't stop bleeding for what seemed hours, then I was left with a faint scar on my face for years after. How we managed to explain that one to mum and dad when they got home, I can't remember. Much like the time when we were teenagers and we had a water fight inside the house; the carpets and walls were soaking wet, but I'm not sure what story we told our parents that time either.

It was, of course, great to get my revenge on Carlton whenever I had opportunity, like the time he offered me what he was passing off as a sweet, when in fact it was a laxative! I'd guessed he was up to something and pretended to eat the so-called sweet, then after allowing a little time to pass, I started to roll around on the floor clutching my stomach as if I were in pain. This actually worried Carlton immensely, so he rushed over to see if I was OK, at which point I ceased the moment and hit him in the nuptials for what he'd tried to do to me!

I was making sandwiches for lunch one afternoon, when Carlton came into the kitchen and started taunting me, I said something along the lines of, "I could stab you sometimes Carlton!" And with that, a bit of a fight broke out between us and completely by accident, the knife I'd been holding cut into Carlton! I was horrified, which I think he found rather amusing! Luckily, his injury wasn't bad at all, but could easily have been worse.

There were days when I could not cope with Carlton's antics and would beg him to leave me alone, which usually bought me a few days reprieve before he would go back to his old ways. I know this makes Carlton sound like an awful brother, but he was very caring as well. It wasn't just me in the firing line either, he also liked to torment our cat, but one day she too managed to get her revenge on him! I'm not sure where mum was but me, dad and Carlton were watching a typical hammer horror film, which we all loved, one night and it was about cat people. We were coming to the end of the film and the credits were rolling up, when a cat came across the screen; Fluffy could not have picked her time better because at the very some moment she decided to attack Carlton's arm which was draped down the side of his chair. He jumped so high I thought he was going to hit the ceiling then go after my cat, but fortunately he came to his senses after a few seconds, otherwise poor Fluffy might have gotten strangled that night.

Carlton has always been the clever one in the family and when I started Juniors, he would help me by teaching me simple things like the days of the week, spellings and so on. If ever I felt scared because I thought, for instance, that there was a monster under the bed or someone outside my window, it was always Carlton that I went to for reassurance. Kind and protective though he was, in terms of behaviour, Carlton was pretty bad as a child, but believe me he ended up paying for any misdemeanours against me later in life, for example when we were older with our own kids' mum and dad brought Carlton's girlfriend and Carl's mum round (remember, at this point in time Carlton was still living with Denny and my two nieces Jamie-Lee and Jodie). It was a lovely day, and we were all playing around and having lunch in the garden, when Carlton popped in to see his son, Carl. Prior to this my son, Thomas, had been playing with his gas BB gun in the garden. Carlton was standing talking to Carl when I decided he was going to pay for all the times he had tortured and tormented me, so I did no more than pick up the gun and fired it at Carlton, hitting him in a lovely soft part of his neck! I didn't hang around, but run straight into the house, pushing poor Lynne out of the way. Carlton shouted at Thomas to give him the gun because, as he put it, "I'm going to shoot your fucking mother!" Being a good nephew, he gave the gun to his uncle, but luckily for me even at 12 years old he was clever enough to remove the cartridge, which saved me from getting shot. I came back eventually, once I knew he had calmed down, but it was well worth it!

I could tell so many more stories of life growing up with Carlton as my brother, they'd probably include things like, wrestling his mates in our East Ham home, me being locked in the garden, my worldly possessions being chucked out of the window, darts being thrown, or the knife down my back, but I always came off better than Carlton when mum and dad waded in, plus Carlton took a lot of the punishments that should have been aimed at me as well, which was him protecting me, as always.

Forest Gate was a great place to grow up back then and we enjoyed a great deal of freedom to play, run around and generally "be kids." One of the neighbours that lived in Westbury Road at the end of Westbury Terrace was a bus driver and several times, he was allowed to use the bus for the whole street to go on a day out to the seaside! I remember vividly that there were sing songs, fun and laughter all the way to our destination…. those were great days out and the sort of thing we might now refer to as "the good ol' days." Carlton and I both have very fond memories of those trips, and it was such a great way for the whole street to come together as a community, spend time and get to know one another; neighbourhoods and upbringings can be very different nowadays.

Also, with neighbours and friends, we regularly visited

West Wood Ho! holiday camp, travelling down in convoy and making the journey part of the holiday fun. One year, dad was working as an appliances engineer, so he put a chair and a mattress in the back of the firm's van for us to sit on, which further added to the excitement for us kids and away we went, something which of course would not be allowed today, what with health and safety rules! Whilst we were on holiday, the group participated in all sorts of games and competitions, ending up with plenty of those crappy holiday camp prizes, trophies and certificates by the end of the week! Carlton was very competitive when it came to the darts and archery competitions, and he won quite a few times. In general, he seemed to behave when we were away, or maybe it was more a case of keeping his head down a little more than usual, but it certainly seemed a nice change for everyone that Carlton wasn't getting into trouble. Mind you, having said that, I used to share a room with Theresa on these holidays and I remember being somewhat suspicious that her and Carlton might have been, let's say, "courting," to use a phrase appropriate with the year of the story! I guess her having a baby around 9 months after that little camping trip was proof enough that my suspicions were correct.

I'm not sure if dad and Carlton used to duck out of holidays abroad that mum and I went on because they wanted to stay behind and do a bit of male bonding, or if our family just couldn't afford for us all to fly. Mum, my nan and I flew back from the USA one time and expected to be getting home via public transport as dad had taken Carlton away with the usual crowd to a holiday camp, but as we made our way through the airport, I told mum I'd seen dad's work van in the car park, which she shrugged off as my mistake, however, as we entered the arrivals lounge, there was dad standing with mum's brothers, my Uncles Tony and Rod and it transpired that whilst we were travelling back, my grandad had passed away. I was 11 years old and Carlton 13, we were all upset, of course, but

Carlton was very strong and supportive towards me.

It wasn't long after this time that we all started to have holidays abroad, mum was working in a travel agent, so we probably got a good deal! To go abroad in the late 60's was quite a big thing and I remember going to Spain with the Gunner family when Carlton was about 12 or 13. The parents all got along really well and I was friends with Nancy Gunner, so was entirely content to spend my time with her, but Carlton on the other hand got himself in with a group of guys from Liverpool, all in their 20's, who for whatever reason, happily took him under their wing…. I dread to think what went on throughout that time! One particular morning, after a couple of hours of not seeing Carlton, we all became worried and a bit of detective work by our parents revealed the strong possibility that Carlton was on a coach bound for the airport, as the Liverpool lads had left for home that morning! Mum managed to board the next available all-inclusive bus headed for the airport and found Carlton there, apparently, he'd just gone along for the ride to see them off; as you can imagine, mum was displeased to say the least!

Although we got on well with all our neighbours and this was East London, there was an incident which landed dad in the dock, thanks to one set of the very same neighbours (who I shan't name) we considered to be friends. Dad had been selling stolen goods for a very well-known East End family and for what I can only chalk up as sheer jealousy, said neighbours opposite us bubbled him up to the police, subsequently, our dad was carted off for questioning and charged with handling stolen goods. When the day came that dad was due in court, mum must have thought he wasn't coming back because I remember her crying and cuddling me in our living room; at about five or six at the time, I don't think I fully comprehended the situation. Fortunately, dad was given a fine and suspended sentence, the aforementioned "well-known family" paid dad's fine and wanted to go after the neighbours, but dad would never tell them who they were as he didn't want anything to happen to them either.

Our family on mums' side are from the East End, apart from my granddad, who came from Bermondsey, so nan moved there and that is where mum and her brothers were brought up, so you can see there would have been a conflict of interests when it came to football and which team to support! Dad took us to both Millwall and West Ham matches, but both Carlton and I settled on West Ham as our team, which was just as well as we lived off of Green Street and not far from the Boleyn. I think it was the excitement we all felt when West Ham won the FA cup in 1964 and watching that coach with all the players on the top deck come past our street…that really sealed the deal for us. It's funny that I can remember that day and all its excitement so well, but I can't remember the world cup in 1966! I can remember dad taking us to a West Ham match and I reckon I might have been about 6 years old. We were standing right at the front and there was some big controversy over a decision the ref made at one point, then at the end of the game Carlton and I tried to join the mass of angry fans in climbing over the wall to get at the referee, but dad held us both back by the scruff of our necks!

Nan and granddad lived in a big, old house on Cathy Street, a basic home with an outside toilet, then through the front door was a curved staircase and chunky wooden handrail, which provided Carlton and I hours of fun, climbing up, down and sliding around. Supposedly, one of the bedrooms was haunted, but as hard as Carlton tried, we never found any proof! The two of us were gutted when, in 1964, the council moved them out of that house and put them in a brand new, modern looking maisonette off of Jamaica Road with my two uncles; the new place had no character at all!

My Saturdays were usually spent with mum while Carlton, loving being left to his own devices, was probably up to his usual antics, or maybe at football with dad if West Ham were at home that week. Our mum wasn't the "stay at home" or motherly type, whereas our dad had empathy, affection and cuddles in abundance. Dad was the one that Carlton and I would always turn to in the event of a problem and whilst my dad can, by no means, be described as "soft," he was a fair man and the epitome of a good father. Mum was great at taking me shopping for clothes when I was in my teens, but she was never too good at the whole womanly advice stuff and her temper was something Carlton often got himself on the wrong end of and as I mentioned, he often stepped in and took blame for me, but I do remember one time when I got a clump from mum which I felt was entirely unjust, so in floods of tears and rage, I took myself off to my room where I proceeded to destroy the Christmas present I'd bought her, but being a Libran I decided it was unfair for dad and Carlton to receive gifts from me and not mum, so I destroyed theirs too! Once I calmed down, I was so upset with myself at what I'd done that I cried all the more, dad heard me and came to find out what was wrong and once I'd explained, he didn't get angry or tell me off, because he recognised that my upset was punishment enough, what he did do was hug me until I managed to stop crying; only dad could be like that: Non-judgemental and immensely loving, even in difficult circumstances.

Through our teens it was our house that everyone congregated at, as our parents really didn't mind a crowd of teenagers, so long as they were relatively respectful. Perhaps they preferred to know what we were up to and who with, or maybe it was just our parent's tolerant nature, but be it me and my friends getting ready for a party or Carlton and his lot meeting before a match, our house was almost as busy as Piccadilly Circus at the weekends!

It was during our late teenage years that Carlton and I finally stopped fighting and started to get along better, then when the time came, we found that we would often frequent the same pubs and clubs as each other, so his friends always looked after me and my girlfriends. For a while, we were living parallel lives; Carlton and I both got married in the same year and moved out of the family home, something mum found really difficult because not only were her kids around far less, our friends were no longer congregating at their house either and what was once a lively household, must have become oddly quiet. As we were both married, dad decided to take the opportunity to leave mum, unbeknown to us two. The first I knew of any issue was when mum called me up crying, saying that dad was upsetting her, so I called dad to see what the score was, but he gave away very little and didn't tell me of his intentions, but in the end, he didn't go through with leaving her, instead opting to stay, the reason for which I didn't realise until some years late: He stayed with mum so as not to upset the family, because me and Carlton were the most important things on earth to him and he knew the fallout from mum would affect us.

Carlton and I ended up buying houses next door but one from each other and now with Carley born we were always in each other's homes, especially when my son David was born and Karen, Carlton's first wife, looked after David for me while I went back to work. Both our marriages only lasted five years, we split from our partners around the same time and Carlton even came to live with me for a couple of weeks while he found somewhere to live.

We gradually went from being in each other's lives daily, to almost the exact opposite, as Carlton became more heavily involved in the club security scene, steroids and other things which I hadn't even dreamt of but would hear about much later on. I realise now that my brother didn't stop bothering or caring, in fact he distanced himself from me and my family as his way of protecting us, which I respect and at no point did I ever feel abandoned by him, actually, if Carlton even suspected I might be short of a couple of quid one month, he'd think nothing of dropping a couple of hundred through the door. Eventually, we must have found a way to be close again, without actually having to be around each other's houses all the time and to this day, I'm really proud of how we've always been such good friends.

It was when dad became ill that our relationship and contact was re-affirmed on a daily basis. I am so grateful and lucky to have a brother that was there to help and someone I could sound off to when things were getting difficult. Dad was diagnosed with Alzheimer's, even trying to get dad diagnosed so that we could get the right help for him was a nightmare. It was difficult for all the family to watch as the father we idolised and the granddad our children adored, just deteriorated, confusion and paranoia taking over him. It didn't help matters that I found I was constantly arguing and complaining to his team of carers, who were supposed to look after dad, but I would turn up to visit him and find he hadn't been showered or shaved for days, something that Carlton used to pick up the slack on and sort out. Our dad wasn't a difficult man, he just needed a bit of encouragement, but anyway, I won't go on too much about that issue as I could write a book on that alone!

After receiving the inevitable news late one night on a dark and dingy hospital ward that dad didn't have long left, we managed to get him into a care home in Upminster where he would receive his palliative care and it was here that the whole family, led by Carlton and myself, would take turns visiting dad, never knowing which visit would be the last. I can't believe how supportive and caring all the grandchildren were; I remember once they came with me to visit a care home we were considering for dad and the manager of the care home must of thought my nieces were my children as well as my son Thomas and she remarked on what a loving and caring family we all were. I don't think Carlton and I would've got through the emotional trauma of dad and mum needing so much care if it wasn't for all of the grandchildren.

Carlton had been to seen dad a day or two before he passed away and I think it was at this time that Carlton said to dad it was time for the big sleep, which I suppose was Carlton's way of reassuring him it was OK to leave us, he didn't need to suffer anymore just to watch out for us. I went to see dad the night before he passed away and that was the first time I cried in front of him throughout the duration of his illness. He wasn't communicating much by this point, but I said to dad, "Do you love me?" and his response was, "Of course I do!" as clear as anything. I was on the train back to London and I would always call Carlton after my visit to update him, and I could not stop crying down the phone as I explained that I didn't know if I could cope with keep seeing our dad deteriorate so much. It was the following morning I got the call that dad had died; I think he knew we had all suffered enough and it was time to go.

During all of this mum still needed looking after and she too was in and out of hospital due to her diabetes. Mum was taken into hospital before Christmas 2016 and due to the fact that I had no car and lived in London I could not visit mum until transport was running again after boxing day, but I knew that other friends and family were there to visit. When I arrived at the hospital after a long journey that encompassed engineering works and a rail replacement service, I got an ear bashing from mum, as it was apparently my fault she was in hospital over Christmas! I walked out of the ward in tears and as always, the first person I called was Carlton, not only did I tell him the way mum had spoken to me, but I also blurted out the stress I was under from the neighbour below who was causing us a lot of problems over the past year. He enquired as to why I hadn't mentioned anything to him before now, the truth being, I had wanted to protect him as much as he has always looked out for and protected me and even as trivial as neighbour from hell issues can be, I did not want Carlton involved, as I was afraid of what might happen. I'd already politely declined Uncle Tony's kind offer of helping the neighbour over his own balcony, because even though Tony was still a force to be reckoned with, I really didn't want him in trouble with the old bill either!

After the hellish neighbour moved out, I could finally invite Carlton over for dinner at our flat again, as he must have been wondering why he hadn't been asked over for so long, but I dread to think of the outcome, had he heard this animal that lived below us! You may say that Carlton and I are as different as "chalk and cheese" and you'd be entirely correct; we both live very different lives, mine being that of a straight and law-abiding citizen! We do have some similarities though, both of us are always described as being very loyal to friends and family, very protective of our family and close friends, plus that strong dislike of bullies! You might find this hard to believe after reading some of my comments about Carlton, but tormenting, teasing and aggravating are not the same thing as bullying.

Over the years, I have met several women who know Carlton and when we're introduced for the first time, they have all commented on the fact that I'm not what they expected…now I'm not sure if they expected the "Honey Monster" or as my husband would say a "Mushmolt!" Either way, you get the picture of how different we are, but at the same time still very close.

I know Carlton has done things that some people would be horrified by, but I'm sure that he's never done anything entirely unjust and for all the mistakes he has made in life, it can't be taken away from him that he has a good heart and a lot of love for those closest to him.

CARLTON - The Final Say

Carlton & Tracy as kids.

On the bonnet of dad's car
- the day of that cup final!

Carlton in his rock days.

On a caravan holiday with our dad.

2 SCHOOL DAYS

Elmhurst Primary School, Upton Park Road, Forest Gate, London, was my start and without question, the most impressionable of my schooling years, nothing but good memories …....and it couldn't have been more of a perfect setting. It was close to home, which mum loved, as it was less than a 10-minute walk from our house, I would be able to get there with little effort to and from any place where a ball was being kicked about, and the streets that surrounded my small world back then were, as much a devil's playground, but to me were an outlet that promoted a life for a young East London kid whose adventures and Peter-Pan mind-set, were limitless.

The housing, buildings and I guess you could say, "face-value" of life back then, was one of basic tones and colours, but what brought it all to life, were the kids playing out and on every street, and not those just around your immediate home, but on the way to and from school… life back then and my early school years, was one that was promoted by the people that came in and out of your day, outside your front door, and my primary school, that by many standards was like a second home….. a toy shop with teachers. I saw primary school as a place to go, learn, meet and spend time with mates, and more than anything, for me to play football. It may be as much a surprise to some, as it will be a disappointment to equally as many others, but I was very well "placed" at school. I really enjoyed all the subjects, did well with my exams, the results and what I achieved. I always got on well with the teachers, who would never have a bad word to say about me, as I enjoyed my time in the classroom and what I gained from being in there, I always understood and accepted what was expected of me.

I remember primary school for learning and appreciating the social aspect of making new friends, ones that didn't necessarily live in the same street as you. Learning your first swear words and what boundaries could be pushed with your boyhood cheekiness towards both, teachers and your parents, but there was never any level of spitefulness, or malice… definitely a time and place of, "boys will be boys," but again, there was a certain level of innocence in your humour, actions and behaviour.

No matter what lesson existed, I always looked for any opportunity to kick a football about in the playground or a flat open space, before, during and after school…and that, "football" was anything that we deemed was kickable and God help anyone if the existence of an actual football was missing, because if you dropped anything that we felt that could be kicked, dribbled and then put between two jumpers, markings or anything that some-what resembled goal posts, then you'd have to wait for either a goal to be scored or a teacher to come along and retrieve what you were once in possession of. It was also a time, that your injuries, falls, cuts, and scrapes where, as much part n parcel of your childhood as the method and cause. My mum would joke, if I was climbing a tree, it would be on the branch that'd always break, and no matter how small a piece of broken glass was on the ground, he'd land on it. The warm summers and riding of bikes, the climbing of trees in your mum and dad's back garden and the snow-filled winters. A childhood that seemed to be consumed with laughs and dares, that you found in any one of the months that filled the year, and it was during these years and your primary school days, that the times, places and adventures that you shared with the same playground-mates, you honestly thought you'd be hanging about with forever; I'm not in touch with a single fucking one now!

If your parents wanted to place you in what was called a Grammar school; a higher level of discipline, concentration on academic achievements and a very strict school uniform, than you had to sit an exam during your last year of primary school that would determine if you met a certain learning or academic standard (I'd have to check into it, but I don't think they even make kids sit that exam anymore). So, to say I was gutted when I sat, scored very highly on my 11 plus exam, then being told I would be attending a (grammar) school away from all of my primary school mates, is an understatement. For the best part, all of my mates were being sent to Sandringham Secondary School, where Tony Tucker went, and I've thought at least once, if not twice, how my life might have turned out if I'd met up with him back then, as I honestly think the meet would've been inevitable… birds of a feather and all that.

Mum couldn't have been any prouder, her little boy had earned his place at the best school in Newham Borough, dad had decided that I was going to Stratford Grammar without question, as he'd already planned, that after finishing school and gotten my O – levels, I was going to be getting an apprenticeship at the docks. I knew it was a lost cause and would be impossible to argue with a man who left school at fourteen and went into the merchant navy, or a mum whose education was that of an all-girls Catholic school, whose administration and teachers were all nuns and of a post-Victorian discipline and mindset. In their eyes, I was being given an opportunity that they'd only dreamt of as kids, and it wasn't going to be passed up.

The first step was opening day; mum came along and was still, "over the moon," but no sooner as we'd left from seeing what everything was and I didn't want to be part of in any way, I found myself attending my first day at a place, that I wish didn't exist. Grammar school was a step in my young life, I think I could never have been prepared enough for, and if I'm honest, for the first year, I never liked it at any stage, as one bad day at primary school, for the best part, was better than any day of the first year of my grammar school life.

My first thought and question when walking towards and then through those gates for the first time was, 'what the fuck have I done to deserve this I noticed a lot of kids about my age, were all bunching together and walking towards a yet unseen, unmarked finish line. With our socks pulled-up, and ties worn correctly covering the top button… our fresh, innocent faces and wide-eyed expressions, couldn't have made us look like we stood-out any more than we already did. We were easy to spot, and being very self-conscious with my new school uniform, I felt like easy prey. What seemed like a swirl of predators circling around the outside of our group, were the returning students and years above us, who themselves had been through this same start and ritual in previous years, you could easily tell them apart from the new kids, loosened top buttons, and ties not as straight, their bags being carried in a less military fashion and more relaxed way. I didn't even want to trade places with them, I just wanted out of here. It was as daunting as it was humbling…...a reminder I had no real pals, and no one to lean on…...it was as if I was in a foreign land…and even amongst a mass of people, I felt totally defenceless and exposed, a feeling of emptiness and realisation of isolation, I believed I'd had a better chance of survival if I'd been washed up on a desert island!

Very quickly and without any warning, I discovered my fun-filled primary school days, were fast becoming nothing more than a distant memory, and it was this shit hole that was committing an unforgiveable crime, one based on hate and empty promises… a place I loved going to, had now been replaced by a prison and a sentence, disguised as a new school with years of forced attendance. What was once a care-free life with mates and cheerful faced schoolteachers, was now substituted by students in penguin looking outfits, with a badge on a breast pocket, acting like miserable old men in young men's bodies. The teachers must've been at least 9ft tall, appeared as black-cloaked menacing un-emotional ghosts, here to suck the life and your memories out of you, then sending you home, a hollowed-out version of a boy who once had a soul. Even going to the toilets had you thinking if the stories were true of these man-sized children jumping out and beating you up. I found myself standing in the corridors, thinking if I was in the right spot, or someone else's… if it wasn't one thing, it was another…. when the teacher said, "The lesson is beginning," I actually heard, "Your life is now ending!" Even morning assembly was a cold experience, some might think a huge collection of kids in one area, would promote and give a sense of unity and strength in numbers, like fuck did it, just another heartless and emotionless hole that reminded me where I didn't want to be, I absolutely hated the place! And the cherry on the cake and something that couldn't have been any worse in terms of timing, was me having to wear glasses! Both mum and dad grafted, and whatever we had was as a result of their hard work, but anything extra meant it was at the government's expense. So, when I needed and had to wear glasses, I was kitted out with what was on offer – the hard to miss and all too classic NHS's thick-rimmed glasses and just the sight of them being worn, made most think I was trying to emulate the puppet character, Brains, off the tv show, Thunderbirds. The fucking stick I got as a result of wearing them things! I tried everything to get rid of being seen in them. I'd break them, hoping for an upgrade, something more "modern," and not so fucking clumsy looking……but my dad would find ways of fixing them…the next move would be keeping them hidden in my school bag, so as not to have to wear them, but then I couldn't see fuck all, or what was on the black board, so I'd end up sitting at the front of the class and spending the whole lesson squinting so I could see what was being written …. an absolute nightmare! All I know is, what worked for Michael Caine, didn't work for me!

But, as luck would have it, I learned one of my pals had an older brother that went to the school and was in the fourth year - Jimmy Colkit, he had some pull and presence, was a good-looking bloke and was a bit of a chap, you could always tell where he was in the playground, there was always a buzz and a lot of people around him…he had a certain energy that people wanted to be part of…and he must have had something else, as he always had girls hanging off of him. So, no sooner as I learned I had a chance of improving my existence and life, I befriended him, and that, thank fuck, started to turn things around for me. Sports was, I thought going to be something I could disappear into and keep myself busy with, but again, as a testament to how much my start at the school was an unwelcomed one, the P.E teacher was Welsh, so you guessed it, his love and obsession was for a sport that had an oddly shaped ball and whose rules were totally backwards, and if that wasn't bad luck enough, the other sport on the menu was basketball!!!!! Both never really fit, and as much as I tried kicking that fucking mis-shaped ball and with the grabbing and hugging of other boys, I just wasn't having it. But, when the opportunity came along, I got into the football and on the school team.

The first year was like living in Groundhog Day; each day seemed to repeat itself, there was absolutely nothing that would make my existence or experience anything worth talking about, or special…… my life and the days there were simply dull and mundane; but being I'd now started going to football regularly with my dad, if there was any chance of a conversation on football, or if someone supported West Ham, that then helped me make a couple of friends at school. It wasn't until the second year of school that I started to find, both myself and my footing. This allowed me the benefit to form a small crowd of mates. There was a field right opposite the school called West Ham Park, a good place for kicking a ball and meeting up with some of the mates that I'd now made over the last year or so.

Up the road was another school called, St Bonaventure's, known informally as St Bon's on the Boleyn Rd, it was an all-boys Catholic school, which meant they had twice the number of boys in their ranks as us, simply further translated that they had a decent number of lads that could have a fight. Now, being that we were a school whose strength was measured by kids who were more accustomed to fighting their way through equations and higher math problems, than having it out on the cobbles, meant we had, at most, 1 out of 20 kids that could, or were willing to have a fight, but St Bons, didn't have such a problem or concern, as they had about 15 out of 20 that could have a row. So much like all neighbouring schools, there was always talk, or a chance of a fight between them and us, but I'll come back to this later.

It was during this time, and my pre-teen years, that I started to work part-time, a milk-round, working on the market stalls, anything to earn a few quid. I was starting to fill out a bit and took an interest in music, fashion and even grew my hair out. Glam Rock was all the rage, I remember the first album I bought was Electric Warrior by T-Rex, they were big at the time, the year was 1972 and they held the number one spot in the charts. The album cost me 2 quid, which was a whole day's money from working, I brought it from a record shop that I'd pass whenever I was walking to or from my nan's house down Old Jamaica Rd. David Bowie, T-Rex, Slade and their songs were topics of conversation. I remember the girls at school would lean against the wall, listening to the popular groups and songs on their transistor radios during lunch break. One thing that impressed and attracted the girls was boys who were into music, fashion and knew, "what was in."

When I hit 13, I was on a mission, and much like a dog in heat, it was the start of my interest in the opposite sex…I was, "full-on girls", and trying to navigate how, and what it took to get around them as much as possible, was not only a daily conversation but also an objective. This then led to making sure we went to as many birthday parties at people's houses as possible and that there were girls there, and no sooner had the parents decided to disappear for a couple of hours, entrusting the group of young party goers with a bit of responsibility, we'd be sneaking in the bottles of gin, cider and cans of lager. Our thinking was, this would improve our chances with the girls, but the only guarantee, of course, was us suffering the next day or two from the drinking. There were a few times of, "fumbling and stumbling about" until finally, you'd landed a girl that was interested in you, as much as you were learning of the female anatomy, and the all-too-common lines and promises of, "it's ok", and you'd, "never tell anyone."

It was also during these years, that I experienced bullying from the much older kids at the school. We'd be on the coaches, going to play other schools for a football match, and there would be kids from either the 4th or 5th year, walking through the coach and beating the younger kids up! For me, it was probably where I'd come into my own, filling out and having a broad set of shoulders, that made them feel I needed to be knocked down a peg or two, but what bothered me as much as taking shit from older kids, was the bully's belief they could simply make anybody's day miserable because they didn't like the look of them, was not strong, or able to defend themselves – I always fucking hated that, and the way they acted. So, one day I'd had enough, found myself standing up, not just for some of the kids being systematically bullied, but also myself, and had it out with one of them. Back then when you had a fight with someone, you'd meet them out of the teacher's sight and not right in the middle of the school grounds, you did this for obvious reasons - you'd want to avoid the chance of being caught and the punishment of being caned. So, after school, you'd more often than not meet behind the school bike sheds, where all of the other boys would form a circle around you and whoever you were fighting. The routine was very much the same each and every time, it'd start with the accusations and reasons for the fight, some name calling and the encouragement from your mates in the circle that had formed around you both. The next part was where things made, break or determined what happened next – the physical contact; more often than not, it consisted of a series of pushes, pokes in the chest and getting in the other boy's face – and from there, consisted of a series of wind-mill punches and wrestling to the ground, but, here like a few times before, I was the smaller and younger of the two in the confrontation, I ended up on the floor, but, as quickly as I went down, I jumped straight back up and shouted, "is that it?" I'd had enough of the bully, and the fact I simply didn't respect them – so no amount of punches, kicks and being thrown to the ground was going to change that.

I think it got to a stage where I learned I wasn't made of glass or going to be held to ransom by anyone at school, so I started to get some back at the older boys, then on one occasion, Jimmy Colkit, got hold of one bully who'd given me a kicking before, pulled him to one side and gave him a good slap in front of me. Not long after that though, Jimmy, who was a few years older than me, left the school. I felt like my safety net and back-up had left me to now sort things out for myself. Being that our school was not known or had a history for "fighting men," I decided that I'd better, "step up my game." With each attempt of someone trying to bully me, or another to suffer at the hands of a bully, I'd row with any kid of any age, and it wasn't long after that, I become someone that wouldn't tolerate it, and was recognised as the main fighter in my year. From here on, I found my own place and standing in the school and never suffered a bad day because of the cowardice actions of a bully.

One fight and caning I remember in particular, was when a kid thought it was ok to go around and simply bash the other kids, so, I took it upon myself to put him in his place. For the sake of the story, we'll call him George. I was standing inside the school gates, and much like most days, thinking about girls, football and having both within my daily activities, when in walks George, but instead of acting like a decent human being and someone of a stable mind, he decided it'd be ok to simply walk up to some innocent, unsuspecting kid and lay into him; punching, kicking and being the cunt that he was (and probably still is).

The unprovoked attack, that if witnessed and much like previous times, was something this evil prick enjoyed doing. They say that if society aligned with, "an eye for an eye, will make the whole world blind," well, tell that to someone whose now been forced to suffer a miserable existence at the hands of a bullying cunt, who'll never make a conscientious decision in being a decent human being. Before I could get to him, George had left the poor kid on the floor and carried on inside the school, all without any thought or care of what level of injury, either physically or mentally that he'd left the kid in. I eventually caught up with George, watching him enter his classroom, and waited for him to take his seat at his wooden desk. As I looked through the classroom door window, I saw him sitting there, with a grin and level of arrogance I was looking forward to wiping off his face, and it was only when the teacher had started the lesson for that class, that I threw open the door and addressed George by calling him out and going at him without any mercy or reservation…. I was going to smash this fucking arsehole into the ground and make him understand, not only how much he'd fucked-up, but how much I detested people like him. I used both my hands, feet and even the same wooden desk he was originally sitting at, and put him on his arse, and I made sure he stayed there. Once I was happy he'd learned his "lesson," (excuse the pun) I left the class, only to be chased by a bunch of teachers that'd heard all the commotion. It goes without question, that the headmaster wasn't happy and when asked, I admitted (not that there was any dispute on what and who had committed this act of violence) and justified my actions because of George's bullying ways that I wasn't going to tolerate…. but rules are rules, and being that I've always been one that has respected the institute of schooling, teachers and those that invest in a child's life, I accepted that I'd done something, that in my mind was the right thing, just in the wrong place, so after a few painful strikes of the cane, I left the room, clinching my arse-cheeks together and telling myself, 'don't show it, don't show how much it fucking hurt', but I was all the more happier, that another cowardly prick had met a level of justified punishment.

Then, it was as if there was a new dawn and age that had come…I was welcomed to hang out with the older kids at the school. Certain privileges come with a status and friendship with an older crowd, the main one being girls that had, "developed" and were more, "experienced" in the ways of the world. Part of my later days of school life, and thankfully a time that I'd found my feet, was as much about music, girls, fashion and ……fighting. School rivalries was commonplace, and there were a few close to us, so it was inevitable that we'd have a big row with them, but one main element that distinguished us from a lot of them; they had twice as many boys as us and never had the prerequisite of being of a certain academic grade to come to the school. So, while other schools had little or no requirements to be allowed to attend, ours and more importantly our ranks weren't fitted out with seasoned fighters! But and it was here I was introduced to what was all too common in most schools around the country – how exaggeration and childhood myths are commonplace.

When word spread through the school that a mob of hundreds, docker-sized men were coming from Forest Gate high, it was like we'd been called to war. A few things went in our favour though, one being I'd gained a lot of confidence and would happily fight with any school, and in recent years, our school had switched from a grammar school; whose policy was once based on the academics and thickness of a child's glasses to that of an 'open door' policy, so if your name was written on a piece of paper, you was admitted to the student body, and I had a few pals from West Ham that were a bit handy when it came to a row, one in particular – Ronny Pyle; a skinhead that could really have a tear-up, who also brought a few pals. When the time came round, what was supposed to be hundreds of docker-sized men, was in fact about 50 teens of the same age, and what was supposed to be a full-on war, fight 'til the death, turned out to be a, "come on then!" and, "fuck off, I'll fight you here and now"…it was more of a verbal row and a bit of a stale mate….it also might have been something to do with Ronny, as he was well known around Forest Gate and wasn't known to be anything but someone who would fight come rain or shine. The remainder of my school year was one of fucking, fighting and becoming who I would be known for years to come.

Whatever was going on at school, home… or in life, the fact remained, that my hormones and body were in full swing and very much in need, and I felt that I had, both a moral obligation and responsibility in feeding those desires, so in an attempt to spend more time around, and improve my chances with the girls, I considered my options and weighed up what was on offer during the school day, and luckily, at the same time, we were given a choice between wood, metalwork or the cookery class… for me, it was a no brainer. Admittedly, there were a few girls, in both the metal and woodwork class, but this was only if you were into girls that looked like they played the cello, wore chunky thick knee-high socks, had thick-rimmed glasses and played rugby with the boys, but for me, I fancied and wanted to be around those that wouldn't necessarily beat me in an arm-wrestle. So, I convinced my mate, Neville to join the cookery class with me. What was a welcome surprise, but being it was a seed planted some years before, thanks to my dad's efforts in teaching me how to take care of myself, I took to cooking and really enjoyed it, so much that I even got one of my O-levels in the class, placing 2nd highest in the whole year and you have to remember that half the school was girls!

Another common trait the girls liked was the smartly dressed, stereo-typical, bad-boy and the image they were willing to portray. So, when I could rustle a few quid together, it was Stay Press trousers, Dr Martin boots and Ben Sherman shirts. Loafers then followed Dr Martins, but you had to have them fitted with Blakey's shoe protectors, they were a horse-shoe shaped piece of metal that would be fitted to the bottom of your shoe, helping to prolong the life and wearing of the sole, but we'd end up skidding down the street in hope of sending up sparks and making a noise. Your shoes had to always be shined to perfection, and you should be able to see your face in them if polished properly, my test was being able to see up a girl's skirt when I placed my shoe below them. I remember going to Granditer's boy's and men's wear; now called Base, and was a favourite of mine, a one-stop shop for everything that a lad wanted and needed; much like a department store found on Oxford Street or Regents Street, but instead of being in the centre of London, it was right on my "doorstep," conveniently placed on Green street. Whether it was my first bottle of Brut aftershave, with its trademark metal medallion tag, or my first Crombie jacket, if you had a few quid, that was the place to go, and after going in there, I looked the dogs-bollocks, but the school didn't have either the same opinion, or view of my new-found wardrobe, but further adding to my "Jacko" reputation, I would get sent home. In the mind of the school administration, this was a form of punishment, as by them sending me home, forcing me to change and then return to school, was a lesson of inconvenience. But, in fact, as it proved, it actually encouraged me to pre-empt being kicked out for the day, as my family had now moved to East Ham, which meant it was a 20-minute car drive, or the bus to get home, this exclusion gave me more reason and opportunity in bunking-off school and doing what I wanted, not to mention the, "climbing up the ladder" of notoriety in a lot of pretty-girl's eyes.

Each and every opportunity I got, I was trying to get my leg over with a girl. Then, when I did land one, we were both at it like rabbits and the world was coming to an end… and I'm not kidding, when I say any opportunity, I went as far in working out a schedule, learning the timings and days of whose parents would be out, and for the longest….and it didn't even matter if it was for just 30 minutes, "let's go around mine, quick, my parents aren't home!" or, "it's Tuesday, you're mum and dad are out, we can get a bit in there!" ……I was at it like my life depended on my efforts and time spent on the subject. Then, what was probably one of the most embarrassing of times, was when we got caught whilst we were, "at it!" My dad had come home early from work, and with that, he came to my door, checking what I was up to and shouting, "Carlton! Why's this door locked, open it now!" I remember saying to my girlfriend, "Fuck, quick, it's my dad" then adding, "get yourself sorted out!" But I'd been sussed, my dad was no fool, and no sooner had we sorted ourselves out, and I unlocked the door, he was all over me, with, "Don't ever do that again in this house" and so on. Dad was old-school, but no number of threats and advice were going to lure me away from the girls or the experience…I'd found a new hobby and was hooked – girls!

My dad never gave up on me, had all the confidence and faith in my abilities, as he still had plans for me and my apprenticeship to become a marine-engineer, counting my O-levels, (14 of them) a planned-out career and future around the East London Docks. I on the other hand, was counting the days until I was free to do what I wanted and simply be Jack the lad. I wanted to relive my primary school days of freedom and not having a care in the world, but from the viewpoint of an overconfident teenager, who thought he had it all figured out.

So, the academics, that was once a large part of my successful childhood, had now been replaced by some of the vices that was there for an East London teenager: music, fashion, girls and supporting West Ham Football Club. My first love was at 13, we honestly envisioned we'd be together forever; I saw it all laid out in front of me, marriage, kids, house, a job for life …the lot. A realisation of my progression from my childhood to adulthood was when I got an 18-year-old girl pregnant, I was just 14, but as said earlier on in this book, things didn't go as we'd hoped.

3 SOME HAVE NO SHAME

On occasion, people say things like, "Well Carlton's made loads of money talking about the Range Rover murders!" but in fact, my angle was the early ICF days, then into the muscle game. What happened to Tony did affect my life because I considered him my best friend, but in the years after it happened, the last thing I wanted to do was put myself into any spotlight, much less capitalise on the situation, I was more concerned with staying alive! My first autobiography, Muscle, didn't have F424 NPE on the cover, it has my photo on there! Like I say, I have spoken about the murders from my point of view, but that makes up just one small part of who and what I am. I've spent the last 15 plus years trying to move on from the whole triple murder thing, move on with my life and crack on with other things, but unfortunately there's always someone lurking with an agenda, looking to gain fame or fortune, often both.

So, let's shed a little light on some recent events, or if you prefer to be melodramatic, maybe you'd call them 'revelations'. There's no denying the level of stupidity that exists in this world; none more than with a certain obsessive fantasist, you know the one; there's several people around exaggerating the truth or using a bit of bullshit, but then there's those that really take it to a whole new level. I've left it alone for a long time, as I was raised with the belief that you don't pick on those less fortunate than yourself, but come on, it gets to a point where you really have to laugh at the efforts of the only so-called gangland boss I've ever seen step out, dressed head to toe in ill-fitting Millet's attire, and even more so when considering the tripe he puts out almost every year. I don't know if I should genuinely feel a bit sorry for him, but what I do know is, we all have a good laugh at Bernard O'Mahoney, as most days, his sheer existence just provides pure comedy. The fact remains that he has nothing else to do with his life and is overly obsessed, even after a quarter century, with the deaths of those 3 men, I must conclude that it is truly sad. Especially if you accept what those in the know have confirmed many a time, that this is a man who never knew Pat or Tony on the level that he claims, was never at any sit-downs or were friends, let alone business partners. Just because the lads used to use Raquels as a playground, didn't make it their H.Q. Desperately arranging to have your photo taken at Raquels, dressed as if you've just come back from an afternoon at the allotment (he really is a scruffy cunt) whilst standing next to one of my mates doesn't mean you're connected or worth an ounce of anyone's time. I mean, who would get too deeply involved with a bouncer who got his arse handed to him on more than one occasion by drunks and straight goers? It should be said that when Bernard was brought to me in an attempt at an introduction whilst I was running The Ministry of Sound, it was that same night that he showed a good few people what he was made of. Even after being knocked back for work by myself, he tried making himself busy when it kicked off. As a result of his typical bumbling ways, he got himself stabbed in the stomach, only to crawl out the back door and have it on his toes, but we'll go into more detail about that later in the book.

It's known as standard practice that when proper people, faces, chaps call them what you will, work or align with like-minded people, they only trust to become properly involved with established firms or known money getters and the depth of involvement depends entirely on how the parties carry themselves and their reputations. It's similar to applying for a straight job; you need a checkable CV and verifiable references, else you're lucky to even get an interview. When this fella arrived from the midlands asking for work, I took the measure of the man and he didn't make the grade to join my team, but down the line, when he asked for an intro to Tony so he could get invoices and remain head doorman at Raquels, Tony knew he could make an easy couple of quid off this guy whilst keeping him at arm's length, plus he and Pat would have a new haunt to get the VIP treatment at! The reason Bernard's attempts to advance into the Essex or London underworld were continually failing, is because no one that had ever worked with him or for him could give reference to that, plus no one, not to mention proper people, liked the way he conducted himself, he was a very odd man to say the least, who acted strangely. For example, look at that photo he uses all the time of him gurning next to Tony or the photo of him outside the club. He'd asked the club photographer to take a photo of him and his pal, but Tony didn't even know he was about to be photographed! Do you really think he'd have had his picture taken in that state (his eyes were almost closed)? I'm not sure if the latest generation even believe the tale of this guy driving down from Birmingham to Pitsea and taking over Essex, not knowing anyone, no crew wrapped round him, just him alone rocking up…next thing he's a top boy running things. Even stranger still is that Bernard regularly pretended to be a woman and wrote to inmates in order to try to trick confessions out of them, so that he could be the one to snitch and get them more bird! He used names such as "Belinda Cannon" in 1991, but there were several others too.

Bernard is particularly consumed and arguably obsessed by the triple murders, and although I thought he was a weirdo before, all these years on I have to wonder if he has some kind of mental illness or even worse, a sexual fetish about the men killed that night. Bernard O'Mahoney is widely referred to as a grass and a liar, his twitter account was set up in 2009 and he only has 5200 odd followers as of March 2021, which indicates to me a lack of interest by the public in what he has to say, something that I think eats him up inside because he seems to have never fitted in anywhere or gained any real recognition or notoriety for anything, especially not as a hardman or gangster.

Bernard once done a documentary and had John Whomes on. John referred to me as "Leach"; something I've only ever known Bernard to do, which makes me wonder if John Whomes was talked into telling the lies about me on that show, but more fool him for working with a wrong'un. He told a concocted story that after his brother was arrested, he called me up and introduced himself, then I shit myself and hung the phone up. Well…I don't know where to start with this one! This was before every fucker carried a mobile everywhere with them, so he's saying he got hold of my home number in Brentwood and called me there, which is doubtful. Secondly, I didn't know who the fuck John or Jack Whomes even were, much less be scared to receive a phone call from either of them. If he was such a tough guy or some proper fella, why didn't he come and see me? It's things like this that keep cropping up that brings it all back for me. When it initially happened, as people already know, I spun out of control; booze, drugs and paranoia were my life for a few years, though nowadays I'm stronger, I still don't want to listen to people's bullshit tales and have it all brought back to me once every year or two, especially not just because some numpty is skint and needs to try to earn an extra few quid on the quick.

To have an idea of how delusional Bernard is, you need to know that it was him who pushed the name "Essex Boys." Never did Pat, Tony or Craig sit down together and say, "Right lads, what shall we call ourselves?" No group of mates doing a bit of graft together ever sat around and named themselves; teenagers have gang or group names, not hardened criminals out to make serious money. The idea that there was a group of grown men going around calling themselves, "The Essex Boys," just further proves it was concocted on a journalistic level. On one hand, Bernard regularly says that he didn't want in on their drug deals and other shenanigans, but on the other hand, claims he's the founding member of the very gang that dealt with vast amounts of drugs – which one is it? So here you have the man who called his book "Wannabe in my Gang", but when 'his' gang gets accused of supplying the drug that killed LB (may she rest in peace), he not only denied any knowledge or involvement, but instead started grassing dealers up; how can you be a gangster and also expect to earn recognition as a 'crime writer' when you're a known grass? Isn't it crazy to think that a big, tough, switched-on and widely-feared bouncer who's running Essex, didn't even realise, thus didn't do anything to stop, copious amounts of class A being sold and consumed in his venue?

Nowadays, his level of resentment and jealously knows no limits, and is easily seen when he has commented from afar, about some of the old boys who have made commendable efforts in projects and given stories about their previous lives in crime. BOM, being the low-life that he is, has referred to them as grave dodgers and all manner of derogatory terms that you'd expect to hear from a policeman or a 7-year-old, bearing in mind he's spent years of his life desperately trying to become one of them, or make money from their names and reputations. That disrespectful nobody should know that these chaps are people that have actually lived "the life" and his continued cowardice is only a sign of his disconnect and discontent. But if we're to play in the gutter, it's better to be a grave-dodger, than a grave robber – nobody likes a turncoat, Bernard! I've come to realise that this person's attempts to stay relevant and to find a new generation of youngsters to believe his tales are all he has left in life.

It's not just the lies that damage his credibility now either, people can plainly see that he keeps doubling back, switching sides, changing alliances...he was up the Kray's arses for years, next thing he's slating them publicly, and the same story is true of others he's latched on to and tried to suck blood from...much like a parasite. On 7th February 2021 in a publication called Birmingham Live, there was an article by a Mike Lockley. In this article, O'Mahoney bitterly slags off Pat, Tony and Craig, which is to be expected, then the article claims that Bernard made his name as a football hooligan (which is a new one on me and a lot of lads from firms all over the country), then there's something about him working as an armed police-type officer (tells us something doesn't it) in South Africa at the end of apartheid, before coming back to the UK to be a feared mobster; I've never met anyone proper who's been scared of Bernard! Does nobody ever stop to question that if Bernard was so powerful and feared, why didn't he take over all the doors in Birmingham, instead of keep moving from one place to the next, trying to find a feeling of acceptance from anyone that would have him? The best part in this article for me is when Bernie slags off the Krays! Yes, you read right, a nobody like Bernard O'Mahoney said that the Krays were a pair of clowns. For all their alleged wrong doings, but known standing in the world of organised crime, I find it a bit rich for a nobody like Bernard, slagging off two dead men who were actual gangsters. Here we have two men known within the criminal fraternity that actually ran east London, who had a criminal enterprise that stretched into other countries, a life and legacy that still lives on to be questioned by someone that couldn't even run a door. Regarding more recent history, take a look at what Bernard did to the family of Paul Massey! Once again, he weaseled into somewhere he didn't belong and fucked people over, but only after the head of the family died, of course, else he wouldn't have had the bollocks to do what he did. Once again, he slopes off into the darkness, but on the plus side, Manchester is probably rid of him now as he'll be too scared to rock up there any time soon. In a similar turn out, I'm told he opened a café in Ireland called Faces, but was politely asked to jog-on by some friendly local lads who must not have appreciated what he was cooking up…

Here's another prime example of dragging up the past

for questionable reasons: December 2020 and we're told that Steven Ellis knows who killed the lads in the Range Rover, but wait! The YouTube Channel needs 1,000 subscribers before the video will be made public; why is that? I'm told that you need 1,000 people subscribed to a channel before you can monetize the content, so is the motive behind this purely monetary? Let's analyse the big confession, shall we? When Tony told me that they were going on that bit of work, he told me they were picking MS up, no mention of any Damien, who also has never been spoken of in any (credible) publication on this matter, that I'm aware of, ever before. Conveniently, this Damien is uncontactable, due to him being a grass. Another point that I've always considered in all of this is that about 9 months before the murders, Tony had gained access to a shooter with a suppresser, just for emergencies. Once he had it, he stashed it away, he didn't walk about with it, but it was there as insurance. Pat also had a small arsenal of readily accessible guns if he needed one. Those three were almost always tooled up, not with shooters, but at least with a blade, knuckledusters or some CS, it's pretty standard stuff in that line of business and especially since they were doing so much gear, they were paranoid as fuck! Strangely, not one weapon was found on any of them by police, nor in the car, which very strongly suggests that whoever took them there that night was known to them and also trusted by them and posed no real threat, which rules out this Damien fella as the one who led them there, for the simple reason that nobody knew Nipper's mate Damo, so they would've tooled up to go anywhere with him.

Having never done Martial Arts in his life, Nipper is sitting in an MMA gym, and I must ask, what on earth was he thinking…about to drop the biggest revelation in Essex underworld history and he's dressed in a wooly Christmas jumper? How can we all be expected to take a man seriously if he can't even take himself seriously? Never once looking at the camera, he answers a series of questions around the subject of the "Essex Boys"; tediously saving the so-called best bit till last. I'm guessing this was to build some theatrical suspense. When mentioning me, he confirms some things I've previously said, such as the fact that I helped him out by speaking to the lads about leaving his family out of their dispute and that he asked me to shoot him in the head because he couldn't cope anymore. Most who have seen the recording will pick up on the sheer contempt in Steven's voice when he talks about me. Now add that to when he done an interview with Bernard and was calling me names, you like me will probably be wondering what his problem is with the only man who tried to help him out. Incidentally, when he called me in tears fearing for his life, why didn't he call his buddy, the self-proclaimed "leader" and "founder" of the supposed "Essex Boys gang?"

A few people have suggested to me that it can only be through bitterness and jealousy that the man wastes his energy harbouring such contempt for someone who helped him. Nipper seems to want to earn money (maybe for some better fitting clothes) and gain recognition, but he's had no success at either. So, I wonder if this could be the source of his problem with me, but do I care? No, not in the slightest! If he was a man I respected, I would have spoken to him about it, but he's no gangster, he failed at everything he ever did; he was a burglar (a very disrespected level of crime by proper villains) that got caught and banged up and when he didn't get caught, he blew his spoils on drugs and became a junkie, he even tried to shoot Pat dead while Pat held his son in his arms – imagine that being the pinnacle of your career and claim to fame. Yes, he tried shooting Pat from the shadows whilst Pat was holding his infant son, where as a man would've confronted him face to face. In his true form, Nipper fumbled and missed the kill shot, then when Tony went to Nipper's house to beat him up for shooting Pat in the arm,

Nipper tried to shoot Tony and Craig but again fucked that up. He thought he'd gain fame through the documentary and book with Bernard, but by Nippers own admission, that was a complete fuck up too! Possibly the biggest mistake of Nippers "career" as a (failed) criminal was what led him to fall out with Pat in the first place; Nipper told the lads that he and his pal had £100,000 worth of some valuable documents that had been chored out of the Post Office, for which I had a buyer. So, I let Pat and Tony put a deal together and said to give me a drink out of it. The goods that Nipper had offered up never emerged and Pat, not pleased at looking like a mug, flipped his fucking lid and told Nipper he'd get him for putting him in such a position.

On to the actual shootings now and we're asked to believe that 2 men in their prime, fit as fuck and paranoid as hell, watched Craig get shot to death in the driver's seat and they patiently waited in their seats as Nippers Dad ran around the 4x4 in the snow to take aim and kill them too. Obviously pre-empting an element of skepticism from viewers, Nipper had an explanation ready for this, in that they were "so stunned" from the sound of the gun shot that they simply couldn't move. Well, a loud bang wouldn't stop many people from at least trying to clamber out of the door and escape, or even at least duck, but we know all three were found sitting normally. I could understand some kind of ringing ears-based concept if the shots had been fired inside the car, but they weren't, they were fired from several feet away in an environment with plenty around to help soak up the noise, like the snow and the trees, plus the windows were closed on the motor. The police already said there was at least 2 gunmen, and I don't believe for a second this could be a 1-man job. So why were spectators of the case treated to this well put together video now, around the anniversary of the murders and 4 years after Nippers Dad actually died? Nobody's going to drop their old man in it while he's alive of course, but I fail to see who benefits from this, aside from Steven, after all, if the wrong men got banged up, why leave them to rot for an extra 4 years! I know what I make of all this, but I'll leave the readers to decide for themselves!

When James English approached my people and invited me onto his show, they reported back to me about their due diligence and what caught my eye was the fact that James once took it upon himself to sleep rough, as part of a homelessness awareness campaign, and I respected both his efforts and the cause, so I agreed to take the interview.

Whilst Jason and I were still writing this book, the podcast host treated us to another Nipper Ellis interview, but this one was even better than the last…well, at least better in terms of comedy value! When I'd met James in person, he seemed like a right decent guy, plus his podcast does well on YouTube, so hats off to him for that and I sincerely hope that his number of views soar after people read this and head over to his channel to see James endure Nipper waffling on at him in a confused, fumbling, buffoon-like state! As I said, from what I know of him, I like James, so I felt for him during his interview with Nipper, as he looked like a man who regretted having put himself in the room in which he was now sitting! Someone commented to me that towards the end of the interview, "James looked like he wanted to grab his equipment and run out the room, straight back to Scotland, as fast as he could!" Even the best show hosts and post-editors in the world would have struggled to turn what he had before him into anything that anyone could consider to be "good watching."

Back in the MMA gym again for whatever reason, but it was nice to see Nipper had dug out a shirt this time, though that was to be the last of the positive surprises! Early in the interview, I found it rather disturbing to hear Nipper say that because his dad was such a big-time, impressionable gangster, he had always wanted him (his own father) to be the sperm-donor so that he himself

(Nipper) could have children! I couldn't help but picture Nipper calling up the stairs; "Come on Steven Junior, we're off to Daddy-Grandad's house now!" I tried to push Nipper's statement out of my mind, but the twisted thoughts just kept coming…was he going to ask his dad to donate a jar of sperm, or was he going to arrange for his father to shag the lucky lady in order to impregnate her?

The mostly recycled tales of botched burglaries just kept coming and even James ended up commenting on Nipper's clear lack of ability as an actual criminal. Jumping all over the place, from one story to another then back again, Nipper even started to appear frustrated with himself when he couldn't get his act together and recall any timelines, or chain of events either correctly or accurately. Nipper had fumbled his way through about the first quarter of the interview, crying regularly, then much like the wall behind him, the real cracks started to appear in his stories! Along came that resentfulness, too, as he's forced to mention me; "Tony came in with Carlton, Carlton Leach, another hooligan" he reluctantly said in a flippant tone, with extra emphasis on hooligan, as though a failed burglar is in some way a better man than a football hooligan. It must have pained Nipper to listen to James going on to say that I'd been on the show and he "really rates me", watch the clip closely and you'll see Steven actually biting his tongue as he says that I'm "Just Carlton" and people don't impress him!

I completely agree with Steven that Craig was Tony's gofer, and I understand his lack of confidence when he sits and ponders whether Pat was actually his true friend or not; "Pat and I…we were friends…and I'm sure we were…we…I know we were…" Well, I hate to kick a weak man while he's down, but Nipper was to Pat, what Craig was to Tony, a gofer, an errand boy, someone to hold onto shit that they didn't want to be caught with themselves, something Nipper confirms with the story of Pat's cocaine in Nipper's wardrobe! Craig and Nipper were both weak-minded men, desperate to be liked and fit in to some kind of family-like unit or firm and thinking back, it was unfair of Pat and Tony to take advantage of them like they did, but they'd left themselves wide open for it through their desperation to be wanted by someone....just like when some arsehole kicks his pet dog, that dog always comes back, wagging its tail and gazing lovingly up at its owner, knowing that a swift kick could be imminent, but that poor little mut just keeps hoping that its owner will eventually begin to treat it equally...someday!

The most revelatory thing Nipper had to say, in my opinion, was that he got arrested for three attempted murders, possession of a firearm, counterfeit bank notes and some blank documents, then his appearance in the dock was in no less than that of a closed court! I'm advised by legal counsel not to share my full opinion on this, and I'm sure there are many reasons for a closed court, but unfortunately, Nipper had forgotten the reason for his court appearance being held in secret...

What Nipper does know, however, is that Tony, Pat and Craig all made statements against him in order to get him sent back to prison and luckily, Nipper's friend pretended to be his brother and snuck into the closed court room with a tape recorder and captured evidence that the 3 men were all grasses. Sadly, Nipper's friend is dead now and no one knows where the recording is...Ah! Here we are again where Nipper does have someone to back his story up, but they're not able to speak!

The most annoying thing for Nipper about me sharing my opinion in this book is that he's sick of talking about the Essex Boys, he wants to leave it all behind him and not keep dragging it up: "Poor Nipper," I hear you say! So that in mind, if I may ask a question: Nipper, why did you organise an entire boxing gym, film crew, director and show host, plus a plea for 1000 YouTube subscribers, in order to release "The Big Confession" to the public, if you don't want to talk about it anymore?

I know better than most, how hard it can be to recall something that took place 20 plus years ago in great detail, though I have successfully done it many times in front of live audiences of hundreds, but during this interview Nipper was giving, James asks Nipper directly about the claim that his dad had committed the murders and I was absolutely shocked at Nipper's blatant reluctancy to answer the questions directly! Bearing in mind, at this point he's doing the rounds on any podcast that will have him, with nothing new or interesting to say other than the big confession and all of a sudden, it seems he's not actually that certain after all! "Did your dad do it?" "Errm…well that's what he told me." I don't think there's anything else left to say on the matter, if Nipper himself isn't even that convinced anymore!

Nipper, John Wholmes and several others have allowed themselves to be used by Bernard and consequently become wrapped up in his attempts to verify himself, but every single person to ever fall into his trap has ended up falling out with him or parking him up, and I've always wondered how people fall for it…Bernard has next to no verifiable background, his whole back-story is effectively planted by himself, much like any undercover police officer would do before trying to slip into an organised crime outfit. I'm shocked that even Carnaby, in their pursuit of a party and a pound note, have stooped so low as to make a film about a doorman who grassed and turned on everyone he ever knew, but in my opinion, their worst crime to date has to be getting Vinnie to play the no-mark! I see what they've done, from a business point of view putting Vinnie's mug-shot on the posters will mislead people into believing it's a big budget film, perhaps even dupe some more of the youngsters out there into thinking Bernard was what he claims, and that right there is the tragedy, they've given the bullshitter another platform from which to spout, even though he's never had an ounce of credibility.

Friend or Foe? Terry Turbo was a known name on the rave scene, one of the boys, one of a few who I considered to be a friend. When I say friend, I mean friend, not a mate, pal or acquaintance, an actual friend. When we were discussing casting for ROTF 1, Terry wanted a major role and he'd worked hard to help finance the film, so he deserved it. He ideally wanted to play Tony and I backed that bid fully, because I felt Terry would do an excellent job, one that would have made Tony Tucker proud. Terry Stone and I spent a lot of time together discussing the role, he really wanted to know about Tony as a person, as a man, which is a sign of a good actor, but more than that, I felt he would go the extra mile to do Tony justice, knowing what it meant to me.

I don't know at exactly what point it went wrong, but in my opinion, Terry sold out. He went from being one of the lads and a personal friend of mine, to being (again, in my opinion) a fame whore. Some of the shit he's been involved in is unforgivable to me. Even before ROTF Origins, he started falling over himself to get in with Bernard O'Mahoney, just to get an acting credit. I actually called Terry up one day to ask what the fuck he was doing working with this bullshitter, and he told me, "Well Carl I'm an actor now and that's what actors do!" Maybe I hold some people in too higher regard sometimes, but I would never turn my back on everyone and everything I ever knew or stood for, then roll out a cop-out line like that.

If I recall correctly, it was in December 2018 when the ROTF producers started pushing a series of promo videos on social media. Jay called me proper early one morning, so I knew it must be important; like me he's always lively in the mornings, but he rarely calls me before I've had chance to have two coffees and a look at the news! He told me he's sent me a link over and that I'm not going to be happy with what I see. I grabbed my coffee from the machine and quickly went about starting the video off and there he was, Terry Stone dressed as Santa Clause and wearing that Tony Tucker wig! Snorting cocaine, talking bollocks and acting like an absolute prick, nothing like Tony at all, I was absolutely outraged. This little lot have resorted to churning out fiction about 3 real men in order to make money and become more famous, but this was just an insult to a man's memory, stooping so low, they clearly never considered that these men aren't around to defend themselves anymore (though their families have to continually suffer this) - so to be making them out to be such morons is muggy at best. Knowing I was seething, Gemma told me to calm the fuck down, then call Jay back. Believe me, more than one way to deal with this was discussed, but I agreed to try Jay's idea first. He was pissed off too, he knows what Tony was to me and that I'm a moral person, therefore I expect others to have at least some moral compass too! So, I shared my feelings on Twitter in reply to where the video was posted, and it turned out that hundreds of people were also disgusted by this cheap attempt to grab attention. The film producers tried to defend their poorly judged move, Terry contacted me to apologise for his involvement and whilst I respect him for saying sorry, it was too little too late for me. There's no reason Turbo couldn't have said no to this farcical, but I think he was too carried away with "being Tony Tucker" to stop and think…. Terry was not the same man that I once called a friend. Public outrage continued in the Twittersphere; seems they'd gone too far in defaming a dead man this time! A limited company cropped up, seemingly from nowhere, to valiantly declare that it was all their doing and that Carnaby had played no part in it, they said that they had removed the video (which hadn't contained their name) from Carnaby's own YouTube channel. It was a small victory, but once again, I'd had about a week of bullshit, all because they just can't be left to rest in peace!

What are you going to do? I don't know who actually shot

Tony, Pat and Craig that night and I don't believe, after all these years, we'll ever know exactly what went on, but I do know that no amount of talking, arguing, debating or investigation is going to bring Tony back. I'm going to take this opportunity to address some common questions that have plagued me for almost a quarter of a century now.

Am I angry about the murders? Not anymore. On the emotional rollercoaster I was on after it happened, anger featured high on the list of feelings, but I no longer harbour such anger or rage, because if I didn't move past that it would've consumed me and destroyed my life, as well as those around me. If I had carried on the way I was going in 1996, I may just as well have been in the car with them.

Am I looking to take revenge? When talk that Jack Whomes was due out imminently, this kept cropping up all the more. As I said, we don't know who committed the murders, Jack Whomes and Mick the Pilot both deny it. I moved past anger a very long time ago and have no firm reason to direct hatred at anyone. In addition, I've asked myself what I would do if those 3 were after me and I can only conclude that I would have done something similar, because Pat and Tony were a serious force together. Not to say that if I met the killers in another life, I'd shake their hands and be best pals, but 'Live by the sword, die by the sword' is very fitting here and I'd love it if just one youngster out there heeded the warning of that proverb and chose a different path.

4 FOOTBALL DAYS

Following West Ham for me was everything - it encapsulated all that I knew and understood about my life and growing up in east London. Being that my late dad was the start, main and most valued reason I went to the games, it has to be said that there was always something special about being from the same neighbourhood that spawned the captain and club, who took us to the top in 1966 - Bobby Moore, a local lad and West Ham, who's players Martin Peters and Geoff Hurst made it happen and us known to the world.

Following and supporting the club allowed for some great times to be remembered, some more than others...... and then there's those that can never be put into words. Being a West Ham supporter for as long as I can remember, I would say gave me a sense of pride; for me, it is something that can never be totally explained and certainly not in a way that would do the experience any level of justice......there really wasn't any other club or sport that came close.

We lived on Green Street; the Romford rd. end, so we were literally minutes from the ground. Everyone in the family including our neighbours was a supporter, which meant it (the club) was in most of what we did and how we lived, and there wasn't a time that someone wasn't having a conversation without the local club being mentioned. So, you can imagine when a local lad took us to the world cup and our voice to be heard in 1966, not forgetting the club winning the FA cup in 1964, '75 and then in 1980, each and every time the whole area came alive, everything was claret and blue. Everyone celebrated and was proud of the place we all called home. A great sense of pride and accomplishment was born of those wins…....and this was all within my childhood. For a young east London boy, this was a magical time. People that went to the same schools, walked the same streets and a club of the same area as you, made it seem that anything was possible and attainable in the eyes of a young working-class boy. For me, it was more than just a game; much, much more – 'it' is something you can't buy, borrow, or adopt, it's simply something you're born with and if at this stage, any part of what I've said, doesn't make sense to you, or you can't relate to the whole 'football thing,' then you'll never understand.

I'm a big believer in supporting your local club, you're maintaining a level of backing for both the community and it's social and cultural identity. The way I see it, when you invest a level of support for your local team, you keep everything alive – so West Ham simply made sense. You were all part of the same infrastructure; the club was seen as much a part of the community and its existence as the local pub your dad and uncles drank in and the shops your parents went to each week. The fabric of east London was made up of everything around you and the team you supported. There was never a question of, 'why do you support West Ham?', it was a question of, 'why don't you?'. Remembering this was a time when lads across the country supported their local team. Certainly, a long time before the cockney reds and plastic armchair-type supporters who now superficially choose a team based on their place in the premier league.

When I've been asked about why that level of violence existed, not only at football (that I was proud to be part of) but also with known and written about villains that came from east London, I think it's just within our DNA, but also some of it has to do with our local history. There was without question, a level of poverty that led some of post-World War 2 England into some sort of villainy and on many different levels, but during the war, Hitler reigned down more bombs on the east end than any other part of London. What was once standing, by and large was destroyed. Families, their homes, culture and way of life was attacked, but the good old British Bulldog spirit is one that made east enders unbreakable. Old film footage will show families coming out of bomb shelters only to see their homes and the community they grew up in totally smashed to pieces. None gave up, in fact it only made east enders more resilient and defiant to that level of oppressive authority. Of course, poverty led some to 'wheel and deal', but maybe that's why we've remained such a tight knit community against what could be perceived as any type of governmental presence in our neck of the woods. For much of London, and east London in particular, everything was a fight, and to be honest, I think most in the east end wouldn't have dealt with it any other way; they certainly wouldn't have given up and moved away. The philosophy and trademark of the east end has always been a shared one of, 'be thankful for what you've got' and being grafters.

I came into my own when I was about 12 or 13 years old. I wanted, like most kids of that age more independence, breaking away from their mum's apron strings and hanging out with your dad. My new family were mates from the same area, who of course supported West Ham and my home would soon become what was once known as the north bank. Being of that age, which was the back end of the skinhead era, we all wanted to roll with the big boys. These were all of a real working-class identity - gritty and as game as they come. To see grown men having it out with the visiting fans in the away end was something to be marveled at. Typically, it was only a handful of West Ham fans, no more than 10 - 15 and surrounded by hundreds of visiting fans, who to be fair, were as game as the local lads, but what made our lads stand out was their level of sheer violence and willingness at inflicting as much damage and hurt on the visiting fans, all the while being totally outnumbered and not giving an inch - it really was something I knew I wanted to be part of and a necessary progression as a hard-core supporter of the club.

Being from east London, there was a certain reputation to live up to. I felt there was a benchmark that needed to be met, the Krays and a lot of serious heavy-duty villains were all east London. In villainy, south London criminals were known for being good money makers; east London villains were known for their level of violence. To support and promote our team in the same way, meant I had to be part of any level of what went on and brought us into the limelight; even if it was by some people's standards for the wrong reasons, but back then, my thoughts were it's better to be remembered as a someone, than a never heard of no one and for me, being from East London and supporting West Ham was like a badge of honour. To me, even pre-teens, I believed West Ham was ours, not only to support, but to promote and in some sense defend. The working class, typically only have their community and what can be held in their own two hands, it was all you had and what you believed in - and to us, West Ham was part of that equation, and we owned the visitors end lock, stock and barrel.

Getting to where I wanted to be, was a fairly quick progression, I matured somewhat quicker than a lot of other lads. I think it was because even though I was not that long into my teen years, I identified more with older lads than those of my own age group. I was now hanging around with an older established firm at West Ham. The Teddy Bunter Firm were the first group to take me under their wing so to speak. Teddy and Bunter were two of their main faces and their firm were knocking about the same time as Bill Gardner and the old Mile end mob, both groups were mostly built up of dockers and factory workers, all grown men who simply enjoyed really tearing into the visiting fans each and every week, who themselves came down and wanted to have a go at the cockneys.

One of the first London derbies I remember going to, and if memory serves me well, was the first time I met Cass, it was when a group of us younger lads went to

Highbury playing Arsenal (their ground). There's something special about going to an away game with all your football mates and jumping on the train, you get a great air of superiority and feeling…. like you're one of the chaps. It really can give you a great sense of confidence, but as we learned that day, that same sense of confidence will be questioned when you come bowling around the corner close to their ground and you're suddenly confronted by much older seasoned hooligans that are growling and screaming for your blood.

A quick lesson was learned for me on this trip. Even though I was on a path of getting a bit of a reputation and recognised amongst a few top faces at West Ham, been amongst and fought alongside one of the main firms, it didn't count for much when you're on your own and away from the main firm, I guess you could say it's like owning and wearing a new pair of running trainers, it doesn't make you an athlete and won't win you gold. I'd be lying if I said I didn't quickly rethink my approach to the ground and ditching the claret and blue scarf that I had previously wrapped around my wrist (which was a common practice back then). Looking back, I can laugh at this event, but there's been similar situations that have resulted in people getting seriously damaged and even killed.

Early days of being part of the ICF: Let's consider the 1970's and early 80's, running with the West Ham lads, even before the ICF was formed, as well as in its heyday, I'm talking before everyone had a mobile phone, never mind the internet and fucking Facebook! The proper serious, core firm looking for weekly agg always travelled by car or train to away games, sometimes we hired vans or jumped in the back of someone's transit, because you were too easy to spot on coaches and the official travel always picked up a police escort on route, which isn't helpful! Plus, when you were herded onto the specials, you were treated like shit, sometimes you were classed and treated less than cattle on their way to the slaughterhouse. We always had good numbers when going up as far as the Midlands, usually about 3-4k, but much further north than that and our numbers could drop to 300-400, but what we lacked in numbers, was overcompensated by people that wouldn't take a single back foot or leave without having caused some lifelong health issues for those that got in their way.

Being that we took what we did and considered ourselves serious supporters, we decided to swerve the normal routes and means of transport and go a bit up market and what better way than by intercity (train). The specials, coaches and small minibuses would be hired and used for the away games, but like most things in business, it was always about profit, not comfort. As working class, football supporters and being from the east end we'd been looked down on for too many years and traveling by the cheapest, dirtiest and less appealing types of transport only encouraged people to see us as nothing more than third-rate, low-class citizens. So, we opted for a service with all the trimmings, like access to a buffet-bar, better toilets and space away from the scarfers. We started using the intercity trains for away games – fewer prying eyes over what plans were being made, a lot more space and freedom and definitely more upscale which we always said was a 'bit of us' – arriving before the specials and mass of fans, feeling relaxed and ready to meet the opposition proved the way to go, and as history has shown the name was born of our choice of travel. Then all the other factions and firms within West Ham came together and started using the same method of transport. What started as about 20 hard core fans on the train eventually grew to several hundred. You could literally walk from one end of the train to the other and in each and every single carriage there wasn't one person that wasn't really up for it – all proper fighters and with that turn out, it proved to make a big difference when you go to an away game. What went from one incident when we were ambushed outside a train station up north and having to fight for our lives, to then coming out mobbed handed and literally tearing through what ever came at you.

Considering what we were up to and being such a tight knit group, one interview that was a bit of a rarity was the one shown on Thames Television back in 1985, titled Hooligan. There was myself, Vince Riordan, who was the bass player for the Cockney Rejects and another pal, Keith all sat around the table giving an insight into what and why we consciously involved ourselves in fighting at football. What made it that much more 'unique' was we never allowed outsiders into our circle and certainly not an outsider with a camera crew – anyone with half a brain knew that would only incriminate you and land you in it, as this was a time of the Thatcher era who's governing body were handing out hefty fines and lengthy prison sentences, but for the ICF, who had now gained a reputation not only in London, but across the country, to a degree this was putting us 'up there' and letting every other firm know about us that much more…… sort of rubbing their faces in it. I remember Cass telling me while we were in the Britannia pub in Plaistow; a pub back then that was thick with proper hard core ICF, again no outsiders, about some bloke who was interested in getting our story and allowing people to see and hear what we had to say. Right off the bat it was a "No!" At every corner and any opportunity, lads were getting early morning police raids and finding themselves inside court rooms, but eventually Cass convinced me this was a good idea and the person behind it was decent and had no hidden agenda. So, we agreed to have a talk with the man behind it, we come to know him as, Butch; he was the writer and director of the documentary. Over a period of time, and in his defence, Butch showed his worth and came to a lot of games with us. He came on his own, and to be in the thick of what we were doing and in the middle of some of the biggest fights we had, I had to take my hat off to him. After it was aired, what was seen reflected who we were and no discrediting to any of the lads involved…. again, this was a rarity at the time and especially for us to be front and centre.

London showdowns were highly anticipated and very heartfelt! For me, the toughest London club we came up against back in the day was Millwall; love or hate them, you had to respect them, they were a tough firm! Like east Londoners, they'd had tough upbringings, the same social and economic backgrounds and a shared, long hatred of a club they were once neighbours with. There's truth in the saying that the closest of opposition can be the one most hated (Tottenham and Arsenal as an example). I considered Chelsea's and Tottenham's firms on par with one another, coming very close in after Millwall. I got chored 3 times at Tottenham away, the most notable time, I was up in court 2 days before my first wedding and as a result of that day out, I found myself struggling at my own wedding. Where my knee was so fucked up, I couldn't even kneel at the alter and most of the guests had black eyes and broken noses! Like I said earlier, football was my life and anyone I was in a relationship with knew that West Ham and all that went along with it was part of the relationship too. Last but not least in London would be Arsenal's firm and just because they are ranked below the others in my list, doesn't mean they aren't up there with some of the toughest football firms in the world.

We had many run-ins with Liverpool F.C.'s firm, usually on Main Road outside Stanley Park and they were game as, but the worst rucks in this neck of the woods, I have to say, were against the Everton lot! As we went near Lime Street Station, you'd get absolutely swamped by them boys, but we held our own. One time we went up to a West Ham v Liverpool match and Everton's firm turned out...unbelievable! I remember it was pitch black and they came out of no-where, started pelting us with rocks and bottles, a broken brick hit me in the throat and knocked me down, I got up and couldn't speak for ages!

Don't think I'm claiming we always came out on top either! All sides fought hard battles up and down the country, sometimes we got turned over, sometimes we came out on top, but either way...it was fucking great stuff and not in a million years do I ever have any regrets! The terraces where I once roamed made me the man I am today. There is no question in my mind, the men I fought alongside and against are the same men you'd want to be there if we ever went to war – some of the most vicious and bravest of men, willing to fight over a patch of dirt, an inch of ground and a stretch of land and all in the name of a club and flag, those are known in ancient times as warriors, in modern times as soldiers and remember, those that are opposed to violence are always protected by those that aren't. Nowadays, loads of the football lads from different firms are friends and we get together occasionally, we also support each other's causes and some of us can call upon each other day or night, if need be.

In conclusion - For me, football was more than just kicking off every week - it was everything from walking up Green street to the ground and the sound of the fans intensifying as you got closer. Standing outside in the queue, then the clicking of the turnstile as you went in. The thousands of people around you, all there for the club I loved. As the years progressed and I got a bit older, it then become about the early morning cafe stop before an away game and the walk to the train station. It was standing in the local pub taking the piss out of each other and the banter that existed between mates. It was having a 2 and 2 in the local pie and mash shop, that only a few years before, the same window you passed and the seats you're now sitting in were once occupied by the older generation. Then of course, the meet before the home game and the conversations about if the visiting firm would have a decent turn out. The Feeling like Billy-big bollocks as you walked into the ground and onto the terraces firm handed, the nods and acknowledgement from others and the sound of your name…. and that feeling never faded or got old – EVER! Each and every week, the same excitement and energy would be there, for me it never got old or felt less than the previous week, I called it, 'the noise of Upton Park', it just sucked you in. There was a concert every week at my football club, and we were the rock stars. Drug addicts will tell you how they have to double up on a fix or look for something stronger for a better high. Adrenaline junkies will be forced to out-do themselves by looking for something a bit more dangerous so they can get the next big rush but going to football and being part of all that went on, never felt any less, week in, week out and you knew you always had to be there. One missed game and you felt you was missing out on what could be compared to something previously not discovered and now being introduced to the world for the first time, and you weren't there or part of it.

Why was the violence and the televised national mayhem part of what I did? Just like the conversations and my experiences that were born of that club following, were all part of the same jigsaw puzzle and not one piece independently would work for me, it was also the friendships and allegiances found there that would last a lifetime. Even away from football, violence seemed always to be there. One night a few of us ventured over to a club in Charring Cross, nothing in mind or on our agenda than a few drinks and trying to see what luck we would have with the ladies. You would think that wearing no colours and being off our manor would be a simple one and of no conflict, but inevitably there was never a quiet night for me. Even whilst minding my own business and having a piss in the toilet, I found someone breathing down my neck, demanding to know what team I supported. So, like anyone from my part of the world, I proudly said, "West Ham," and with this announcement I found myself turning around and having to floor this loudmouth. Now any other time, that should've put an end to his aggravating attempts, but as we found out, a good few Chelsea were in there that night and exit and what unfolded is something that still makes me laugh to this day. The exit of the club was a narrow hallway, so as they came out, perfectly lined up they walked straight into one of our firm who'd armed himself with a fire extinguisher. One by one they fell, as he was smashing them in the face. Unfortunately for the man coming out, it was too late to see what had happened to his pal who'd come out before him, as he'd not had time to turn around and warn him as he'd been knocked spark out. What remained was a bunch of pissed up, gobby cunts lying in a pile outside the club.

The reality of it all was football, our firm, the people around us and all that I saw was part of that, and it was something that we'd created - we lived and was in control of. Football hooliganism and the ICF was of our making, a private club - it was one that we didn't need anyone's permission to form or exist - in some respects it was us sticking two fingers up at those that would never allow or accept that we were part of the same human race as them. At the time, there was very little else you could do or say to get any recognition; those that wanted success and coming from east London, did so by either fighting, football or villainy. You had to make nothing less than great, if not exceptional efforts to gain just an inch to climb that ladder of success and acknowledgement and it was through my actions at West Ham, I felt I'd found that. I'd earned my place through what I guess you could call an apprenticeship; having a row with visiting firms or traveling to away games and having it every week, come rain or shine…. I was there.

Some might say that, back then a large part of what we did was as a result of boredom – as now kids have the Internet, play stations etc., and there may be some truth to that - but the game of football was something that everyone I knew identified with and West Ham was the place to display and promote what and why I carried on the way I did. The east end and football were the perfect platform for promoting what and who I was and my agenda.

The young working-class kids of the 90's and today, they'll never experience what we had as a weekend addiction. In addition to over policing of the grounds (and not the streets late at night) and CCTV, there's too many distractions from what we knew as boys. A poorly substituted existence is shoved under the noses of today's younger generation with game consoles and laptops, and it's here I'd like to commend any parent who takes the time with their kids, encouraging them to have a healthy childhood, one away from the influences and toxic nature of anything that keeps their kids glued to TVs and the like. We made our own entertainment - a football and a patch of grass, or even a football and a wall was all that was needed; it was simple, and everybody could be part of it - it really was your mates and jumpers for goalposts. There's also some truth that if you didn't have an older brother, who may even have led different social interests or even a father figure, there was nothing like football and the crowd that would be a healthy substitute and the biggest family you could ever wish for. In our crowd, there was always someone to watch out for you.

The other issue I want to raise is what I believe was and continues to be the belittling of us as a collective. So, let's put a few things to bed - the first of their claims being that people that fought and carried on at football, aka football hooligans, did so because it was solely down to tribalism, a lack of education and boredom. What a load of bollocks! As I've mentioned, we did so for a sense of belonging, something of our creation and we could control. Pre- and post-match having it large on and off our manor, did they honestly think we went to football and rowed because people identified with a tribe, didn't excel in school and we were bored? As far as I know, the only thing 'tribal' was Birmingham's mob that were known as the Zulu's, a lot of lads gained success before, during and after the ICF and there's never been a single day in my life where I'd say I was bored. Being branded a West Ham/ICF football hooligan was, in a sense, for me and many others a badge of honour and we wore it as proud as a peacock. The fact we'd created something, and they were trying to take it away from us only encouraged lads that much more. The academic and tribalism comments along with them referring to our behaviours and beliefs associated with race, ethnicity, language, religion, that is such an outsider's view and an uneducated look at it. Like most firms, no one gave a shit about race, religion or language at West Ham – FACT! The only colours that mattered were claret and blue - end of!

Only someone who's never truly identified with football fans and or firms would try and compartmentalise us by saying such ignorant small-minded comments. It's just another typical university bod's attempt at looking down on us and at something they have no idea about with their upper middle-class view and interpretation. Also, for those relying on the internet for an insight and some half-wits view or claim to what went on and who was there, won't do you any favours either. Reading Oliver Twist won't allow you to relate or understand an orphan's life; it'll only show your ignorance. Only known people will ever be able to give verse and testament to what and how it was. So, if you've never stood with working class lads, was about from the 60s through the mid 80's, save yourself the embarrassment, take a seat and be quiet!

What I think is closer to the truth is, no industry or commercial enterprise would've had the level of creativity or originality in what we had made in terms of terrace history. As an example, anything to do with real terrace history and then shown in tv, film and the daily rag is laughable and a far stretch from reality. Only when the lads themselves have put themselves out there has there been a commendable result (but please don't quote Green St.) and believe me, if 'they' thought they could have taken what came from working class lads and the football days, much like they did with the 'casual' era and bastardised and earned from it, they'd capitalized on it and run with it all the way to the bank. Their continued efforts at name calling and labelling is only a reflection of their wishing to have been behind what we created and another example of their lack of involvement – the sheer lust and wish of inclusiveness that they would sell their souls for will always be treated with contempt from those that were really there – So, a message from myself and all the original lads, go fuck yourselves!

Steve Guy – "….he's the father and big brother I could've only wished for and he's a man who could not be traded for all the tea in China."

For those of my era, the early '80s will promote conversations and memories on their first pint, football match or buying of their first pair of trainers……not influenced by their parents – mine was meeting up with Carlton and with a man like him, the saying, "I am not led, I lead," doesn't even come close. Looking back and thinking about how long we've been around each other, the things we've gotten up to and into, I'm surprised we don't have more scars than we actually do.

It has to have been, since '87, that I was first in Carlton's company; and that alone makes me feel old but going to football (West Ham) at a time and place, like most working class and the communities that we grew up in, was a home and refuge for me. It was also a time that you learned the value of what a friendship was, those that you could really count on, who you could walk and talk with, and that'd ultimately show people for who they really were and it's since then, Carlton has never changed, in either who he is as a person, the strength, beliefs or the character that he is.

He is someone that has never judged me on the things I got up to going back over 4 decades; as it was a time in my life that I would indiscriminately, and without any thought of repercussion take from those (firms) that had it, and if they didn't tie it down, it was mine! It was also at this time of my life that if I had a row with someone, no matter their standing or place, it was never asked what it was over, or with, as Carlton never allowed people to be around him or his family (for too long anyway) that he wasn't willing to call out, and I never was – the saying, "Proper people never suffer fools lightly," tells you that after 40 plus years, that he doesn't have friends, as they come and go, but family.

My relationship has been one that has seen him for, as much as his strengths, as his weaknesses; and that's something I have trouble accepting - the "hanger-on's." I feel he lets people take advantage of what has to be one of his (many) admiral qualities, and that's his willingness to help people…... and he's helped a lot! They eventually take the piss, but their selfish and personal agenda only then says more about Carlton and what he is all about – and that's helping others before himself. If the truth is known, he's put a great deal of food on a lot of people's tables, and many of those same people, that have short memories, are the same people who will enjoy a free meal, but to further add insult, these cheap liberty takers, don't even have the common courtesy to "leave a tip," let alone a kick back to him. He's a man that will allow someone to live and survive from his efforts, more than their own. He has always helped those that say they're in trouble, simply, and as I've seen first-hand and more often than not, out of loyalty.

I've seen him when he's been on top of the world, and when he's been at his most vulnerable. One of those times was when he lost his dad, and for a man that many will see as someone who is allegedly, as a cold, ruthless and heartless "gangster," then confide in me, says a lot about a person, as only a man will truly let his guard down when he has to. The bond and closeness that was lost after his dad passed, greatly affected him, as it did me, as this was a relationship that I only wish I could've had with my own dad, but what I took away from Carlton's loss, was how involved his dad was with Carlton as a father …. to see that bond is more than special, it's something I didn't see as a rarity, but something that was a compliment to both Carlton and his late dad - Norman was a proper gentleman and a lovely man, a loyal husband and a dedicated father.

Dawn raids in the mid-eighties, prison sentences and myself getting pulled in '88, pushed not only me, but a lot of people in different directions, but it didn't matter what time passed, or where we all ended up, Carl' was only a phone call away. I guess you could say I'm an independent, stand on my own feet kind of person, but like I said, it didn't matter how much time had passed, my time away from football or time spent behind the wall, our friendship has been as strong, if not more so as time has passed.

So, there's no way I could put into words, what and how much he is loved and respected, as it simply wouldn't translate, but all I can say is, he's the father and big brother I could've only wished for and he's a man who could not be traded for all the tea in China.

Dave "Robbo" Robinson – QPR – "That's one thing with Carlton, he will always make time for people."

My friendship with Carlton all started through a mutual friend of ours, Steve Guy. A well-known and respected face at Upton Park over the years. My first meet with Steve was in a cafe in Plaistow on a Saturday morning, talking a bit of business before a home game against Leicester. Anyway, to cut a long story short and before you know it, he tells me, "You're with me today, bruv!" I made a call to a good pal of mine at West Ham by the name of Dale Matthews, who seems to know everyone in the East End and with the mention of Steve's name, he commented, "Good stock, Dave". That's all I needed to know. Well, I can't remember what hour I returned home on the Sunday morning, but I was in a right old pickle. After that first meet, I would regularly go over the Boleyn if I wasn't at Rangers and meet up with Steve and the chaps making some good mates over the years and being accepted into the West Ham family but, known as "QPR Dave". I first met Carlton before a night game against Tottenham. Steve and Carlton are very close.

Everyone seemed to be out that night. It was a blinding atmosphere. Steve introduced me to him outside the Boleyn. "Carlt', this is Dave I was telling you about" which drew a grin from Carlton followed by a firm handshake. We went for a drink in the "workies," more commonly known as East Ham Working man's club. It was mobbed in there, but somehow, we managed to get a section of the outside garden. Everyone was coming over wanting to shake his hand or have a photo, but more than anything just to say hello and have a chat with him. That's one thing with Carlton, he will always make time for people. Nice to be nice as they say, unless you've pissed him off! This can also be said of Bill Gardner, aka Mr. West Ham himself and someone Carlton has always looked up to. It wouldn't be right not mentioning Bill in my notes as they are of the same stock, two proper Gents you would trust your life with and as Loyal as you get.

My affiliation with West Ham has been strong over the years, so much so, that whenever I'm down the Bush (Shepherds Bush) I always get a bit of light-hearted stick from the Rangers lads.

Some of those same lads in question I've taken over West Ham with me, before they moved to the "Fish Bowl" in Stratford, and I tell you what - they all loved it! At the end of the day, I bleed Blue & White, I was born and bred a mile away from Loftus Road and although I'm part of a different club and part of the city of London, I see so many similarities between the two clubs. There's a mutual respect, as both have and identify with a working-class background, no glory Hunter fans, a tradition of maverick players and teams playing attractive football….as it was meant to be.

Football has changed massively since the good old days of the 80's and 90's and so with it the social element. For me it's all about the meet with the lads before and after the game. If QPR actually win the game, well, that's a bonus as we accept it's about the day and all those in it, as much as it's about the game its-self…… a big proportion of my mates, some of whom I class as "family" have come from the football world, be it playing or watching on the terraces. Lads from all around the country and into Europe, like-minded people with the same core values, who identify with the traditions and values upheld by the greatest people in a land that gave the world the world's biggest and best of all sports. And that brings me back onto Carlton - I've had the pleasure of being in his company on many occasions over the past few years along with his other half, the beautiful Gemma, and my missus, Sophie. We love each other's company. From Boat party cruises on the Thames, live chats he's hosted, his 60th Birthday party in Essex or visiting them both in

Spain. Sometimes in life you just click with people and it's like that with us. Don't get me wrong, he drives me fucking mad calling me going on about Inter Milan; he's Inter, I'm AC, and that's one thing we don't have in common, but in life, as you get older, your inner circle gets smaller but stronger and Carlton is bang in the middle of that inner circle. My only regret is we never met years earlier, having said that, I'm always here for him and his, as he is for me and mine. I'm grateful and honoured to know him and call him, not only a friend, but a brother he knows.

Dave Walker - "He has always been there for me and I learned very quickly that if you're in his circle, he will do anything for you….."

I first met Carl when I interviewed him for an online fanzine I was running called Sex, Drugs & Carlton Cole. To be honest, I didn't really know what to expect because in the films he's portrayed as a very serious character, so I was surprised to see how funny and jovial he was. We had such a laugh that day and we've been laughing ever since.

Aside from our mutual love of West Ham, we also have another thing in common - our Dads are our heroes, so when I heard that Carlton's had passed away, I felt his pain. I was honoured to be invited to Norman's funeral, where Carlton done him proud. It was also an opportunity to meet his friends and family and I soon realised that he is surrounded by such a lovely group of people, including his partner, Gemma.

One good memory I have and remember well, was when I met him and the boys for a drink on what was the final game at Upton Park before it closed its doors. We agreed to meet at the East Ham working man's club, I got there first and when I arrived the queue must have been a mile long! The guvnor came out and said, "Lads you're looking at least a 2 hour wait to come in!" At that point Carlton and the boys arrived and I told him what I just heard. His response was, "Fuck that" and we walked straight to the front of the queue, past security, through the doors and had a beer in our hands within 5 minutes!

I've enjoyed a few nights out with Carl. He is always the life and soul of the party and if you're in his company, you're having a good time. He had a boat party on the Thames once and there was so much coke on board I'm surprised the fucking thing didn't sink!

If you like your sleep, then going out with Carl probably isn't for you! His 60th was a fantastic night, I took my wife, and everyone made her feel so welcome. I knocked on his hotel room door the following morning to drop off his card and Champers and he looked like a zombie! The sign of another good night.

I have got nothing but love and respect for Carlton. He is a very selfless man who despite his success in life has always stayed very humble and down to earth.

I see him as family now. He has always been there for me, and I learned very quickly that if you're in his circle, he will do anything for you, never asking for anything in return.

5 OVER THE YEARS

The conflict between friendship and business…....it's inevitable, over the years and during your life, you will witness people you know feel the pressures or find themselves in financial hardship; sometimes that wasn't of their making. I felt it an important topic to discuss as I'm sure as the day is long, most of you will have come across someone that tried to confuse your ability in helping them in a business deal as a free meal ticket, or even worse still, they should be given a pass. I've been nothing less than humbled to have been around and worked with some of the most principled people, not just in organized crime, but also what mainstream society has to offer, but as much as I've gotten to work and meet the best, but also the worst. For me, and my chosen type of work, the simple fact the 'worst' exist can in some respects be of benefit and a reminder that greed sometimes knows no limits. It's not that their bullshit and cowardice conning ways are appreciated, but it highlights there are good people in this world, and that level of good is something I value and respect. Money is something that can easily change a weak-minded person's view on integrity and their (lack of) morals – others already had a stain on their soul.

Over the years, I've helped out countless people, some have been friends and so-called friends, with others it was strictly business. I've introduced parties, helped people get funding and investment, licenses and permissions, land and premises. Sometimes the bit of business doesn't work out, which is understandable, but when it does, and everyone involved earns a big lump of cash or an ongoing income, I expect to be looked after a little bit for my efforts, bearing in mind that if it wasn't for me, it wouldn't have happened in the first place; company share-holders and investors get paid and a return for their efforts and invested time too. People have come to me more times than I care to remember and said, "C, I've got

A, B and C, if I can just get XYZ we'll make a fortune." Half the time, when I deliver them the XYZ, they become far too busy to call me, or it turns out that actually, there wasn't quite so much profit in the deal after all and the "we'll make a fortune," suddenly becomes, they'll make a fortune. There are several ways to deal with this scenario and sometimes, I use a combination of them. The first is to demand my cut and collect on it, which is fairly self-explanatory. Why would the agreed rates that you shook on, that guaranteed your return now be less? Can you imagine taking a flight and after successfully and without incident arriving at your destination, only then saying, "yeah, not bad, but I'm only paying half of the agreed ticket price!" The way I look at it is I've trusted you on your end of the deal, I've successfully delivered on my end, so now pay up – services rendered! The second is to shut the work down all together by making a call to the other party, because one out of the two sides will usually have loyalties to me. I'm known for getting results on every level, and that's why people come to me. The third method, is to never, ever, open another door for that person again! Believe it or not, I have had people with the audacity to call me up years later and ask for another favour; when they don't get it, they suddenly wish that they'd done right by me in the first place, because the move currently on the table is always worth even more than the last one was, so it costs them dearly in the long run.

It's not always money on offer; in return for helping people out, protecting people and putting deals together, I've been promised shares and partnerships in all sorts of things, both legit and otherwise. A common line is, 'If you help me with this Carlton, I'll set us up in business, you'll have a regular income for the rest of your life.' The most popular businesses on offer have been a legit debt collection agency (I've been promised about 20 of those), pubs and bars, flipping properties and land deals. Needless to say, 9 out of 10 have been bullshit.

There are of course several stand-up people I can count on and for whom my phone will always be available, and it's the likes of these that keep my faith in humanity – as it's been said, "integrity and principles aren't reserved just for a few, most people know the difference between right and wrong" Sadly, the list of dependable people is far shorter than the list of let-downs! If I wrote the let-down list, I imagine I'd have Greta and her eco-warriors at my door for wasting paper! But my MO has always been one of quality over quantity.

When me and Jay were lining up new bits of work, one of the people I called was Jazz, a former club owner who I'd met back when I was running doors. Jazz owned Shades in Graves End, Kent. We'd hit it off and remained friends for over 18 years by this point. Jazz and I had some great times over those years, laughs, parties, successes. When the 3 of us met up we had a great catch up, Jazz told us how he'd just been pulled over on the way for speeding and had had to put on an American accent when talking to the old bill because he was using a US driver's license, having been banned in the UK! Jazz was a rarity in that he was very clever, a great businessman, but also, he pulled in people he could trust to come along for the ride, even if he wasn't 100% sure he'd need them, because he was happy to 'share the wealth' if it meant keeping a group of mates working together, this wasn't bad business sense it was long term thinking. Unfortunately, he didn't have a need for the setup we had at the time, but he told us details of what he was working on, which was to be kept an absolute secret. He'd bought an old distillery and all the equipment to make his own vodka, he'd also contracted 2 big names in the UK rap scene to front the brand, he took us to his car and showed us the proto-type bottles and labels he'd had made; "Carlton, I want you with me on this one, it will be a good thing for us over the next two years, then I'm 99% sure that one of the big groups will swoop in to buy the brand up, we'll be set for our retirements mate." It sounded great and Jazz was no bullshitter, I told him we should let the youngsters crack on with the leg work and the two of us would be there to oversee and steer the ship. I told Jay on the way home how confident I was in Jazz's plans and in the months to come, Jay met up with Jazz or his people at least once a month. Now money isn't earnt until it's in your hand, but this was looking good. One afternoon I was sitting in the conservatory when my phone rung, I looked and it was Jazz's wife's number, I figured he was calling me from her phone, but no, it was his wife and she sounded terrible in her voice. That feeling of impending doom came over me, I thought she was going to say he was in the hospital after a heart attack, but she explained that after feeling unwell, Jazz had been taken into hospital, turns out he had cancer and he never came back out of there. I don't know what happened to the vodka plans, I guess they died along with Jazz, but that was irrelevant. I was absolutely gutted to have lost an old friend, one who would always call me periodically just to chat, one who would tell me straight if I was doing something that he thought I shouldn't. A mate who whenever I saw his name flush-up on my phone, always made me smile. It's a sad thought knowing that I'll never see that name come up or hear that enthusiastic and welcoming voice with a, "Hello, C! What's going on, brother!" Rest in Peace Jazz.

In business, there is nothing worse than a combination of a man's ego, his ignorance and a belief that corners being cut, won't come back to bite you in the arse. This next story is an example of just that. It all started when an accountant I know called me one day and asked me to go to his offices. He said I might be able to help a friend of his, so we set a meeting for later that week. At the meeting I was informed that this chap, Harry, had recently bought 50 acres of greenbelt land in Essex and even though greenbelt isn't worth as much as normal land, it's still a fair few quid, so money wise, I took this guy seriously. His problem was, he'd over stretched in buying the land, leveraged his other business, his house, the usual stuff and subsequently had needed some short-term cash to stay afloat, I could guess what was coming next in this story! Harry had fallen into the big dark hole that is underground money lending and was, at this point, under serious pressure to meet repayments. Usually, there's nothing that I'm prepared to do to help in this situation, because you borrowed the money, so you have to pay it back, morally it's a difficult case to argue on the borrower's behalf, but with the potentially development value of the land perhaps I could help him to renegotiate his debts. The next big problem when providing services to someone in money trouble is, how the fuck do you get paid! I put this to Harry, and he told me that if I helped him, he'd make me a legal partner in the business, so when the land eventually got planning consent, we'd both be quid's in. Dubious, I ran the concept past a few people I know in the property development arena, and they came back with fairly positive thoughts, it wasn't going to be too difficult to renegotiate Harry's repayments and buy him the time he said he needed if I just called in a favour or two, so I accepted his offer. If I could turn back the clock, I'd would've had to politely decline the proposal and leave the fella to sort his own mess out, but hindsight is a wonderful thing, as they say! Bearing in mind, the plan for the land was to have planning consent within 18 months, then sell the land to a large house builder and be out of it all inside two years, you can imagine my dismay when the saga was continuing 10 years later! I can't go into all the full details, but across this decade of ups and downs, I've had to go and have chats with councilors, my guys have delivered numerous envelopes, I've supported Harry in several bids to keep renegotiating his street debts and buy him 'just a little more time', all to no avail. About 2 years in, I started to wonder how this Harry guy could be so unlucky, after all, he had it all worked out? I got my people to do some digging, even interview Harry and ask to go through the paperwork, it emerged that he didn't own the land at all, he had an option agreement on the land, meaning he paid rent on the land whilst owning the sole rights to broker a sale with a good commission built in. So now we know why he was getting into debt; to pay the rent on 50 acres! With all the money down the pan, we could have been flipping 4-5 house renovations a year and making a great living, but people just have to go in for the big time, wanting to become a millionaire overnight. The number of times he'd spun me a yarn and said, "We're almost there, Carlton, by the end of the summer we'll be exchanging sale contracts", then it was, "Just before Christmas, Carlton, bear with it" and "In the new year, Carlton, as soon as the solicitors are back at work…". Around the time I was thinking about an exit strategy, Jay came to see me, he'd become more suspicious than usual of the most recent story from Harry and not wanting me to be getting mugged off, he had done some finding out. After some desperate stunts Harry had pulled with the landowners, they had gone to court to get him off of the land, he'd lost the lot! I was insulted that Harry thought he could pull the wool over my eyes like that. Why did he think I have handpicked people wrapped round me, I mean, I don't need to be everywhere and looking into everything myself, I have people to help me keep on top of things. I'd given him squeeze after squeeze for his lies in the hope of this thing actually coming off, although each time I had let him know I knew he'd lied and that I wasn't actually falling for his bullshit, I was just letting him off lightly. But that was that! I would take my severance pay and move on, I'd come out up, but what a lot of waisted time and an absolute fucking headache.

When people try muddying the waters in a hope of hiding their true intentions, but also in an attempt to con me, they're always best to know that me being a born and bred working-class east-ender, I, amongst a few others, not only invented and mastered, but also own sole rights to the same game they're trying to play me at. Talk about insulting my intelligence! Let me tell you a tale of two such chancers. Neil and Martin were being extorted. A pair of straight goers who had tried to cut a corner in business and unwittingly become entangled in the underworld. They'd been pressured and bullied over the course of about 10 months, handing over thousands of pounds in a series of final settlements. The more the pair of office bod-types resisted and tried to state their case, the worse the threats became from these bullies. The straw that broke the camel's back for them was when Martin's elderly father got a visit from these thugs and luckily for them, they were able to get themselves a sit-down with me. I don't fucking like bullying, I equally dislike extortion, if a genuine debt is owed then it's a different matter, but it's morally wrong to be taking money you haven't earnt from people who don't owe it to you. Someone might get away with this practice for a while, but they won't find much support when someone higher up the ladder steps in. So, I agreed a fee with the pair for resolving their issues with this low-level local villain and told them I don't want a penny until they are satisfied that the guy was off their backs - I didn't think I could be fairer than that! They were over the moon, so I made a call to the bullying twat and explained that I think his practices are rather unfair and that I would be representing Neil and Martin in this matter from now on. I suggested that perhaps we should meet up, an invitation that was declined, so I simply left it that should there need to be any further discussion about the issue, it should be done via me and me only. I gave Neil and Martin a phone number, explained that either Jay or myself would be on the other end and they should call if they hear anything, but other than that, we'd be in touch in a fortnight about payment. 2 weeks passed and not a word, Jay called one of them and asked if they'd been pressured by anyone, which they hadn't, so Jay organised to meet them and grab my payment. When he went, however, they had less than half the agreed amount! The pair of them were very apologetic and they also had an idea about an alternative way to pay the owed balance; armed with fancy brochures and a sales pitch, they explained that they had obtained a load of Carbon Credit Certificates through one of their businesses, which they were going to cash out within a few weeks, if I could kindly allow them some extra time, they'd pay what they owed with a hefty drink on top. Now, they were businessmen and we had already checked them out to make sure they did actually own these companies. So, I agreed to give them a bit of extra time, after all, I knew I'd get it in the end, one way or another. When their time came around again to cough up, Jay met with them to collect the money, but now there was another problem! The funds hadn't cleared yet. Jay marched Martin to an ATM to get a balance and prove their story and sure enough, there was an uncleared balance of over £100k showing. Previously completely skeptical, even Jay now thought that they might actually pull this off! As sure as day turns to night, the pair of plonkers let us down again each Friday for the next 2 weeks. On the Monday morning, bright and early, Jay dropped a birthday card into Martin's letterbox, then went to Neil's house to have a photo with Neil's Alsatian in his back garden. Within a couple of hours, we had a text message from Martin thanking us for the card and enquiring as to how we knew his date of birth and address, then Neil was on the phone pleading for an extra 24 hours to pay. The next morning, they paid the balance of my money. Jay convinced Martin to tell him how he'd dummied the ATM balance that day and we couldn't believe what we heard! He'd paid himself a cheque in, knowing that it would just show as uncleared funds until it bounced, clever really! Another few weeks wasted on bullshit and unnecessary broken promises! I'd been double fair and would have preferred for them to just tell me from the off that they needed a few weeks to pay. Even with the bit extra I'd charged them for the fucking around, they were still financially better off having come to me for help and they were happy that they'd no longer get extorted. So, you can see that even 'straight-goers' will try being dishonest. With me, honesty paves a way of making good of a situation and that same honesty would've been a cheaper experience for them both, but all's well that ends well.

At times, I've wondered why the majority of these things haven't worked out and I concluded that it's a combination of things. First off, I've always been pretty well placed to help people out, so I get asked a lot more than most. Secondly, perhaps I've been too nice or too patient at times, people have pushed me quiet far before I've eventually had to turn on them over these things, but never let it be said that I've bullied or extorted someone, because I've only ever collected what was genuinely owed. Finally, nothing ventured, nothing gained! I.e., if you don't try these things, none of them will ever work out, will they!

In life, you live, and you learn, but what you do with life's teachings is the important thing, as the saying goes, "fool me once, shame on you. Fool me twice……! The good news is that I have educated people around me. None are of the mindset of fools when it comes to this line of work. My family and close friends are clued-up enough never to put themselves in a position where money becomes an issue or causes conflict. The decades of networking and social structure I work in and amongst doesn't allow people to take the piss – that's a fool's paradise and I simply don't allow for a loss.

Contrary to what some may conclude from reading this chapter, I'm not bitter about these fucktardians, I'm actually angry at myself for allowing their treachery to take place and for so long. There's been genuine people that I could've helped and made their lives a little easier, but instead they've been pushed to the back of the line as a result of the frenzied mass of judases and ponces.

At this stage of my life and career (and as this book drops) what better time than now to change my phone number and drop out a whole load of people who call me up regularly, pretending to be my friend or looking out for my best interests, yet we both know that they aren't! Their list of wants and demands, favours and needs are reeled off like a kid with their Christmas list. They'll never be useful to me, they'll never bring something to my table, they're hanging around like a bad smell because I'm only useful to them; well not anymore! And that's not to say that I require to earn money from a person in order to have them as a mate, because a 2-way valued and honest friendship is more than enough for me and something I respect more than the wishers and demanders, but when I know that a person has gone behind my back and hidden something from me to avoid giving me a drink, they can jog right on! There are people that have lived vicariously through me and my name – claiming to be a business acquaintance or even an associate; that has been a regular practice by a few. It's been a common routine for many, but it's time to be honest with yourself, don't try and be something you're not! It'll only lead to disappointment by trying to emulate someone else and live off their efforts; my life experiences and time in the game are what I've earned… and largely at a cost.

As far back as when I was running doors, I can give examples of people I've looked after, brought into the fold, fed, clothed, given work or money to. I've taken in people who'd just left prison and had fuck-all, blokes on the run, lads coming from the coast to find work in land to feed their families. Sooner or later, most of them have taken advantage of my kindness or stabbed me in the back entirely. I've acted with my heart instead of thinking with my head on far too many occasions throughout my life and as I look back now, there have been many a time when this mistake has been at a cost to my family. Think about it; I invest my time into helping out a guy who's in need of a hand up, then I help him out with some cash, or I split some work and share the return with him; I could have been selfish and spent the time with my wife and kids or my parents, spent the money on them too and ended up far better off all round, not just financially. Effectively, I've let certain people into my house, and they've robbed me of time and money, in a roundabout way.

I found that as I became a bit of a commodity, more vultures circled, as did people who wanted to see me fall. People I knew personally and people I didn't know at all, would turn on me, either for selfish gain or out of jealousy and spite. There are many people out there who have and do to this day, benefit from having been around me, but for most, their memories are very short and yet expect my pockets to be deep! They know who they are, some are sitting in big houses in the Essex countryside surrounded by piles of cash and shiny things, but are their consciences clear? Are they fuck! If a chunk of that change was earned off of my back, don't think I don't know, because I do, and karma will come around in the end. I won't print these people's names, not through fear, but because they don't warrant to share my platform, but if you're reading this, then thank you for the tenner you just put in my pocket.

I once took the wrap when a bit of work went wrong, and I was looking at a few years away. Out of sheer luck and due to a technicality, everyone got away with it scot-free in the end, but do you know the thanks I got for risking my liberty in going forward and taking the blame? You'd think my family would have been looked after with a few quid, or some plane tickets might have been at the ready in case I wanted to go on the lam, but no. In fact, some of the very people who I was saving from jail time started to say that I was a grass! Without any fucking evidence, they tried to tarnish my name with the worst insult there is in the underworld. By rights, if they genuinely believed that I'd grassed them up (they all got off remember) they should've done me, I shouldn't be here today, simple. But they didn't come for me, they didn't kill me or even bash me, no one did – EVER!

It's because deep down they knew they were just slandering me with no truth behind their nonsense. This is a common play by people you've helped out in life, calling and accusing you of the lowest of actions in organised crime and by doing so, they honestly believe they've lessoned the moral obligation they have, or they can relieve their conscience of the money you put their way. Some good loyal people would tell me about anyone on the street gossiping and passing the lies on. Some of those doing this would still come and work for me, drink and eat with me, never saying a fucking word to my face! So, the ones using the term 'wrong un' turned out to be the actual wrong-uns themselves, because if you genuinely believe a criminal is a grass, you certainly don't continue having it with them and if you don't genuinely believe it, don't say it! I know that 99% of these judas's would jump on it like tramps on chips if I put a bit of lucrative work under their noses. My well-known stance has always been the same; no matter how hard a man is, how big his firm is or what run of the ladder he's on, if you have a problem with me, let me know to my face and what will be will be. Don't be a weasel or a snake and talk about me, come talk to me, but make sure you're in the right if you're accusing me of something so terrible. A common trend I've identified is that the rats deflect from their own wrong doings by flinging mud everyone else's way, something I recently discussed with a well-known and respected face, Mr. Paul Ferris, who picked up on this tactic much sooner in his career than I did. Paul is a proper staunch, old-school gentleman with whom I have had several mutual friends for many years (if only there were more moral men like him in crime these days!), but more about Paul later!

Whether you want to call it dirt, intel, info or compramat, I've got that much of it on so many villains that, if I wanted to, I could change the landscape of the underworld in the South East as we know it, but that will never, ever happen. Those sorts of things will die with me and frankly, people who know me, know that that's why I'm trusted in my world.

If I had a fiver for every time one of these mongrels, who previously slagged me off behind my back, ran into me and started offering to buy me drinks and rack me a line up, I'd be rich! From the bottom of my heart, I truly wish them all a long-lasting, ill health and a lonely death which they are more than deserving of. If you thought that this book was going to be confessions of the old-time gangster who repents and forgives every fucker who ever tried to screw him over, you're now up to date and realise you got the wrong man! Again, they hold a lower than shark shit existence on this earth and there will be not a single tear shed on my part if they died as a result of contracting a painful and incurable disease.

I can adapt to most situations and settings, I can (and have) travelled all around the UK and much of Europe, either with a mate or a woman. This is in direct contrast to most of these so-called villains out there who won't or can't leave their manor. They operate and live from either the safety and sanctuary of their armchairs or local patch in Essex and won't leave unless it's 15 handed. Most of them hate going out of their comfort zone, some are just hiding in fear, but I've never been difficult to find if someone had a genuine problem with me.

The whole underworld and crime scene has sickened me over the last few years. All of the old school chaps are dying off and our moral codes and way of life is dying too. Look at the stark difference between, say, 1960's East London vs. the same place today! We've been on a downward trajectory for decades and I dread to think what lays ahead. If villainy and the old school is to be represented by the so-called criminals of today – drop me out!

Paul Ferris – "…. he holds a quality that would be favored in the company that I keep"

Whatever the type of business we are in, and for those involved in certain businesses, can be as defining as the friends we keep, the choices that we make and what we all stand for…... but what isn't, are the views and negative opinions of others - believe me when I say, no truer a phrase is spoken when a man's alleged notoriety proceeds him, and a conviction is given based solely on his reputation.

Carlton Leach is a name that I first heard from my old friend Wilf Pine. Wilf, a very heavily respected man, whose judgement, counsel, and experience I trusted more than most will ever know, spoke highly of Carlton - if there's one aspect and element in my life that I respect, it's the word of my own including those that maintain or have had a life in and around organised crime. Carlton's name has reached the most northern borders and spoken of within trusted circles of wise men; the same wise men who could never suffer the mistakes of fools or others, as sometimes those judgments and stories made by others can be an early conviction.

North, east, south, or west - the lines in a map, the dialect spoken and the alignment of social or religious practices that some have chosen to live in and by, can instill certain disciplines and understandings, but when a conviction that can be counted in its entirety by a generation, what is measured more, is when it comes to how a man is trusted and respected within our own community …. the size of a jailer's frame or the keys he has turning in a cell door, don't make the years any easier to count because of a person's poor judgement, only his recognition and understanding of what's deemed rights over the wrongs, as well as the good from the bad. Carlton is of an era that holds that standard – that's why he is known and respected throughout the UK. Someone I've not yet met, but he holds a quality that would be favored in the company that I keep - even if he does choose to put that green stuff over a pie and mash instead of gravy, but in the end, we are all from the same tree – just different branches.

Lew Yates – "He's a gentleman, not lairy or loud and I can't fault him, he's a good man who never once let me down…."

I have always had a lot of time and respect for Carlton, and I know he feels the same way. A powerfully built lad with a good physique on him, I knew that if it was kicking off, Carlton would be right by my side, he proved to always have my back and I could trust him one hundred and ten percent. He's a gentleman, not lairy or loud and I can't fault him, he's a good man who never once let me down, we got on very well and had plenty of laughs together.

Lautrec's was a very "active" club let's say, there were always plenty of fights, both inside and outside, so Carlton and I got to know each other a lot quicker than two blokes would normally. Carlton had absolutely no issues in dealing with violence or confrontation at the club, I could never have asked any more of him, I always felt that I could trust him 100% with watching my back and we all knew he would step up whenever there was a problem, and that was most nights to be honest!

There was another place we looked after called Starlights, and I remember going down there one night to make sure everything was alright. Johnny was on the door on his own, so I asked him where Carlton was and he said, "Have a look inside Lew!" When I went in, I couldn't bloody believe what I saw; Carlton was on the dance floor enjoying himself, throwing shapes and having a right dance! So, I pulled him back to the door and told him to stay there with Johnny, then off I go to see the manager about a few things, but when I've come back Carlton's gone again…he's back on the dance floor having the time of his life! I pulled him back to the door again and this time he stayed put (thank goodness)! I hope that when Carlton remembers that night he laughs as hard as I am writing this!

Can't shake that look: Some people always look like they're up to no good!

6 THE NEW GAME

The collection of a bad debt is something that has existed since the dawn of time in one form or another, but the processes and methods of resolution, legal and illegal, have evolved over the years. I've collected many debts myself, but by this point in my career, I tend to keep in the background a little more, unless I'm needed to step in on a situation. I'd get jobs in, find out about the debtor; is he a face, is he a nobody, is he related or connected to someone in my world and my findings would determine how we went about dealing with the situation.

Thinking about the last 10 years, I'd say that when you're collecting an underworld debt, believe it or not, it's usually easier than when I'm asked to collect payment from a straight goer for a business debt. This is down to several reasons, the first is to do with respect with the commodity at hand…..villains actually, in a manner of speaking, respect money, as it's a large part of their (obvious) survival and only form of income….they have to remain within the world of villainy, so they have to play by the rules, it's not like he'll be able to go and claim unemployment (which is actually never done by proper villains) nor will they be able to get a regular 9 to 5 job to feed their life style and social interests. A lot of villains look at how they got the money with a certain level of contempt – easy come, easy go and there's more where that come from! Plus, the villain, by and large has to have a moral compass, as it's not right to fuck one of your own over! The second is because there's always someone higher up the ladder, so whilst it's one thing to knock an average Joe, it's a lot of hassle to knock another villain, as there will always be someone that's going to keep coming for what's owed.

As for the average businessman who's not involved in the underworld, other dangers and threats exist and he needs to be careful, because nowadays so many people are setting up companies with the sole intention of not paying their contractors or bills, they know the law to a T, are ready to hide behind it and hang on to every last penny they just stole. There's a whole industry for it, from the accountants and lawyers who help keep everything "above board", to the mailing addresses that just have hundreds of letterboxes on the wall. Like I've said, I've seen and heard of people that have loaned money or goods on promise of return; that couldn't otherwise have been gotten from a bank, but, when it comes time to repay on the loan or up-front purchase, the supposedly respectable business has now gone under and largely protected under the guise of many laws, one in particular and favourite being 'bankruptcy'. These fuckers know how to play the system and the infrastructure, plus UK law is on their side. The once moral fabric seen in business and their respective transactions, have been removed by scumbag owners, who are now brazen enough to even try and rip-off gangsters! Their intention was never to build a business on trust and with an honest, long-term agenda, and as I've seen, it was to try and rip people off. The moral obligation in repaying the debt, has been poorly substituted by the belief they have some sort of moral superiority that now allows and justifies the 'straight goer' to threaten running to the police and screaming 'extortion'…...and society calls us criminals!

What's either forgotten or ignored, is the simple fact that success, in both legitimate and other means of income, stays with a person a lot longer if they stuck with the accepted ground rules. That's not to say that a group of people meet up, take long walks and drink tea together on a regular basis, it simply means that by people operating with an agreed set of principles, translates to everyone involved getting ahead and earning – after all, that's the whole point isn't it!

Once a huge part of my income, underground debt collection was changing for the worse. Crusher and Jay, my two main grafters, were very 'creative' in their methods, but the odds were starting to stack against not only us but the whole entire money collecting infrastructure: CCTV, Traffic Cameras, ANPR, facial recognition. Even bystanders now have the police at their fingertips thanks to mobile phones and on top of all of this, people's cultures, ways and morals have changed entirely. There was a time when joe-public wanted nothing to do with the underworld, if a villain was putting it on some other crook, the average person would quietly cross the road and keep what they saw to themselves, most people today would raise their smart phone and start recording, or live streaming or some other bollocks that's going to land you right in the shit! Have you been in a local shop recently and seen a poster in the window urging you to call the hotline and dob in a school kid who's bunking class? There's a hotline for just about everything nowadays and grassing has been bred into people, it would seem, from a young age. I've done some things in my life that would be considered terrible by many, but I can't imagine trying to knock someone for money, then when they come looking for repayment, calling the police to help me duck out of coughing up! But that really is the average mentality now, people who think that they're owed a free ride or that someone else should pay their way for them. If someone owes any kind of debt to me personally, I'm still going to collect at any cost, but when it's purely business, collecting someone else's money in for a cut of it, the reward needs to outweigh the risks and these days it's rare that that is the case. Up until very recently I was still collecting, but I was picking and choosing which jobs were worth my time, effort and risk.

After many years of looking after people and cash, I have a good reputation for being fair and reliable, plus of course, I get the job done! Sometimes I can ensure the safety of you and your cash by making a phone call, other times it requires a bit more presence, but ultimately, those who have engaged my services over the years have been satisfied customers and nobody on my watch has ever lost a tenner. I've overseen transactions of many kinds and in lots of ways, occasionally remotely, often in the obvious types of places like car parks, woods, closed up clubs and pubs and alike, but these things have also taken place in public, too; you yourself could have been right next to a massive underworld exchange while you were shopping, driving, walking with the family or eating a meal. I've been on jobs from 20k to over a million quid and treated every one with the same sense of urgency and potential danger.

There was one job in particular where I was entrusted in the handling of a million pounds. A million quid (or a bar as we refer to it) in used notes, as you may, or not can take up quite a bit of space, you can carry it in a big holdall, sure, but it's not easy to hide in your car, if you get a tug from the old bill you really don't need them asking to look in the bag so I always made sure I had my license with me, the car was taxed and insured and it all looked well kept. The police were an occupational hazard that you got used to, but the biggest problem of all was, I didn't really trust anyone enough to put them fully in the loop, after all, this is a life-or-death situation! Yes, the client trusted me with their funds,' and they knew I'd deliver, but people who can pull up that kind of cash can pay to put you in the ground if you fuck up or try to have them over; it doesn't matter who or what you are, there's always someone who would pull the trigger on you, either out of craziness or desperation, for some cash. So, without giving away any details, I arranged for 2 of my guys to wait around the corner from the pick-up location in a van, if I were to call them, they had instructions to come over and put down anything that moved, but if I just drove past them, they were to follow me until I gave them a sign with my hazard lights, then they could head off. This tactic has 2 purposes, the first is security; if anyone tried to take the cash from me, I had 2 extra guys with me to surprise them and back me up. The second reason is to make it much harder and less likely for the police to pull me over! If the second car stays behind me, a police car can't really get between us and pull me over for some silly reason. It was arranged that if the police were behind, my guys would stage a breakdown to let me continue on, or if that wasn't appropriate, they'd pull a terrible driving manoeuvre and get stopped themselves, leaving me to casually disappear. I made it back to my place without any issues, but there the hard work started! I had arranged for my Mum and Dad to be there waiting for me to help me count the cash, because as I said, I couldn't trust anyone else with the money or the knowledge of it, plus, I did not want to sit and count £1,000,000 twice over on my own! It took most of the day to check and I managed to head out, tooled up to the teeth, to go deliver the cash before it got too late into the night (police wise, it's best not to drive cash in the dead of night, especially when you look like me).

I'm sure that there will always be some form of cash or physical method of payment, especially in the underworld, but I believe 9/11 changed the game entirely, with new laws brought in to protect nations from global terrorism being used (some would argue this is heavily misused) to catch crooks. Everyone has, at some time, imagined what they'd do with £1,000,000 if they came into it, but now imagine that million was in cash? Trust me, that makes life much harder! With new EU laws, you would struggle to even go and buy your dream car with that money, never mind a house.

There will always be people who need to get physical cash into their accounts, then there are others who will want to get readies out of the banks (without the aid of a shotgun), those that will want funds sent to far flung islands, a few back into the UK from overseas…and that's (largely) the new game, and for anyone reading this that's clued-up in such business dealings, will know that this was a new direction ……and for the right brains and outfit should've lit up their eyes like a Christmas tree! Luckily, some great work with several different parties and good earners came from the closing and end of one type of business, and someone who I once considered an old friend; though, much like the Judas that he is, would later foolishly stab me in the back – but I'm getting ahead of myself, so let's introduce someone who I'll simply refer to as, Maxi.

Years ago, I'd looked out for this young kid a few times when I was running security at raves, he was a cheeky little fucker, but at the time I liked him, as he was a hard worker, he had fuck all back then and was hungry to move forward. I got him in with an Indian family who I was providing protection for, they were smuggling fags on a big scale, and I got Maxi a job with them, which at the time he always showed his appreciation for, whenever I saw him, he would give me an expensive bottle of something and fill my boot up with Marlborough lights! Over the years Maxi worked his way up through the ranks with these guys and became one of the top 3 earners in their organisation. By now they'd been investors in bars and nightclubs as well as other businesses, the tokens of appreciation from Maxi had long stopped, but to be fair, anytime I wanted a night out or to entertain a little firm from off the manor, I was well treated in their venues, so I didn't mind. Anyway, this lot were all pleased that I would allow them to use my name and be a known person within their organisation and new business venture, Maxi said that with us now on board, they would without a doubt turn over some serious money each year and agreed to my fees and terms straightaway - we were set to start work shortly after.

Jay dealt with all the day-to-day and just gave me a roundup of all the important news every few days. He had built a group of a few really good people to facilitate our business, people he'd known a while, knew their backgrounds and were gradually proving to be trustworthy over time. Jay would find ways to get the guys around me for a day, or even an afternoon, later we'd catch up and I knew he was looking for a nod or a knockback on that person, my seal of approval if you like. One of the first big deals that would be entrusted to Maxi by his new colleagues, and it would appear, on the surface, that he made one of the worst schoolboy errors of his life, however, many would soon consider the possibility that it was no accidental fuck-up! All he had to do was deliver a 280k payment to a supplier for a delivery of bootlegged goods that had just arrived, but when he pulled into the pub car park, instead of calling the supplier to come outside as he should have, he went into the pub for a cheeky half, to be "one of the lads' for a short time. In a miraculous stroke of misfortune and in a packed-out car park, within that 15-minute window his vehicle was unattended, some thieves happened to smash the rear window of Maxi's old banger and stumble across the bag full of cash! From the supplier's side, who hadn't seen or been handed the payment, it looked like a set-up, the oldest move around and it looked pretty much the same to those who had allowed Maxi this chance to prove himself. Things were looking bleak and at best, he was about to get badly hurt, but I honestly thought at the time that Maxi wouldn't do something like that, so I stuck my neck out to do what I believed to be the right thing and risked my own professional reputation in the process, to protect and vouch for him, in turn, saving him from the grim reality check that was undoubtably coming his way.

In the absence of any evidence, but the main suspect having me in his corner, a plan was formulated to work together, between supplier and buyer, to replace what had been lost over a few future deals and continue trading as before, albeit with a lot more suspicion in the air! A few months down the line, Maxi asked to meet me and take me out for a meal, at which he handed me an envelope stuffed with Scottish fifty-pound notes, he explained that he didn't have a lot of money around him given what had happened, but this was a token of appreciation for what I'd done for him. At the time, I took this at face value and really respected his actions and for going about things the right way where I was concerned, this action further reinforced, in my mind, that I'd made the right call, although, years later I happened to have a very interesting chance conversation with someone on the buyer side of that deal, who mentioned that they no longer dealt with the supplier who liked to be paid in Scottish notes!

Slowly but surely, business got back on track, and things were going really well with Maxi and the family run consortium of smugglers, when one day they called me and asked me to go to their offices right away. "Ok I'll come by tomorrow before lunchtime" I told them, but they couldn't wait, "It's an emergency brother, we need you now" Maxi declared in a panic. I called Jay and told him we need to go to the warehouse because something must be coming on top, so we met near the tiny train station at Battlesbridge, in Essex and headed to London. When we arrived at their warehouse, we screamed into the car park expecting to see World War 3 going off, but there were just the usual people hanging about and nothing alarming happening at all. We got out, looked around and went to the door, Jay asked one of the staff to get Maxi, he looked at Jay, looked at me, nodded and scuttled off through a security door, shielding the code as he punched in the numbers, as if we were going to rob them or something. "What's the deal with that office up there anyway C, they trust us with tons of their cash, hundreds of thousands more in bank accounts, yet we aren't allowed into the main fucking office?" "Mate, it's been that way since I've known them, they tell me I'm family, yet I'm not worthy of a sit down in the office." As I replied to Jay's question, the guy appeared again, closed the security door, looked at the floor and scurried off elsewhere. We waited for about 10 minutes, I looked up towards the mirrored glass of the forbidden office and said, "Fuck this, they called me and dragged me up here, we're off!" We headed towards the car park and as we reached the door, we heard Maxi shout, "Brother! Come mate, come with me let's talk!" We followed him out the back of the warehouse to their shithole staff room, where I opened the conversation; "If you want my help, don't ever leave me standing down here in the freezing fucking cold like one of your little minions again, alright!" He replied with the usual bollocks, along the lines of "Sorry, bhaji, you know it's not like that, you're family, you want a drink?" I explained we didn't have time and we should be elsewhere, so he got to the point in explaining that they'd fallen out with some business partners in the chain and that these people were trying to extort them. "Brother, you know what Richie's like, he's up there shitting himself! I told him fuck them, we'll get AK's and meet them anywhere, but him and his old man insisted I call you straight away!" "Never mind AK's, what the fuck do they want and who are they?" I asked. Knowing how ridiculous it was and sounded, Jay had rolled his eyes and started wandering about the room at Maxi's mention of AK-47s, but I know he was still taking in every word. Maxi said that these former business associates had sent text messages demanding 150k in cash by the next morning, stating that they were watching Richie's mother at her home.

It was here that questions started to formulate, and none more towards those that understood the infrastructure and those within the family business. Being that Maxi had been looked after very well in terms of an income, it had also crossed my mind that he might be trying to play, not only the family that'd taken him in, but also me – greed is always a factor you must consider when you're dealing with certain types of people. I ran this same level of questioning over with Jay, who with his own reasoning, began to question the overuse of, "we'll blast them with AK-47's," and "let's just go to war with them!" it all seemed a bit 'over-kill' and dramatic to say the least…. plus, when I arrived, I'd managed to get eyes on at least half of what was being demanded, was now being counted and ready to deliver. I insisted that from here on out, that only I should be dealing with the threats and people applying the pressure. Something just felt off…I had started to question a few things, but like I've experienced on many occasions, give it time, and the truth will come out.

So, when it came to arranging a time and place to deliver what they thought was going to be a bag of cash, instead got an address and a time to meet with me. I needed to have them meet on my terms and a location of my saying. I decided on a small wine bar south of the Thames, that would work well, as we'd used it for some firm meetings in the past and I knew the layout well enough for what we needed to do. In the meantime, I put out a call to find out if the names given were part of any firm or were connected in anyway – nothing, and no one had heard of anyone involved or branching out away from known families.

As it got closer to the meeting time, Maxi had been on the phone several times, in fact it must've been at least every other call he was ringing me, insisting that, "we deal with these people in a way they'd never return again," or maybe it was a lot simpler if they were, "simply paid off," as he said his boss and the family that was being extorted had expressed a lot of concern, but as I stressed with him on each and every phone call, if there's one thing I know, if you pay once, they'd not be happy with just that one (large) payment, as greed knows no limits, especially when it involves people whose arse falls out with the first threat of violence. It was also then, that Jay proposed what was an obvious question and statement, "Was that Maxi again? …...for fucks sake, anyone would think he's owed the money himself!" My suspicions and gut-instinct were rarely wrong, but now further amplified by what was becoming even more questionable behaviour by Maxi.

We arrived early and pulled into an adjacent parking lot, Jay walked in ahead, followed almost immediately by two members of the firm, so as to check the obvious hiding places, just in case someone thought they could jump out and surprise us. Jay came out shortly after giving a signal that all was good. When the meeting time came and went, at first, we thought it was a no-show, but like the amateurs I suspected they were, arrived late. Wheel-skidding into the car park, with their car windows down and music being played loud was a statement all in itself and further testament to what and who they were. Following them in, and no sooner had they sat down, I introduced myself. I instantly noticed the fake Rolex watch with the part water-filled facia and their matching faded gold chains – I'd seen enough! Jay then stood up and excused himself and left me to hear what they had to say. Jay is very good at what he does, not only in finding people, their backgrounds, but also knowing where they're going after a meeting, so while the two lumps from our firm had eyes on the inside of the wine bar, the main firm was plotted-up outside, making sure Jay could get to work uninterrupted, placing tracking devices on the vehicles so that at any stage of their lives, or until an MOT inspection, we'd know where and when they could be visited if need be. The meeting went exactly as we suspected, claims of what they felt they were owed by Maxi's bosses, as they were operating on their manor, and as they put it, to sweeten the deal, their guaranteed protection would be part of the price. I said I'd have to speak with the people in question, as much as I acted as the mediator, I was also the one who gave advice on certain finances.

When it came time to leave, their over confidence and sense of security was cut short when one of them said that he'd caught my first name, but not my last, which I humbly told them. I can't quite put my finger on it, but the look on their faces and the urgency of phone calls as soon as they left the wine bar, strongly suggested there was some sort of issue at hand. Standing across the street and watching their erratic behaviour, brought a combination of smiles and chuckling from Jay and myself. I then asked Jay if what had unfolded had been enough of a warning, but his smiling and the look on his face said, 'not in a million fucking years is it!' So, the very next morning the two 'top' members of their firm got visits at their homes whilst still eating their cornflakes and thinking, 'how the fuck do we get out of this mess?'.

A few questions remained with me even after that day. Why was the money being counted even before I'd gotten to speak with Maxi, and why the urgency to deal with those and their demands without my questioning? The way I saw it, for someone who was spouting off about the use of AK-47's and being a gangster, his so-called trigger-finger was seen to be more eager and active in the counting of money, than use of alleged firearms. Also, how did they learn where the family's homes were, and how did these low life's learn that such a large sum of money would be given up without little or no resistance? For now, as much as I had my suspicions, I'd chalk it up to a few local scum bags who'd simply gotten lucky with their intel, and whilst it's true, that paper beats rock, scissors beat paper and bullshit baffles brains, there's no denying that proper people and muscle outweighs chancers and wankers!

Even though I may not have been a 'squeaky clean' citizen all my life, I have a sense of pride in the fact that, throughout my years in the muscle game and having had to regularly deal with the dregs of society, I've always conducted myself in a morally correct fashion. That is to say that I've never been a bully and have consistently been fair when handing down a verdict, dishing out a punishment or deciding what time a debtor has left to pay.

Unfortunately, not everyone has such a precisely configured moral compass as I do, and I've been paid several times to politely ask a liberty taking arsehole to kindly leave his current victim alone! One such occasion was when an estate agent was being forced to allow certain types of gardening projects to go ahead at his properties, but after he was left to pay to fix extensive damages on 4 of the properties, as well as the fact that the green-fingered firm of Albanians hadn't paid any rent and had somehow racked up, let's say, 'above average' electric bills, the estate agent found his way to me for some help freeing himself of them.

The Albanians were running a mock in their area and were having their strings pulled by a local face, who was obviously getting a cut of the proceeds. The front man, or as it turned out, the mouthpiece of the operation, was invited to a meeting to discuss the vacating of the properties for a final time and of course, he was welcome to bring his team of hedge trimming, seed watering, fan adjusting gardeners, if he liked! I arrived to the estate agents' offices an hour early with 4 of my most trusted associates and entered round the back, Kevin and I sat in the boardroom waiting, my 3 other guys sat in the next office with the door closed; if they heard anything out of place, they'd be through the door getting stuck in faster than you could say 'grow-house', but Kevin is seriously heavy-duty, a one-man army, so it was always likely that we'd be just fine.

The local hardman arrived a couple of minutes ahead of time and full credit to him, he had just 1 of his minions with him. I'd found out about this fella beforehand and he was known for a good ruck, fair play to him, but bullying isn't accepted in the higher tiers of criminality, and you can't be wrong and strong! I let the gardeners and the estate agent have a little bicker for a while, back and forth over who fucked whose girl and who knew what about the activities taking place at the properties, right up until Kevin and I had heard enough and it was time to announce exactly how this needed to end, but after I'd amicably said my bit, the hardman revealed his complete distain and contempt for me by going into a rant about my being there. Clearly, his reign of terror over this bod was coming to an end and rather than find some other poor fuckers flats to wreck, he wanted one last try at hanging in there to rinse this guy…shame really, because up to this point, I'd given him a level of respect and credibility. I calmly asked him if he had a more personal problem with me, to which he replied, "I fucking 'ave actually, Carlton!" As he reached into his pocket, I leant into the plant pot next to my seat and pulled out the combat knife I'd planted (no pun intended) there earlier and lunged across the table at my now target, who proceeded to try to clamber out of the first-floor window! Having heard the chairs and tables going up in the air, the lads next door burst into the room too, but they weren't to be needed after all; Kevin stepped in to stop me from plunging someone, then he helped spiderman down from the window and stood him against the wall, like a head master and a naughty student and as the colour continued to drain from the man's face, Kevin asked him in his usual sincere tone, "How many children do you have?" "3" came the reply. "3 kids just nearly lost their father because of your big mouth; you do realise that don't you?" It was an epiphany-like moment in the room for what probably lasted less than 10 seconds but felt like a minute and finally ended when Kevin advised them to sit the fuck down and try again to deal with me in a more sensible and respectful manner.

Many reading this will know that when you're in a violent conflict, everything feels as though it happens extremely fast, almost like someone put the world on 'fast-forward x10', meanwhile you're experiencing intense tunnel vision and a heightened sense of focus, thanks to adrenalin. If you've ever stabbed a man, you'll know that the knife also goes through the skin very fast, from there on it seems as though you're in slow motion, gradually pushing the blade deeper into the flesh, and if you hit bone, it's a feeling comparable to when you hit the brake pedal in your car but your pads are worn so you're met with a vibration through your foot via the pedal. As you pull your blade back out of another man's body, you feel the grease of his flesh helping you to slide it back out, the blood starting to spill acting as extra lubrication in the process.

Luckily, the situation was resolved that day without anyone losing their fathers, or anyone having to go on the LAM to Brazil, but it could have been much worse.

CARLTON - The Final Say

Jay – "If you end up leading this life, your choices concerning the people around you are very important."

I started working for Carlton at a young age via his then right-hand man, Crusher. I'd been knocking about in the local gyms and nightclubs for so long that he thought I was much older than I actually was. My 'apprenticeship' (as it were) started out on a casual basis; I'd get a last-minute call from Crusher when he needed an extra body on a job. In the beginning we spent maybe 1 or 2 days per week collecting debts all over the country. I would hear the info and instructions from Crusher and in turn, he would handle everything else directly with Carlton, who we only referred to as 'Mr C'.

As time passed and trust grew, I started to be brought in on other work, for example, C had a Client from whom we used to pick up a holdall of cash and deliver it to a little office on an industrial estate in Basildon. One time, I learnt that the bag that day had £400k in it and I remember thinking "Fuck me, they must trust me." Whereas C and Crusher had previously kept their meet-ups between the two of them, they'd started to have me along, too. Having grown up in Essex, in a family who were mostly West Ham fans from East London, I knew who Carlton Leach was, even before the Rise of the Footsoldier movie. I was in my 20's and being sent on jobs by a man who was effectively a living legend, a man who moved in the shadows and people locally traded rumors about. I loved the work and had cash in my pocket, what more could I want! I didn't give a fuck about anyone knowing who I was, I just wanted to get the job done, get paid and have a good crack with these guys while I could.
Work didn't seem to stop coming in and we were up to all sorts of stuff. On a few occasions, Carlton would lead a meeting because a name had been dropped or another face was involved…there was never a dull moment! I remember Carlton saying to me once "You're a paranoid

cunt ain't ya! Keep it up." I just laughed, I didn't really know exactly what he meant by it at that moment, or how to respond! One night, I was told there was a meeting and me and Crusher were going along with C to a restaurant called Marrakech in Surrey. On the way up in Crusher's car we pulled into a layby behind Carlton's Mercedes, got a thumbs-up and followed him from there to the place. I'd been told it was an important meeting, but to be honest I was expecting maybe 6-8 people…I was way off! I won't say who, but our section was full of chaps in suits, almost everyone I recognized as either a film actor or a villain from the South-East. Part way through the evening C came and sat to have a chat with me and Crusher, it was the first proper, lengthy conversation I'd had with C and I think we were both taking stock of one another from a new angle. The details of any conversations I was privy to that evening will be taken to my grave with me. Carlton introducing me to his associates along with Crusher as one of his men was a notable point in time, and I kind of felt honored to be there and grateful for the level of trust that was being given to me.

I was delving deeper down the rabbit hole and people I knew away from C's circles started to warn me about who and what I was involved with. When you're in your 20's you don't heed many warnings and I really didn't give two fucks what people had to say, in fact, if anyone told me I couldn't trust 'those sorts of people' it got my back up. I was going my way regardless, so I never stopped to think that I was actually at a junction in life, there was no time for a 'take the red pill or the blue pill' kind of moment. I was going along for the ride and enjoying being part of this thing, whatever it was, or however you choose to label it. If you end up leading this life, your choices concerning the people around you are very important; if you fall in with the wrong people or allow yourself to be taken advantage of, you can easily end up in deep shit. Point being that, in this regard, I was extremely fortunate to have had the opportunity to work for Carlton; he only kept decent people in his inner circles, so I learnt a lot, especially in my first 10 years. Collectively, I believe we're always learning, and I'm pleased to be in a position where I can turn to Carlton for help or advice if I need it. In fact, the level of street wise that he has is comparable to any academic degree from any university, except Carlton's skills can't just be taught, they have to be gained through experience as well.

Although C was obviously well connected and had plenty of mates, it was interesting for me to observe just how many new people suddenly appeared around him after ROTF came out! The movie made no odds to me, I didn't want anything from C other than the chance to just keep working, something which I believe he realized over time and appreciated. I continued grafting and took note through the years of all these people coming along and then slowly dropping away again. The same surge of 'new friends' came along around the time of ROTF 2 being made, but again I witnessed the inevitable exodus over about 6-12 months after that. People looking to try to gain from being in C's circles was not a new concept, it happened on the regular, it's just that the films exacerbated the numbers over a short period of time, but Carlton is far from stupid when it comes to spotting these users, and their successes are very limited because he's seen their moves a thousand times before. I guess being a good judge of character and trusting cautiously are necessary traits for criminals and if we look at Carlton's track record, it will demonstrate that he's done well in this regard. Of course, some business deals will inevitably go wrong, but C has lived the life to the max into his late 50's without being banged up for a long stretch or getting killed, one or two minor regrets aside, he's very happy in life. Perhaps if he wasn't so generous and didn't have the morals that he holds so dearly, he might be a millionaire by now, but some things are worth more than money to C and that's one of the things that people lucky enough to call him a friend, love about Carlton.

I've got some great memories of funny and interesting times with Carlton, from going on jobs, training in the gym, days out, nights out, plane trips, road trips, meetings and meals. Probably some of the best times were in Ibiza for opening in 2017, what a mad fucking week that was! Carlton still partied like I've heard he did when he was 30! Times like that are absolutely priceless.

One year, Carlton organized a night out for my birthday; he tapped up a client of his for a table at one of their restaurants and about 15 or so of us went. By the end of the evening, we were the only ones left in there, but I'm not sure any of our lot noticed as everyone was so pissed! We only needed to pay for our meals as C had organized all the drinks to be laid on. Apparently, one person in our group tried to duck their share of the bill, but Carlton, as slaughtered as he was, was a step ahead and he rounded up all the cash from everyone, plus a tip for the good people who had served us all night. That's C for you, no matter how relaxed he is, or how much booze he's consumed, his mind is so conditioned to watch out for sharks that he's still a step ahead!

Fast forward to 2021 and I feel privileged to have Carlton in my life. It's not all about graft and it hasn't been for years now. I consider C to be family, a term thrown around all too much these days, as is 'brother', but I don't use the term lightly or meaninglessly. We've been through ups and downs, on both business and personal levels, but we've always managed to laugh, look to the future and move forward. I have mates and I've made many acquaintances over the years, but I can count my true, dependable friends on one hand. Carlton is the definition of a friend, but to me he is family, even my son lovingly calls him Uncle Carlton and always gets excited when we're going to visit him. C's been in my boy's life since he was born, in fact, Carlton's 'baby advice' was brilliant (probably as he's had so many of his own) and at a time when so many people have an opinion, he was one of about 2 or 3 people that me and my missus ever actually listened to!

If I ever need sound advice, guidance or help, I know I can depend on Carlton for it and likewise, if he wants an honest opinion on something, he knows I'll tell him exactly what I think or feel. Good job I didn't listen to those warnings earlier on, else I wouldn't have the friend I have today in Carlton.

I hope that this book achieves the closure of certain topics that C hopes for and leaves the legacy for his family that he wishes it to.

7 THE WHITE ISLE

It's very difficult to put into words exactly what Ibiza is and means, and it's equally as hard to convey why she's been part of my life for so long, but I always seemed to find myself returning to the calls from The White Isle periodically throughout my life, but, basically, for me, Ibiza itself is a drug, it's highly fucking addictive and after you've experienced your first trip, you either hate it and don't go back for more, or you're hooked and have found an inescapable new lease on life. You might have already guessed, but I got addicted to 'the home of dance music' almost instantly! It's not just me either, I know scores of people who will tell you the same and Ibiza Chris is a prime example: He went on holiday almost 20 years ago and has stayed ever since! He tried to move back to Manchester twice but that move lasted about 3 weeks before he found himself bolting straight back to The Island, that's how powerful the magnetism is. Anything goes in Ibiza, and everything is so out in the open, almost as if people leave all their inhibitions and taboos on the plane at Aeropuerto de Ibiza.

Once a small fishing village in the Balearic Islands, there's been a loyal following of people that have visited Ibiza, in my mind, for the same reasons you'd want to visit an island that promoted such transparency and for all the right reasons. Since the 1930s, the island has been a bohemian affair for many. The 1970s saw a subtle change in the scenery and clientele. A few hotels emerged, but as a whole the island still allowed and promoted a 'breath of fresh air' for those that wanted to loosen their top buttons and take off their belts…. to be freer than those that had subscribed to a life-long commitment in a conservative lifestyle in the modern world.

Before I go any further, one promise I will make here and now is I won't start rattling on like an old man at the bus stop, with stories in tune with, "when I was a boy, all this was just fields", as the truth is, even before my love affair with the island, people had been coming to this jewel in the Mediterranean for a long time, and the fact remains, the largest of changes (along with the obvious scenic one) is the crowd size. When people came here, it was typically for the same reasons, and who wouldn't want to be with thousands of like-minded people all on the same vibe, but I will be honest and question 'why' people now come to Ibiza? The beautiful island can be a 'one size fits all' destination with those that want to embrace its culture, music and the experience, but not at the cost of losing its true deep-rooted meaning and identity and all the while being the best party island in the world.

When I first started visiting Ibiza in the late 70s, the Hippy mentality and live music scene was still extremely prominent, on the whole the revellers weren't youngsters, and the island had a massive gay and transexual scene. The most heterosexual person on the planet, with zero exposure to explicit scenes in his life, would walk past a gay sex show in a club window without even batting an eyelid! Inclusiveness is a buzz word today, but Ibiza was the definition of 'live and let live' in the 80's and 90's.

Something I've noticed that has never changed and remains reminiscent of the 70s and 80s, and that's people sleeping on the beaches all day, and there's 2 reasons why this happens. The first reason is that people are on holiday and whilst they do want to party all night, they also like to enjoy some sunshine while they can. The second group of people will have their bags with them as they sleep on the playa, simply because they don't have any accommodation booked! This is probably the hippy mentality of Ibiza at play; why waste money on hotels when you can sleep on the beach! Although it's not a bit of me, this isn't actually as trampy as it may sound, because the beaches have showers, toilets and changing facilities, plus, as I said, nothing is seen as strange there. Back in the day, it wasn't about hotels or luxuries, it was more about the music, partying, drugs and sex, generally having the time of your life, without judgement. Ibiza was your mistress for however long you wished to stay and believe me, she's a temptress with the deepest and most honest of intentions that she'll allow you to find if you let her. I believe that you don't find Ibiza, she finds you.

If you held a gun to my head and forced me to isolate just one example of an incredible memory from Ibiza, I'd have to tell you about the best night out I've ever had, which was at Pacha when Roger Sanchez was DJ'ing. Every single track he chose was a proper tune and each time he mixed the next one in it was as if the crowd got a surge of energy. Sanchez didn't fly in to smash out a 30-minute set and fuck off, he played about an 8-hour set, which is massive for a big-name DJ; he must have loved playing and it really showed through his work. This particular time I was staying at Pikes (hotel), as was my mate, Jason. At the end of the night, we went outside, where it was still just about dark. Knowing that we stood no chance of getting a taxi, we walked to El Divinos, where I knew one of the doormen and we bunged him 100 euros to drive us back to Pikes, because it was literally in the middle of nowhere, real Spanish-style middle of nowhere! The madness of the night wasn't quiet over yet though. As the pair of us slowly came back down and longed for our beds, the journey ahead was to be a surreal one that we could've done without at the time but looking back it was funny. The doorman I knew was a top lad, really friendly and loved to chat with us lot, but that said, he was a big fucker! He was originally from a country in Africa, so you can imagine our surprise when this mountain-sized big black man said to us, "Good job you didn't get in an illegal taxi with one of those African mother-fuckers, they'd have ripped you boys right off!" It felt like an eternity ago that we'd left the motorway and headed down these back roads amongst some fields, when me and Jason simultaneously spotted the turning we needed and shouted it out, but it was too late; our doorman-come taxi driver had missed it. I thought, 'Great! Another few precious minutes of sleep lost before the chance of getting us back on track and in the direction we needed to go'…but no sooner had this thought gone through my head, when things quickly went in another direction…. literally! I quickly discovered our taxi had now become a stunt car as I felt my world violently and completely going in another direction, one that under normal circumstances, would've been questioned by the laws of both physics and gravity. He hung a hard right through some hedges and into a field! I said, "What the fuck are you doing, man?" now trying to find something to hold onto and steady my somewhat fragile state of mind and body. There are ways of coming down quickly and prematurely and this was an unwelcomed one. He shrugged his shoulders, I'm guessing to assure us it was the sensible and justified move on his part, by adding, "It's ok, we can go this way, it's a 4x4," all the while remaining completely calm and relaxed. Bumping through these fucking fields I just wanted to throw up, I don't know how I didn't actually! Imagine you're a bee, trapped inside a bottle, shaken aggressively and not knowing when the confusion would end, then that would be close. As we finally approached the doors of the hotel, we were blessed with the famous Ibiza sunrise, something that millions of people get up early to enjoy, while millions of others only see on their way home whilst feeling worse for wear! As calming, heavenly and angelic as it was, I was of the mindset, "Yeah, great sight…. now where's my bed?"

Pikes was an experience in itself. Sadly, the legendary exclusive hotel is no longer run by the man himself, since he died in February 2019, but Tony Pike and his establishment certainly earned their place in the Ibiza history books. Under new management the resort continues to operate to this day. All of the rooms were unique and most of the suites were themed in styles ranging from Moroccan, to glass walls next to the swimming and even a cave! 5 nights here could easily end up setting you back 4k on check-out. One time when I was staying there, Muscle had just been released and someone told Tony who I was. He came over, introduced himself to me and we got chatting. He took me to his son's grave, which was marked with a specially planted tree in the grounds of the hotel. The next time I stayed there, I took Tony a signed copy of Muscle, which he was made up with! Me and my crowd had arranged to go to a club, so Tony said he'd come too, and he was more than welcome. He said, "Let's go in my car, Carlton, I'll drive us." When I thanked him and said I'd get the others, he said that only I was allowed in his motor! Thinking maybe he had some business or something to discuss with me, I arranged to meet the others at the club, but as we arrived in his BMW, I realised that there was actually nothing specific! Halfway through the night, someone came to me and told me that a guy just gave Tony 3 Jack Jills and I thought 'fuck off, he's in his 70's, he could fucking die!' I rushed through the crowd and brought Tony over to our VIP area so we could keep an eye on him. He was a fucking party animal that man, even in his 70's, can you believe it? He was completely out of his box when he offered to drive me back to the hotel, an offer I politely declined as I'd already seen enough hedges and fields during a car ride on this trip and didn't fancy dying in a crash that night! He never even had a driving license; the local police used to stop him regularly for drink driving, but I think because he was such a well-known businessman on the island, things were left to slide a little. I have some fond memories of Tony and Pikes Hotel; he was likeable and a very easy person to get along with. He wasn't complicated or difficult to understand as a human being. I found he had no ulterior motives and was approachable on any level. If you ever see or hear Tony doing an interview and talking about his life on the island with the celebrities he knew and spent time with, I have no doubt that all are true and if anything, the stories he never told, would've been enough to make even a sailor blush. A legendary Ibiza playboy, the Hugh Heffner of the Balearics and an all-round good guy. RIP Tony Pike.

Ibiza can hold memories for as long as you want them to be part of your life. I remember the year that 'House Every Weekend' was big and listening to Martin Solveig play at Cafe Mambo. In fact, I sat there that evening, drink in and hand listening to his set and reminiscing about this exact spot years before. Mint Bar & Restaurant now joins Mambo and Cafe del Mar, which was famous for euphoric dance records, as does the selection of small boats bobbing about waiting to be hired by couples who want to enjoy from the sea. They've each made the most of the excellent location that their bars undoubtably have, by lining the outside area with tables, seating and patio heaters, allowing guests to sit in comfort, even warm themselves up if the sea breeze gets too chilly as they take in the vistas. Back in the day, there had been no such modern luxuries and people happily sat on the rocks that separated the 2 venues from the sea, gathered together to adore the skyline and watch the sun slowly set, seemingly falling between 2 large rocks a few miles out to sea. Twin the experience of an Ibizan sunset, spurious amounts of drugs, some banging tunes and not a care in the world – then you'll get a taste of why I always tuned in and dropped out – good times!

There was a big group of us out there one year, mostly couples. We were walking to the bars after dinner one evening when we heard this horrific screaming coming from an alleyway. We told the women to wait on the main street while a few of us fellas went to check it out. I honestly thought a woman was being raped down this alley. We found that the screaming was coming from inside a non-descript door, so we burst through it, ready to smash up what we'd imagined to be a man attacking a woman. We had actually charged in through the emergency exit of a tattoo studio, where the screaming woman was having her neck tattooed! The tattoo artist stopped working and looked at us, completely bemused. We just turned right around and briskly marched back to where we'd came from!

When Nigel Benn was DJ'ing, I went to Ibiza with him as his minder, shortly after Tony died. I took Lyn with me and some of the other fellas, who had partners along for the ride too. We all stayed in an incredibly trendy castle themed mansion while we were there, which was cool. Nigel played at a big club one night, and when he finished his set, we headed for es paradis; a famous club on the waterfront that is recognisable mostly by its glass pyramid roof and The Ibiza Slingshot sitting next to it. It was always a plush venue that went all out; there was always something special happening to enhance the atmosphere, such as dancers overhead, water spraying and sometimes they did the neon paint thing, but this particular night we walked in about 20 handed to a foam party! In true Ibiza style, there were couples romping and frolicking in the foam and on the edge of the dance floor, while the rest just partied all around them. Recalling the memories from that night, reminded me just how many footballers and 'celebrities' you used to meet in the VIP areas and how even the most famous of DJ's used to mix with the revellers at parties and in restaurants. Making the most of the long weekend there, we also partied at Amnesia and Manumission on other nights. Amnesia was good, but Manumission stands out in mind as being a fucking mad one! The place wasn't even full with 8,000 ravers inside, the tunes were blinding and the atmosphere, insane!

I've got too many tales of great times in Ibiza to even put into a book! Sometimes I'll even hear a track on the radio, and it will take me back to a specific moment on The Island from years ago. Across my many vacations to Ibiza, I've taken copious amounts of coke, chewed through E's like sweets, sank vodka by the litre, jumped off of balconies and roof tops into swimming pools, dived off of a fast-moving boat and fuck knows what other crazy shit I've done, and all the while under some of the best mind-altering chemical-enhancements. By rights I probably should be dead because of it all, but somehow, the worst that's happened to me are hangovers and some week-long comedowns. If I had my time again, would I do things differently? Bollocks would I! I absolutely loved it – this was an island, where your own personal experience could be one of your own making and natural rhythmic fashioning and if I could handle a little bit more, 'mind-altering chemical intake' than the next man, then lucky me. But would I want my kids or Grandchildren to do half the things I've done in the name of clubbing? Most definitely not!

In all the years past, I've barely clenched a fist in Ibiza, never mind had to have a tear up. Maybe it was because I was 20 stone of muscle or maybe it was due to my reputation, but I think it actually speaks for how the Island used to be. I do believe that ecstasy made the rave scene, but cocaine spoilt it. Hopefully, as with most trends, we'll see a full circle on this and go back to the start, back to times before the flashiness and showing off, when it genuinely was all about the music, dropping out and fitting in – everyone on the same vibe.

Whilst we're on the subject of fitting in and being on the same vibe, now is as good a time as ever to mention and re-introduce someone that was never on our vibe, in my league......our league and out of his fucking league until I opened all of the doors that he's stepped through and been given a great deal of wealth – Maxi! Maxi needs to remember that he's got no real backing or bollocks, he's truly trying to walk in shoes that don't fit him and like most people that have tried walking in both my shoes and the path of organised crime, there is no rite of passage – unless you're willing and able to bite back, people, real proper people will soon see right through you and your bark...... and the hired help won't be able to protect you from the big bad wolves that are out there.

So, when I invited Maxi to come over to Ibiza (many times) with me as my guest to enjoy both the island and all that she had to offer, like the small-minded person he is and the same traits as an insecure child, he always found an excuse to cower away and work the same deals that I'd set him up with. After some heavy convincing, he followed, actually stumbled is a more accurate description, along for his first trip to Ibiza, all the while hiding in my shadow. Much like a kid who's never been exposed to anything other than what was handed to him, he really was like a fish out of water. At first, it was a bit embarrassing - I thought it was a mistake bringing him to the island, he never fitted in and was clearly clumsy and awkward with the people I gave him introductions to and the settings that he wasn't accustomed with - talk about trying to make a silk purse out of a sow's ear! When finally (again after being assured he was in safe company) he actually followed my advice and opened his eyes a little, he saw the opportunities on offer from me and my circle of people. Then after his first ever pill, a sip of the good stuff and loosening his top button, he realised that there was more to the island than just the stories he'd heard about – Maxi had taken the next (small) step in becoming a man. In business, especially businesses in island communities, people talk, and it's quite common in certain types of business ventures, those with no backing, money and muscle are taken advantage of; where there's lots of money, there's people that are quite happy and capable of taking it from you.

It was around 2011 when, knowing that I have connections and people all over the place, Maxi asked me to find out about a firm of Spaniards that they were considering buying out of a nightclub deal in Ibiza. To ensure a smooth business transition, and no liberties taken, my name was put forward as a person of 'involvement' and part of the 'equation'. I got them the info they needed, and they went on to do the deal with both security and confidence. They told me to treat the place as my home, come and go as I liked, do what I want, pay for nothing, they were just grateful things had happened as a result of my involvement and to have me behind them. The first year of them opening their club, they flew me out for the grand opening – an all-expenses paid deal and nothing was too much effort for them to make me feel welcomed. Of course, they had their own agenda, being that they'd now parade me around the VIP section, an obvious move really, they had to show there was validity in my 'involvement', word would now spread that they really had me in their corner, both back home and on the famous Spanish party island.

The following year, my daughter Carly flew out for a weekend to see what the new venue was all about. Our last night there together ended up being crazy for all the wrong reasons though, as egos and alcohol mixed can be a proven recipe for disaster – especially with those that can't handle either in the most basic of settings. It all started with some club and bar owners arguing and fighting who just happened to be in the owner's VIP section. I was completely out of my tree, when the argument escalated from name calling to actual threats involving both violence and my name! "I'm gonna pay Carlton Leach 10,000 euros to break your legs, you prick!" with a reply of, "Well, I'll pay him 20,000 euros to throw you off your fucking balcony!" and so it continued, with the childish, silly rich fuckers going on and on, as did my faded dancing. That was until Carly couldn't take any more and put every single one of them in their place, like the bunch of children they were: "Listen to your-fucking-selves would ya! None of you cunts are gonna get my Dad involved in your stupid shit, or I'll do you myself!" That pretty much settled that to be fair! But my take-away from that little turn out, once I'd come back down to planet earth, was the way they talked about me like I was their property, like some attack dog that would work for a treat! The cheeky bastards. I've worked with money and violence most of my life, but I'm no one's pet, nor do I fetch on command.

My most recent trip to the Island was once again spurred on by an invitation from Maxi and I don't need much convincing, so I said I'd happily see him there for the closing parties, but this time, that invite, and stay was a lot different and as I quickly found out, it was a far cry from my treatment in previous years. As we headed through Ibiza's only commercial airport to collect our luggage, my phone started pinging with missed calls and messages, I thought, 'Fuck me, I've only had it off 2 hours!' I almost didn't bother checking it, but luckily, I did as I had a WhatsApp message from my "brother," and "good friend" Maxi, saying that he wouldn't be able to pick us up after all. I was pretty fucked off, but I decided there and then I was always going to enjoy my holiday here, as no matter the change of mind or level of friendship once offered, and regardless of Maxi's changing attitude towards me, Ibiza was an island I had been visiting for decades and it was mine to escape to, not from. As we stood waiting for our cases at the belt, I told Jay of Maxi's selfish and impersonal actions and he said, "Don't worry, I'll call the Judge, he won't let us down." Bags in tow, we came out of the terminal building and found a shaded spot to keep out of the Balearic sun while we waited for our ride.

As I stood there in my shorts and shirt ready to embark on another big Ibiza adventure, I couldn't but think and ask myself, 'why would you invite someone to fly to another country, only then to treat them so disrespectfully, and to add further insult to injury, then tell them via a text message that you're now letting them down?' You had to question this mongrel thinking, as even a simpleton would see that Maxi had an ulterior motive from the start. What further proved how low this person was, I watched how courteous and accommodating the cab drivers were in their white Mercedes taxis picking up the same passengers from our plane…... even here, total strangers had been given a level of courtesy and reliability from someone they'd never met, and this was in a foreign land. Then there were people's friends pulling up in BMW's and Range Rovers to take their waiting pals off for a good time…... and then here I am, invited over and left out to dry, standing there like a plank...waiting. There was only one person to blame for this scenario and the little wank-stain that he is, couldn't even be bothered in handling the situation like a gentleman and give a justified reason, or even muster up a coward's excuse for not turning up or at least sending someone. "What's the Judge driving mate? Is he in that G55 again?" As I finished my question to Jay, I hear some music from a car stereo and looked across to see a Land Rover covered in grass, slowly approaching us. Now when I say grass, I don't mean this thing had gotten a bit dirty, I mean it was covered in artificial fucking grass, the cars paintwork was entirely concealed by green plastic grass, only the windows were visible. Before I could even finish thinking, 'what the fuck has that guy done to his car' Chris Judge's head comes out of the window; "Ay oop guys, I got here as fast as I could for ya's!" Don't get me wrong, it was brilliant of Chris to turn out for us at short notice, I really appreciated it, we all did, but as I climbed into the back of this thing, I was just hoping no one had recognised me! Chris was driving this motor due to a work thing and in actual fact, he ended up proper looking after us all week, taking us to see new places and parts of the island, driving us to bars and clubs, making sure we always got back to our hotels no matter what time, so even though I would've preferred a 'grass-free' mode of transport, thanks to Chris for being there for us! Chris didn't just run us about; he's a right nice fella and it was nice to have him party with us throughout the week too. I've never done business with Chris, I know him through Jay and Bill (aka The Missing Man), but the no-strings-attached kind of friendship and level of respect from Chris, who I barely knew, puts the likes of Maxi and his ethics (or lack thereof) to shame.

One lunchtime, a few of us went into Eivissa, or Ibiza Old Town as it's commonly known amongst the British tourists. We strolled in the Balearic sun, around the artisan market, through the cobbled back streets, mooched in and out of some cracking shops all around the town, just generally soaking up the atmosphere. You pretty much forget about 'time' when you're in Ibiza, you don't check your phone every 15 minutes and it's rare I look at my watch, you just eat when you're hungry, sleep when you're tired, swim if you fancy and party the rest of the time! We went into the Hard Rock Café that day for lunch. Hard Rock is kind of like an international institution, there isn't anywhere else quite like it and I love the food. After my meal I went into the gents and I nearly fell over; the walls and floor were tiled in the trippiest pattern I've ever seen, the cubical doors the same so you couldn't define the two, all topped off by carefully placed mirrors to freak you right out! I'd only had two drinks, but I turned and walked straight back out the door, which by the way, wasn't that easy to find. Whoever designed those bathrooms had a proper good laugh at the thought of all these tourists with hangovers having flashbacks and freaking out whilst trying to find the toilet! As we strolled back towards the taxi rank, I thought back and considered how much even Eivissa had changed over the last 20 years. The atmosphere was still brilliant, don't get me wrong, but there were a lot more pubs full of people just drinking to get drunk, rather than drinking and enjoying the Ibizan magic. I'm sure when half of those hanging out of both the pub doorways and their arses the following morning, couldn't tell you one bars name from the next, only how many times they fell over or threw up. When I walked these same streets years before, I had enjoyed street artists, live performances and more colourful surroundings. There had been more eateries than pubs, although, great restaurants are still plentiful in The Old Town.

One morning, I made it down to the restaurant around 11am, Gem had gone ahead about a half an hour before, so she was already at the big corner table with Kieron, Kayleigh, Chris, Sam and Jay. Lenny, I presumed, wasn't out of bed yet. "Ready to order lunch now, Carlton?" Jay was taking the piss due to the time. I don't know how, but no matter what we drunk the night before, he was always at breakfast by 08:30! I replied, "I'm not sure if I can even stomach breakfast to be honest, I feel fucking terrible, fuck knows why, I only had a few drinks and 1 pill!" They all rolled up laughing at me. Gemma explained that at one point in the night I'd turned to all our lot in the VIP area, poked my tongue out to reveal 4 pills, then proceeded to wash them down with vodka straight from the bottle! I denied it, but I knew they were almost certainly telling the truth! As Chris started recalling the previous night's events including a story about a short bald man in hotpants, it all started flooding back to me like a crazy trip! Let me go back to the day before at the club…

Day clubs are a new thing in Ibiza and as you may have gathered, I'll try most things once! I know now that it's not for me, I much prefer proper clubs, but I gave the concept a right good try-out before deciding! We'd been at Maxi and Rana's venue since mid-afternoon and Maxi hadn't bothered to show his face. He sent me a text saying he was ill, but I knew for a fact he was at a different venue with Tamer Hussein. Here, his choices and actions were gradually revealing his contempt for me. As I said previously, people seem to have short memories and as the saying goes, Familiarity breeds contempt. Coincidently, that afternoon would bring another prime example of this! An old friend of mine, who we'll call Scouse had flown out from Essex and met up with us. There was a crowd of people sitting together chilling out when Scouse made a nasty and uncalled for comment about Gemma. It might sound ridiculous to some to even consider reacting to this, but he had broken unwritten rules and was testing me! If you know me and have something to say about me or the woman I choose to be with, you should speak to me directly, man to man, not make a childish attempt to make her feel small in order to make yourself feel funny or tough. Scouse has now laid a challenge down to me and I wish he hadn't because we'd been mates for years. He was a football player and DJ, I'd put him in on earners over the years because I liked him, but in hindsight, that was my mistake as he wasn't of the ilk required to operate at my level of criminality. I thought about phoning Scouse, but that wasn't me, next I considered taking him to one side and having this out with him but given that his disrespect was so public there was only one way to deal with this. I spoke the scenario over with Lenny, who by the way, is a sound fella (I did him a turn 20 years or so ago and he's been there for me in return ever since). Len agreed that I'd come to the correct conclusion, and I asked him, Jay, Kieron and the other men to keep back as I went over to see Scouse with all his pals; I didn't need them to back me up. As I walked over, I hoped he would just do the right thing and apologise, but his ego prevailed and when I called him out, he got proper lemon! I smacked him straight in the mouth, which is exactly what he deserved for being a gobby cunt! As natural reaction took place, he clutched his mouth and turned his face away, at which point I decided not to weigh him in, it didn't warrant it. In my mind, I'd made my point and was willing to leave it there.

Security quickly circled and some of the casual acquaintances with our group tried to calm things. For me it was finished and just when I was about to go back to my table, spraying blood from his lip he shouts, "What, is that it?" Maybe his ego had fuelled a reaction within him, and he wanted to try and hold onto what little credibility he had as a man, laughable really! Anyone worth their weight wouldn't have walked away from that comment lightly and I'll fight anyone, win or lose and that's fine by me, so long as it's known I don't back down. But at that time, a flash thought was a simple truth, I was in my 50's with absolutely nothing to prove to anyone, and I'm not going to waste my energy rucking with youngsters high on coke – he wasn't even a challenge. But the fact remained he'd now pushed things, so, fuck that previous flash thought, I pulled out my blade and said, "Have it your way, come here now, I'll open you up like a fucking can of beans!" He wouldn't step to me, he quietly muttered something under his breath and shuffled away nursing his split lip as his pals again moved closer to try to calm things. Big W put a hand on my shoulder and said "C, he ain't worth it mate, don't do it, you'll get banged up!" I could've stabbed Scouse and probably got away with it, I doubt many people there would've given evidence against me and I had the clout to lose any CCTV too, but it was enough, job done, as there's no glory in kicking a dog when it's down. I'm sure he went back to his room, playing over in his mind what he should've done, but he caused and brought on more damage and injury to himself that day than what I did; he showed he didn't have the arsehole to back up what he thought he could get away with, anyway, fuck him…the Ibiza sun was setting over the sea and it was time to crack on with my true agenda…... party Ibiza style!

Late into the night and everyone in the VIP area is absolutely smashed. Everyone was having a great time and if the magic of Ibiza can get Jay and Lenny dancing, then my point is proven, and she's worked her magic once again! I remember vividly, I was dancing about on the edge of things when I saw Sarah lift off the ground, seemingly 3 feet in the air and in movie style slow motion, she flew towards the swimming pool, crashed down every one of the stairs and just fell short of landing in the water. I started dancing towards her (the dancing was out of my control; I just couldn't stop) as the rest of our lot ran in her direction to help. As she lay by the pool unconscious, Lenny went ape shit! He's not small and he can raise his voice, so I can understand why the normal folks who had paid to be in the VIP area started to move away as he roared; "Who the fuck done that to my missus, I'll fucking kill you!" He was spinning around looking for the culprit to fight, whilst undecidedly trying to make his way to check on his wife. Again, I saw everything in slow mo; "Saaaaaaaarraaaaaaaah!" Through my eyes, Len was doing a Baywatch style run towards the scene. The ladies in our group quickly organised a medic and saw to poor Sarah, while the blokes grabbed Lenny and informed him that, in fact, it was he who had just knocked his wife crashing down the stairs in his attempt at throwing some shapes, so there wasn't anyone to fight! We learnt the next day just how battered and bruised Sarah was, she couldn't even get down the hotel steps for the next 3 days, so we kept going to the bar by their hotel pool at lunchtime to see them. Lenny did feel fucking awful, but unfortunately for him, that didn't stop us ribbing him for months to come about his dance moves! You could say he brought break dancing to a whole new level.

A quick warning to anyone visiting these new day clubs: Stay out of the pools! If I had a fiver for every time I saw a man or woman look at the queue for the loo, then only wander into the pool up to their waste and do a little 30-second-long jig, then proceed to fuck off back to their mates, well I'd have come home with more cash than I went with! The dirty bastards…

A few nights later, we celebrated Kieron and Kayleigh's anniversary by crawling a few bars, then hitting a club. When it was time to leave, Kayleigh unwittingly went outside to try and get a taxi. Now if you've been to Ibiza before, you know how hard it is to get a taxi if you haven't booked one or organised a Private Car or 'Pirate' as they're called by local Police. Kayleigh returned to our table looking pretty pleased with herself and announced that everyone should hurry up because the car is waiting outside. "It was proper lucky, this man said he could take us all to the hotel, so I gave him 50 euros and he's pulling his car round to the front!" Needless to say, we didn't rush to the exit, but once we finished cracking up with laughter, we did explain Kayleigh's faux par to her!

After another great night out towards the end of the week, me and Gemma got back to our hotel in the early hours of the morning. I was still buzzing, so I poured a large brandy, but just as I sat down at the dining table, there was an almighty crashing sound, the room lit up with a bright white light and I thought 'what the fuck?' We rushed to the balcony to take a look and we could hardly make out the swimming pool due to the torrential rain, I'm talking like the sky had opened up and the earth was being replenished; a real tropical down pour, it made the heavy rain back home look like a shower! The thunder and lightning continued for hours, and I sat and watched the storm from my balcony in absolute amazement. I've never experienced a thunderstorm quiet like that, I remember as the lightning struck, you could see that it stretched for miles across the Mediterranean. One of Ibiza's many magical natural moments was unfolding in front of me, it looked like she was stretching her fingers across the dark sky, if only for a few seconds. In all honesty, I thought some of my enjoyment was probably chemically enhanced, but the next day I learned that Jay and his missus had sat up watching it too, so I wasn't a complete lunatic! That was the year I saw Anthony Joshua in Lineker's Bar and went over to meet him. He and his mates were all chatty enough and I told AJ he'd be world champ within 18 months. By the following year, it turned out I was right!

Our final night out that year was a closing party. Closing parties in Ibiza are a powerful experience, it's as if the whole Island is experiencing a mix of emotions, sad and nostalgic that it's the final party of the season, but elated at the same time, knowing that it's going to be such an incredibly special event that your part of. The evening hadn't turned to night yet and our waitress sheepishly approached our VIP table and somewhat unwillingly handed me the bill. As I looked down at it, she explained that I'd hit the limit set by the owners, and we should start paying for our drinks. Maxi's sheer rudeness, disrespect and short memory were not the young lady's fault, so I politely explained that she should get him on the phone. She went back to the bar and fetched someone else to have a try at explaining the situation to me and that they hadn't been able to reach Maxi by phone. "It's ok, I'll sort it out with him" I explained, "You're only doing your jobs." Maxi answered in 2 rings when I called, with the usual bullshit "My brother, how are you? Are you having a good time? I'm sorry I haven't seen ya!" I set about reminding him of a small sample of the things I've done for him over the years, some of which contributed to the fact that he was now an Ibiza club owner in the first place, about how he had paraded me around the club in previous years and told me that it was my club as much as his. "I'm going to hand my phone to this nice young lady and you're going to correct the situation, yes?" Before he could finish apologising to me, the waitress had the phone to her ear and when she handed it back to me, she confirmed that there had been a mistake and there was no limit to my drinks. The ladies in our group that night were very down to earth, proper decent human beings, they could have easily been a bit flash, but they actually had more class and character than the stuck-up millionaires we were surrounded by. Recognising how awkward the waitress felt, having to request money and being asked to get one of her bosses on the phone, our lot chatted to her and made her more comfortable coming to our area than any other in the club that night. She probably got treated better by us commoners than by anyone who had frequented the VIP area all year. For the exceptional service we received all night long, we had a whip round and organised a nice tip which she was blown away by at the end of her shift. It shows you that you can't buy class or humility and I maintain more integrity than those with short memories and big bank accounts.

I don't consider myself to be famous, but I do tend to get recognised from time to time. When you're in Ibiza, people are always looking out for famous stars because it's well known that the place attracts people from all walks of life and when you're in a club's VIP area, people really look and study who's in there, wondering who can afford 'that table'. This is especially true when you're pumped up on steroids, wearing shorts and sporting tattoos all over your body! As Ibiza has become flashier and posy, full of pretentious twats and table whores, this trend became accentuated, as I learnt in the 2013 season when we arrived at Blue Marlin by yacht (I'm not claiming this was my yacht, by the way)! Big vessels can't get close to the shore there, so Blue Marlin send small boats out to collect you and bring you to their venue and as we headed to our area, I realised that there were scores of stuck-up bell-ends in £300 shorts, looking to see how much my watch was worth and thinking 'My goodness, who are these riff-raff and how on earth can they afford to be in here with us!' Back in the day I did used to get recognised, but I've noticed this strange new phenomenon emerged. On at least 5 occasions over my last 2 visits, someone has held their smartphone up in line with my face to compare me to a photo on Google! 'It is you, ain't it, you're Carlton Leach, right?' I don't mind at all, and my usual response is, "I hope so!" but even so, what a strange thing that people look you up online to see if it's you!

During the summer season, Ibiza has always filled with party goers from diverse backgrounds, all with a mutual love of dance music and a hedonistic culture, but I can't help but feel that some of what we used to go for has been lost to time and youngsters are now chasing a 'version' of the real Ibiza; a pre-planned, package deal with an all-in-one magical experience. That unique magic may have passed on, or perhaps it hasn't passed on and the day will come that the chavs will congregate elsewhere, trying to impress each other and following the cultural trend of saying, "I went to Ibiza, and it was amaaaaazing!", letting Ibiza go back to its far less commercial roots once again. People didn't used to party for 24 hours a day, we used to party at night, then sleep and eat (a little bit) through the day before going again. Maybe a lot of people didn't get the memo that you can't sustain partying in good spirits without any rest!

It's an incredible shame that probably 90% of visitors to The White Isle won't ever get to experience the other side that Ibiza has to offer, the beautiful and equally magical side that 'The Island' discreetly reserves for those who are adventurous enough both in body and mind to explore and discover. If you find yourself at a loose end and considering a last-minute weekend away, even in winter, please consider Ibiza. Any time of the year, hire a car and drive into the mountains, get a taxi driver to take you off the beaten track, or go on a boat ride and ask the captain about the coves. There is so much that only locals know about, but if you start to ask the right questions, they'll help you discover things you otherwise wouldn't and remember that life and the island is more about the experience and adventure, not social media and bragging rights.

Gemma - "….I'm sure If I were to say, "Ibiza" to him, he'd soon be listening, as that's a love affair for him that's spanned most, if not all of his adult life"

I'm a fairly private person, so it's funny how I ended up being with a man who'd published an autobiography and subsequently had a film made about his life, but they say opposites attract, so perhaps that's true. Carlton has been well known for bodybuilding, boxing-training and the muscle game; so, he's always had an interest in keeping in shape, something we did find to be of mutual interest – although, perhaps, nowadays I take fitness more seriously than him and I find myself giving him a good kick up the arse from time to time where training and (especially) his diet choices are concerned!

I've been with Carlton for a little over 6 years now and like any couple, we've had our ups and downs, but most importantly we've made some amazing memories, like our trip to Belgium a couple of years back. Belgium isn't "the place to be", nor is it party central - two key elements that meant we were able to spend a lovely few days' there, simply relaxing and taking in the city atmosphere. Spending most of the year living in Spain, has allowed us to visit much of the country, as one element of life I enjoy is exploring different areas. When you're away from the crowds and distractions, you can easily find that each city or town has something different to offer or discover….and although Carlton doesn't display that much energy, enthusiasm or keenness as me in this pursuit, I'm sure he "plays along" just to appease me. Saying that, I'm sure If I were to say, "Ibiza" to him, he'd soon be listening, as that's a love affair for him that's spanned most, if not all of his adult life. We've visited his beloved Beleric island on several occasions and had some fabulous times. The VIP treatment we received at some venues was incredible; I remember thinking, 'I'd never pay the prices they charge for all this!'….but it goes with the territory and has become part and parcel for Carlton. The down side to being at Carlton's side in a place like Ibiza isn't an obvious one, it's something that I figured out once I'd spent a lot of time around him; he struggles to be himself within certain environments or crowds. If I was asked why this is, it could be down to the years of continued and relentless pressure of people's expectations of him, not forgetting Carlton having to watch his back all the time; staying sharp around strangers, yet all the while having to appear relaxed and "normal", well…that's enough to take a toll on anyone! Thankfully, there are certain friends and family members with whom he can be his "true self."

Not many people meet Carlton for the first time and go away disappointed, I'm sure of it. He doesn't need to flex within any circle in order to gain respect, as the fact remains, he is a decent, and respectful man. I've seen so many people walk away after meeting or chatting to him and they're either made-up or in shock, because he has this way with people that leave them feeling like they're his new best friend. This outcome is both a product and testament of Carlton's kind nature, but it can lead to issues from time to time, especially when the "new best friend" starts expecting just a little too much!

Spain is probably the best place for Carlton over and above the UK; when he's in England, it's as if stress and problems are only ever a moment or phone call away…. and if it wasn't for his children and grandchildren, I think he'd rarely return. If you were to think about most people's pet-hates in their day-to-day "British life," one of the more consistent ones would have to be traffic! You can't get away from it - you have to plan your entire day to try to avoid it and it drives (excuse the pun) him mad, but outside of the major cities, "mucho trafico" to the Spanish is 4 cars ahead of you at a red light! Throughout our entire time in Spain, people are on Carlton's case to go back, and there seems to be two types in particular. The first type call him up with lines like; "If you were here Carlt we could do…" and "I really need to see you in person Carl, there's a lot going on!" These are almost always the ones that, once he lands at Gatwick, are not to be seen or heard of for the entire trip, they bring nothing good his way and must just want to ensure that they can get access to him if needed. The other kind are the ones who want him at all the parties, the weddings, the funerals. He literally gets invited to birthdays, weddings and funerals of people he's never even met…can you imagine? A handful of people are, of course, genuine and love to have him about the place because he's a good laugh, but most want only to parade him around. It's great to have people pay for your hotels, meals and booze for a weekend, but it will never benefit anyone where the important things in life are concerned, those being health, family and financial interests.

I look forward to Carlton being able to leave behind the vast number of no-mark users he's managed to accumulate over the years; the selfish people that drag him down daily with their wants and false promises, and for us to be able to enjoy many more days spent together in the sunshine; going off the beaten track, visiting random places, and most importantly for Carlton to be able to relax, let his guard down and be whoever or whatever he wants to be. You might annoy me sometimes Carlton, but you know I truly love you!

Gemma & Carlton

Ibiza Chris in the grass covered Land Rover!

8 WORTH A MENTION

I may not be so heavily involved in the game anymore, but my roots run deep in the underworld. When they cut down a mighty oak tree to build those new carboard houses, they never manage or are able to totally completely remove the trees' roots, or the knowledge of where they once were, those will always remain in the earth, as their very existence will always be a blueprint of strength and is one that will always ensure that we know of what was, and that they're there somewhere!

Crime and violence have been my life for over 40 years and now that I'm in my 60's and have taken a conscious step away from it all, I feel a kind of relief, like a heavy weight has been lifted. I'm now more relaxed, mainly because I'm less likely to have someone coming for me, I don't feel like a bullet or a blade is so imminent now, more importantly than that, I feel like I can be closer to my family, be there to enjoy the moments that I might have otherwise missed whilst keeping them all at a safe distance from both myself and my activities. I don't deny or even denounce my life of crime, as through it, I have formed solid friendships and unbreakable bonds with good people, people who I'm still in touch with today and will be until the end. If I needed to, I know I can still count on certain old school chaps, they know that the same is still true of me too, and through this book I wish them safety, security, and happiness.

There's an old adage, way of doing things or more a "code", that many live and are willing to die by and there's some that also give claim that it doesn't even exist. Those that are of the latter and live by no code, are the same that don't have any morals in much of what they do and how they live. I consider those same nay-sayers and people that aren't willing to live by the known and respected underworld's code of ethics, are the same that feel they can then live without repercussion, or be held accountable for an ill or wrongdoing; as even proper villains have principles, as during your apprenticeship, being around some of the old villains and old school will have ingrained within you of such rules, like never involving women, kids or straight goers, never grassing and without compromise always loyalty…..very early on, you make a choice and pick a side – you go, "left", or you go, "right"…you either go straight or you operate on the other side of the law……and accept the rules of that world, as it's said, "if you sit on a fence long enough, you'll eventually get impaled by it!" To say there's never been a code is as ignorant as it is arrogant, and simply insulting to many of the greats, Wilf Pine, Frankie Simms and Roy Shaw, to name but a few, all who lived and died by the code. Speaking metaphorically, there are lines in the road for a reason, and as much as for most of my adult life, I felt the "speed limit" didn't apply to me, I still picked a lane and accepted the consequences that went along with that same choice and decision. The same standard applied to how I made and kept friendships. Keeping your friends close, but your enemies closer is something I've never understood or lived by; save that for the movies and entertainment, as we'd never, EVER let someone of the wrong type or standing to be amongst us – who the fuck would willingly drink, operate and entertain from a "poisoned well?" I'm a huge fan of history, always admired and had somewhat of a fascination with Emperors and generals of old, and I can't think of a single one, that in times of battle, where a general would lead men whose Modus Operandi was one that lacked character but promoted cowardness and deceitfulness, or an Emperor who gained any level of success, health and prosperity for his family and kingdom, whose counsel's advice was one based on dishonesty and an agenda that conflicted with the best interests of his master. The litmus test with those around me has always been on honesty and loyalty and those that are within my circle, are not just friends – they're family and they're for life.

There is no better start in a young boy's life, than being taught the rights and wrongs, and as I've experienced, there's none better than my father; as it's also my belief this should be any dad's moral obligation and responsibility, but there's an undeniable truth that some of the biggest influences will be our peers. There's been people that I've considered 'top of the tree' and impressionable men that I've either worked with, known from childhood or through association, that have instilled as much a moral compass in the workings and existence of the underworld, as much my father did in terms of the rights from wrongs.

I'd mentioned earlier that my dad had an association with the twins, and like a lot of people that worked or had business dealings with them, being on the pay roll or dealing in matters of goods that found their way off of the back of a lorry, if things went sideways, you paying your fair share meant certain protections could be extended to you. When my dad got his hands burned down to the actions of a grass, and a stretch behind the wall was on the cards, like any man worth his salt, my dad accepted that he could be doing a lump of porridge; and even after an invitation from the Twins, stepping in to help defer or sway someone's memory and witness statement, my dad said, "No, I knew the risks and will accept the verdict." You don't need to be a seasoned villain or chap to know that you never speak….rules are rules. And that's why, the teachings and lessons of a man's integrity and his morals should be never on auction or up for debate.

There are simply too many chaps to list and for me to say, from my personal experience, that one is of more 'standing' or 'measure' than another is something that simply can't be done. It's also not a question of who I respect more, or less, or the amount of work they've done 'on the pavement', as there's a good few people, that understand the workings and rules of the underworld, have never done a stretch or been involved in anything 'heavy', but carry the same level of moral integrity as the staunchest of villains that I know, but, again from my personal experience I will say there are some men, that as much as they've left an impression, have also left a mark on me.

There're a few names, that when I think back on, that no matter what's going on in my life, always make me smile, give me a sense of pride in knowing and being able to call them family. The same were also of such impact, that to this day, are as impressionable as they were, in some circumstances, thirty or forty years ago.

Back in the 90's, when I was managing scores of contracts for different types of security and door-work, a man's ability in handling himself was an essential part of what he did, but also reliability, loyalty and respect was key to an overall level of success, as this would then promote and ensure the longevity, as it was as much about business as it was earning a pound note, of what I did. One thing that I was always willing to do was give someone a chance; barring they wasn't a wrong-un or a total fuck-up, and to a degree, what with the established firm I had behind me, it worked well, and it wasn't long before my reputation and name spread through-out, not only London but surrounding areas too. We were very good at what we did, and very strong, but, with that success, there came times where there was always some that would simply try and take liberties, and as sure as I'm sitting here, as it did back then, it would be beyond mind-numbing how many would comfortably try and take the piss.

With brawn, there has to be brains, and with the sizeable, good earners on the books, and as you may of heard, and as much as I've experienced, anyone can say they can run a door or be able bodied enough to work in a minding capacity, but it takes a lot more than a pair of bulging biceps and a nicely pressed shirt, to not only do the job, but also maintain a level of professionalism and reliability, and part of that same reliability and professionalism has to be extended to the same person, who not only employs you, puts money in your pocket each and every week, but also extended a hand allowing you a seat at the table. I couldn't tell you how many people, who I'd taken care of, not only consistently, but better than most, if not all, with weekly paychecks for security work, taken both them and their misses out, or girlfriends and family, never allowing them to put their hand in their pockets once, making sure they all had a good night out, only then to be treated with contempt. But as proven, true loyalty isn't based or measured on a contract or a price, as I always carefully picked the type of venue, people and place I'd do business with, and it'd always be with the preconceived thought that they and the venue was reliable and one that'd prove they'd wouldn't be more trouble than it was worth. So, when I got to hear from trusted clients that they'd been approached by the same people I'd given an opportunity in earning very good money, had very foolishly, tried to either undercut me in price or nick the contract behind my back, learned very quickly that there can only be one head at the end of the table, and another person's reputation won't help you when you stray from the pack!

It was a big change from the 'football days' of the 70's and 80's; to that of 'clubland', the irony being there was no money or big earners and fighting with other football firms (unless you consider what was taxed by the Under 5's as an income), but in terms of loyalty and integrity, the respect and trust with the terrace crowd was in some cases, of more value than any door contract and had no price tag. There were a good few people that were a proper handful, I mean real menaces on the terraces, some are sadly no longer amongst us, but their names will forever live on.

Bill Gardner is a person, that from my first meeting, is a man who I took great pride in standing alongside and will forever be one of absolute legend. It doesn't matter whether it's a day, week or a year that has passed, we can call each other on the phone or meet up and it'd be a welcomed and trusted conversation, that's based on a level of loyalty that started in my teens…. and without giving away anyone's age, that's a friendship and an unbreakable bond that goes back some 50 years! Money, to a degree can buy a level of reliability and dependency; as the best soldiers don't come cheap or work for free, but when you have a handful of men, that when they are relied upon, and I mean you're really up against it, the very thin ice beneath you is about to crack and it looks like this could be a bad one, those same men with an unquestionable level of loyalty that fight and stand there, not giving an inch - that is something that can never be bought or borrowed – it's a type and level of comradery I've rarely seen away from my days at West Ham or within any of the proper football firms.

Another name, as much as some, but a lot more than others, who without question, was as impressionable, as he was leaving a mark on me growing up, was and remains to be Vic Dark. Vic, who I know won't mind me saying this is, marginally, older than me, but the authority, weight and standing he carries is one of the best representations of the old guard I've ever seen; and I've met them all. I grew up with Vic, who as a rarity, was a close and trusted friend both at and away from football (most of the people in my life were either friends at OR away from the football crowd). Vick was a package deal; he was what everyone wanted to have as their big brother: he oozed charisma, could cut a rug and had some serious fucking bottle, and growing up in East London, one thing you had to have was either some serious brains or the willingness to take it to any level – that man would never budge or give so much as an inch, he was as game as they came and then some…..fucking dangerous under any circumstances. We'd go out at weekends, clubs, discos, pubs, birds he knew how to handle anyone, size crowd or situation. As a teenager, I looked up to him a lot; in fact, I'd have to say he was the most impressionable person I was around during that time, he was everything I wanted to be and could've wished for if I ever had a big brother. Some people align and identify with the teachings and writings of a divinity, a king, or a political leadership – for me it was Vic Dark. It was whilst I was still in my teens when he got his first bit of bird, and I was absolutely gutted when he got handed that stretch! It felt that a large part of me had been taken away, part of my strength had gone and the safety net that existed for a long time was no longer there…. I'd go as far in saying that it was like I'd lost a limb or part of my sight. I remember I would go with both his brother and mum to see him on visits, and conversations we had where he'd give me an honest insight to prison life, or lack of, and "Never end up in here, Carlton…. it's total shit." In my mind, only those that respect and have your best interest at heart will tell you the falseness of people's claims of living in a concrete box being one of simplicity, or how easy their life is, and they have it made behind the wall. He made sure that I understood the truth of it and where he was and would impress on me the cold reality of his own situation and the loss of years behind the wall ……. his mentorship, friendship and advice had now progressed from that of previous years - he was now playing the role of a big brother in every sense of the word, now teaching me new, invaluable lessons, that couldn't have been given when we were two local lads, who once walked the shared streets of our East London neighbourhood, when we were all out on a Saturday night or during daytime ventures. It was during those visits and seeing a close friend in that situation, that helped me stay out of prison…....the cold and soulless existence of a human being whilst in prison, who against all odds, would never fold or be beaten, now being treated and held in the same capacity of a man with no life or future. Vic is 'a man's man', his loyalty is both unbreakable and unquestionable……. he is someone who'd stand and be willing to give his life and soul when defending both his name and the very morals that define who he is and the underworld code that remains as much of him as his own beating heart.

Wilf Pine is and will always remain on another level. Wilf, who was born in Newcastle, had an upbringing that was typical to a lot of hardened villains, but there was something that made this man so respected and one-of-a-kind in terms of his standing amongst the absolute cream of the crop; they really broke the mould when they made him. He simply was one of a few and a rarity in terms of his scope and ability, not only as a businessman but a chap at every level of the criminal fraternity. He was a man who knew how to operate on any level and of those that are within the top crime families and members of the whole criminal infrastructure, who's had dealings directly with Wilf, will not only tell you of the respect they have for him, will of equal measure never allow a bad word to be said. As I've said, power and respect are something that remains very difficult to not only get within crime, but also to maintain and hold on to, as once you've been given, or 'taken' the reigns, competition never allows you to take a day off; friends as much as foes can come knocking 24/7 – but Wilf did this with apparent ease and with great success.

His skillset was something that allowed him to relate and identify with the single family run corner street shop as much as being able to shake the hand of one of the most powerful men in all of crime – again, as a testament to his ability in working within any crowd or type of business, even after he did a stretch, living within the confinements of a prison cell and life, when he first came out, he successfully managed one of the biggest names in rock history. This was attributed again to a skillset that was unique to him, and let's be honest, if you can keep a rock star and his band of real rock n rollers in check, you know you've got something!

Wilf had connections throughout much of the known and unknown underworld and it can't be said enough how he was a very heavily respected man, who I can comfortably say was on a level that should be used as a benchmark for anyone within organised crime. Wilf became the adopted son of Joey Pagano, the head of one of the major New York crime families and had his life written about in a book; there's even a written account of Wilf "fighting shoulder to shoulder with John Gotti" in a gun battle! To this day, Wilf is known and accepted as the only Englishman and person of non-Italian blood to ever have been a made-man and being a full-fledged member of the American mafia. Wilf is as many top-tier villains will attest, part of what can only be accurately referred to as Gangland elite, an absolute legend within a world that can never be fully explored or talked about.

I first got to hear of Wilf's name through a good few of the chaps and villains, who all spoke of this man as if he was some sort of myth and urban legend, but it wasn't until I got to actually meet and spend time around him, I learned and saw first-hand how much of an enigma he actually was. It was during some work of shared interest's together, I got to see how intelligent and immersed he was in every aspect of not only the British and American underworld, but life and all those involved in it. He had this aura about him, and it wasn't that you were scared of him, only that you were conscientious of the fact to be in his company was something special and was something of a privilege to be included in any capacity or amount of work. You may have seen and heard of young actors speaking of their experiences around seasoned greats, and the unmeasured level of respect that was given without thought, simply down to their presence and voice in a crowded room of any size, when Wilf spoke, his voice was empowering to the point where he never had to raise his voice or shout to be heard …. it was also the way he carried himself, it simply made me drop whatever I was doing to listen to what he had to say. To this day, and conversations I still have with those close to him, I will always consider it an absolute honour to have been called a friend by Wilf, to have been in both his company and spent time with him. To be extended a hand, an invitation and being vouched for so as to meet those much higher up the ladder and on an international level is something that's beyond any amount of appreciation or gratitude from me.

His known trademark was his walking cane and the gold top set upon it, but it's only his voice and the way about him that will be remembered by those that knew and were actually around him. Some have to work at becoming legends, only reaching the halfway mark, Wilf Pine is someone that was born with all the natural abilities of a general of armies, a captain of industry and a man of great stature who championed many ventures in many lands.

Frankie Sims is a fellow native East Ender and a man who's stood in the Tibb's corner as much as a lot of highly respected, heavy-duty men. When Frankie spoke to you, it was with the knowledge and invested insight of several generations, advice and learnings that if missed, was on par as losing out on the winning lottery numbers. Another man, who when I was in his company could never bore you with the wealth of experience he had and was willing to share with the right people and like any of those within the circle of respected villains, had plenty of bottle and would never back down. His principles, amongst many of his other admiral qualities are something that I've always respected – The times he got served some serious bird, he never moaned, not once, he simply got his head down and dealt with it. When he's come out from doing some serious porridge, and like a lot of connected people, if and when he's been offered a bit of work that'd taken him clear to a stay of luxury and an easier life, no matter the size of the prize or amount of gold, he's chosen to take care of his family first – EACH AND EVERYTIME. No bag of money was big enough nor any number of shiny stones could ever take the place to that of his family.

Frankie Sims is one of those that remains very impressionable on me, and as much as there's very little written on him, a lot is known by the right people and for the right reasons. Down to me living in several places and with business dealings having me move about a lot, If Frank hadn't seen me in a while and learned of where I was, before I got time to put a pair of shoes on and be out the door, he'd already made his way over to where ever it was I was staying, and it didn't matter how far or where it was, he'd make that journey just to say hello and make sure I was ok. A man who didn't have to speak to be heard or respected, and until this day is someone that I have an unconditional amount love, respect and hold in the highest of esteem.

Roy Shaw is a man who has to be included, not because he's a legend, known and respected man in many circles, including mine, but simply because he's someone I always had a good night out with, and we enjoyed each other's company. Back in my teens, there wasn't one of his fights that any of our crowd didn't attend. It was always a big deal, and it was part of who we were, going and supporting one of our own. His fights were truly legendary, and as entertaining as the fights were, the after-party's that were always held at The Circus Tavern were as good. When it came to a fight, Roy was a very dangerous man, inside and outside the ring, and anyone that had it with Roy on the cobbles, if being honest, will tell you he hit very hard and the only way to stop a man like Roy was to knock him out – and good luck with that! One of the biggest misconceptions and untruths out there, largely at fault and fueled by the newspapers and those that had never even met or knew Roy, was his business sense. He was a very clever man when it came to earning and investing a pound note. On and under the surface, Roy was unquestionably a very tough man, had a look and face that'd make any judge reconsider a potential conviction and enough to even get the hairs on the back of a ghost's neck to stand up, but again, it's only after you've spent time and been around people that you learn who they really are and how they tick. Of the many things I always enjoyed and appreciated about Roy was our nights out, and believe me, he had the stamina and will power to out-do any man in either his teens or twenties when it came to enjoying himself - he was simply unstoppable and a machine…. he was always fired up and could only slow down (not stop) when the last person had left the room or dance floor. There was one occasion when a lot of people were going to an event being held at The Cats Whiskers night club in Streatham, South London, and as always, we made sure everyone was sorted getting picked up and taken to the event. I was in a limo with a bunch of people, when I was called and asked if I was anywhere near Roy's place. Even if I wasn't, Roy was someone I would always go out of my way for as his energy and dry sense of humour was welcomed and appreciated by me, and like I said I always had a good time when we were out. As we pulled up outside Roy's place in a leafy suburb of Essex, he came out and climbed in. One thing about Roy was his presentation - always impeccably dressed and on time.

There was nothing ever cheap about Roy, in either his looks, manners when around women or his taste and lifestyle. As soon as Roy climbed in the limo, he made a b-line straight for me and no sooner had Roy sat down next to me, he looked around him and said, "No disrespect to anyone here, but I don't know any of you, only Carlton and he's my friend…...so I'll only be speaking to Carlton from here on out, Ok!" No one was going to argue and if I'm being honest, I took this as one of many compliments I'd gotten from Roy over the years. But, as soon as we started driving away, one of the lads brought out the 'party favours', and with that Roy jumped right in with, "oh, I'll have some of that!"……both the situation and Roy had gone from 0 - 60 in a matter of seconds, and the stern but calm nature of a man, who just seconds ago, made it clear of his need for privacy and space, well, that was now 'completely out of the window'. What unfolded was the beast and party side of Roy......and for all to enjoy. The fun and energy didn't stop there though, as when we pulled up to the event, and being we were coming as VIP guests, and if anyone that's been to The Cats Whiskers will tell you, you have to enter from the side. Before any of us could get up the steps and knock on the heavy reinforced door, Roy was bouncing and leaping up the steps, hitting the door, that only allowed the person on the other side to assume it was either the Hulk, a police-battering ram or a hurricane trying to enter with full force. Now to most, when entering a building or an event, and if there's a door placed in-between you and gaining entry, it's accepted it's been put there as an obstacle or a barrier, but not to Roy! As soon as it opened, with the inconvenience of that same door, stood a mountain-sized bouncer now in his way, Roy was instantly fired up, it was like a switch had been pushed and it was pure 'fireworks' - he was as ready to go as if he was fighting at the event himself and believe me, even in his 70's, Roy was someone that still had a lot of power and was a handful. Quickly calming the situation and leading Roy in, I accepted Roy was of mind and had it in his heart that he was here for a good night, with me and whoever else was along for the ride....and he didn't want it spoilt or slowed down, no matter the number of steps leading up to the entrance, the size of the door or lump on the other side of it. Roy was as staunch as they come and game right until the end - a fearless man on every level.

Charles Bronson to me is someone that also encapsulates, a commendable level of integrity and respect, but much like Roy, there's more untruths and lies written and talked about him, and none more, again thanks to the press and people that don't know or have taken the time in speaking with him. Now, the first thing that a lot of people forget is Charlie is heavily isolated from the WHOLE world; so much of what he hears is via mail or message. So, when he puts a lot of trust in someone, only then to hear that he was let down, taken advantage of or spoken ill about, being that he has always extended his hand, done a lot for people, many that wouldn't help him in the same way he has them, he takes it very personal.

The man has been misquoted and lied about more times than I can begin to explain and by a lot of people, but being Charlie, he wears his heart on his sleeve and always helps people. When it comes to a charity, and especially one that involves a child, he will dedicate an enormous amount of his time and energy into whatever is asked of him….and then some. It wasn't long after the release of Muscle back in 2002, that I was living in Noak Bridge when I started getting letters, cards and also items that people wanted signed being sent to me via the publisher, and the one that really surprised me was from Charles Bronson. When I first opened the envelope, the first thing I noticed was the picture he'd drawn and put in there, the next was the letter he'd written to me. What took me back was the fact he'd taken the time in writing to me, telling me he'd read my book, Muscle that had been sent to him from Blake Publishing, complimenting me and saying how he'd really enjoyed it! On the back of the drawing he'd sent, he wrote, "You're a true warrior, and anyone that's a friend of Vic Dark will be a warrior too" and it was signed 'Chaz'. I was told some years back, that when Vic was away, both Charlie and Vic used to train together, and when Charlie was holding the bag for Vic to punch and work out on, it was with such a level of impact and a type of mannerism being displayed by Vic, that impressed Charlie to his core. From there, I would often hear and read that Charlie had mentioned and spoke well of me in several of his books, which I took as a massive compliment. The first opportunity I got, I helped raise some money for an event that was being held in an effort to try and get him a release. I also had the privilege of looking after his mum and family at a few events – lovely people.

Paul Ferris is a man, who as of yet, I've not had the pleasure of meeting, which is surprising being we have mutual friends and business associates, but from the people that I'd consider very high in terms of their credibility and standing in the criminal fraternity, all speak very highly of Paul. Like I mentioned earlier, Wilf was a man who was "top of the tree," and he never ever kept or allowed fools around him…..... and if Wilf spoke, not only well, but also extremely highly of someone, then you knew they were of a gold standard. When Paul's name came up, it was without question in the most respectful and with the highest regards.

Tony Tucker is as much a name as he is a person, who will be remembered for reasons other than the man I got to know as one of my best and closest of friends, and no number of films, documentaries or conversations have, or will ever truly reflect either him, or the person he was….and definitely not either the relationship or friendship that was prematurely ended on the 6th of December 1995. When deciding if Tony was to be written about, it was without question he should, but one of a few things I had to decide on was what, and how he should be remembered. It's a given, that people will always expect me to talk about him, but it's going to be solely mine in what way and how I share the friendship we had.

We both grew up in Forest Gate, East London, and as much as we went to different schools; Tony attended Sandringham, I went to Stratford Grammar, and there's a good chance we unknowingly brushed past each other in and around, if not the same shops, but even stood in the same pubs and clubs at the same time, as the shared company and circles we moved in, at one stage or another all knew or worked in a shared capacity during their reign. It wasn't until a chance meeting at an after-party at Epping Country Club back in 1990, that started, what was a simple introduction and conversation (and the sharing of some pretty potent Jack 'n Jills) that then led quickly to a very strong friendship. It was one that instantly ticked all the same and right boxes, and it was from here that strong bond, that I believe, is what made his death that all the more painful. It was an instant and automatic liking for each other, we really were two peas in a pod, like the most mischievous boys sat next to each other in the same class, and no matter how many times the teacher separated the two, they would still defiantly find ways in communicating with each other across the classroom, and their efforts and success at being the schoolboy class-jokers could be heard by the consistent giggling. A lot of friendships, especially close ones, are much like two brothers; one will inevitably take the lead and that is one of the big brother role, the other will as much follow as he will stand beside him… like a mechanic and the oily rag, each knew their role, except with Tony and I, we shared the roles and platform and it was never a competition between us, every conversation and plan simply complimented each other. We shared so much in terms of our personalities, likes and social interests. Everything from food, drinks, a lot of the same mates and the areas we'd visited separately over the years.

With Tony, it felt like I'd found a brother who'd been separated from me at birth, there wasn't anything we weren't willing to share when it came to a conversation; fears, concerns, ambitions, dreams there was no inhibitions……and that's what I honestly feel bothered people, they never knew Tony, were and remain jealous of the friendship and bond we had, and if anything, their poisoned opinion and cowardice malice was more destructive than the drugs that changed Tony. We planned a lot of what we did on a social level together and as much as it still pains me, I can remember the promises we made together for our shared lives in the future. As a person, Tony was a very powerful man, and he could have a row, but he wasn't indestructible and I'm sure he went down a few times, but to me, his strength was measured by his willingness to swerve using weapons, as we both were of the mindset, if it takes a man to beat you when he's firm-handed and still needs a tool, then Tony would rather lose fighting just one man with his hands than beating thirty with a weapon.

Tony wasn't a tool merchant, but he wasn't stupid either, so one day he asked someone (definitely not me) to get him a little insurance policy, which this someone, who wasn't me, was able to get him pretty quickly. When I was sat in the offices Tony and I shared one afternoon, he locked the door and removed a ceiling tile, pulling out (what I now think could possibly have been) a pistol with a suppressor on it. "What the fuck are you doing keeping that in here, you silly cunt?!" I asked. He replied, "Well, I couldn't keep it in the shop, could I?!" He went on to tell me that he wanted to take it home and keep it indoors (whatever it was), so I agreed to follow him back to his house to make sure he didn't get a tug and once I'd seen him and his sports bag go through the door, I fucked straight off home to Brentwood. No sooner had I closed my own front door behind me, Tony was phoning me; "Fuck sake Carl, get back here quick will ya mate, I don't know what I've done here!" I stopped him there and told him I'm on my way. My Saab 900 turbo saw 3-digit speeds along the A128, and I probably made it to Tony's in Chafford Hundred in about 10 minutes flat. He had a big new build house, which he came out of as soon as he heard me screech up outside. I approached him thinking, 'he must have killed someone', but I didn't say a word as he ushered me inside and up the stairs. The master bedroom was pretty big and in the room across the landing he had a full-sized sunbed, the type the tanning shops have. Tony pointed at this little hole in his bedroom wall and beckoned me to look, well when I looked through, I could see across the top of the stairs and into the opposite bedroom, where I could also make out another hole in the top of his sunbed! "What the actual fuck Tone...are you starting up a peep show now?" I enquired, as I turned in disbelief to investigate this hole once more. He explained that whatever had made the holes missed his missus, only because she was laying down on the sunbed, had she stood up, the scene would have been very fucking different!

There are plenty of absolute morons out there that can't be trusted with so much as a butter knife, never mind a decent bit of equipment, but this was a clever man stood before me, I couldn't believe what he'd managed to do, but he just wasn't that way inclined, he didn't have the first clue how to handle the thing! I advised him of a few basic principles, shall we say, including a few do's and lots of don'ts! We had to get a plasterer round to fix the walls discreetly and I took the piss out of Tony for many months to come about that incident!

What would typically take a lifetime to build in terms of trust, good memories and an unprecedented number of laughs, we accomplished in those years, and he remained closer to me as a friend than a people from my childhood. I was at his side right up until the day I helped carry his coffin and lower him into the ground. And yes, to a degree, the Tony I knew, did change as a result of drugs, but our friendship didn't, and as I did back then, I do today, I disagreed with him on a few things, but to me, that's one way of measuring a friendship and that's by a person's willingness to tell someone they're 'off' with some of their actions and I often did. What we had to say and had shared with each other, was never openly expressed or was it written about, as back then we'd made life-long plans, we never knew any different because as far as we were concerned, we were in it for the long haul ....and to the end.

I remember I'd always give him shit about his scruffy hair, and I never understood how a man who would go to such lengths and make great efforts in his appearance with nice clothes, would then make no effort with his barnet! Tony was obsessed with the clothing brand Moschino, and it was on one occasion that I remember mimicking Al Pacino who played Tony Montana in the film Scarface … but instead of saying, "Hello, my name is Tony Montana," I'd say, "Hello my name is Tony Moschino" …in the same Cuban American accent. I had all sorts of nicknames when I used to dig him about the state of his hair, one in particular was 'wiggy'. There was one year that we'd all agreed that we were going to meet at a pub and have a drink with a few people. Not long before, I'd gone out and brought a mannequin's head and fitted it out with a wig. I even had the wig 'styled' (if I can even use that word) and cut to the same length as Tony's. I then had the wig placed on the mannequin's head and wrapped in the box. So, when Tony arrived with some of his doorman and employees, I insisted he open his present before we all got on one. The look on his face and his reaction was comedy gold when he saw it, he fucking loved it, he was absolutely pissing himself…as we all were, and it's these funny times and memories that have been bitter-sweet for me in helping me remember a man who was thought and portrayed to be an outright menace and spiteful bully, but to me, Tony was, and will remain to be someone that I shared my life with and I'll always remember him and the good times…. more than the bad. Those laughs and the shared sense of humour that we had, I'll always keep as one that only we knew and understood.

9 FAMILY LIFE

Chances are, the last time you had a substantial update about my life, it was via a TV documentary, at which point I was happily married to Anne, but things didn't work out between us, and we haven't been together for several years now. Though, from our time together, I'm very fortunate to have been blessed with two sons. I can't take all of the credit, what with good breeding and the Leach gene providing me with two more good looking heirs, as the results they provide are both a testament and result of a healthy home and good parenting. Frankie and Alfie, both of whom I am very proud of; they're good kids who are being given all of the necessary building blocks to a healthy childhood. They work hard at school, go to kid's clubs, are involved in a lot of sports, socially active and have lots of mates.

Like all of my children, I miss Frankie and Alfie when I don't get to see them, and even with the continuous calls, messages, amounts of work and challenges that are thrown my way each and every day; many of which aren't of my making, there isn't a day that passes that, much like all of my family, they're not in my thoughts. I'll continue to help and provide for them, and I'll be there for them as long as I live, have air in my lungs and should they need me. Something I hope for, what I'd love more than anything, is to be able to pick the two of them up, take them for pie n mash, then over to the London Stadium to watch a West Ham game together, just like my Dad did with me!

I've had other relationships since Anne and I separated, some longer than others, but they didn't last. There's no big or interesting story behind any of the break ups, or any specific point to be made, just that in life people grow apart, realise that they just didn't click, and it wasn't meant to be. I'm with Gemma now and have been for what has been 6 good years. We get on really well, she keeps me in check and on the right path and to be fair, anyone that has been around me, will tell you this can be a mammoth task. We share a lot of the same interests - she's a qualified personal trainer with a keen interest in diet, healthy living and fitness. It's no secret and as my birth certificate will prove, I'm of an age that dictates you have to make some, let's say dietary changes, not to mention certain vices and habits that played a part in both my social and recreational life, but don't worry, even though I don't kick the ball as much as I used to, I still keep my eye on it, can watch where it bounces and am able-bodied enough to put it in the back of the net. So, we exercise a lot, train regularly and eat right…. mostly! I've tried to get her into watching West Ham, but so far it hasn't happened, but as I can attest, no one's perfect, however, she is a good cook, so I'll let her off!

One of my few weaknesses is a good bit of food, so when Me and Jay were on a bit of work and found that the yard arm hadn't long passed the midday mark, I thought there was no better time than the present to get a plate of the good stuff. Weighing up our options, location and hearing Paul Konchelski had opened a pie n mash shop in Brentwood, and as I was in the pilot seat, I decided we should stop in. So, we came off the A12 and slipped down there to try it out. Whenever we have half a chance we always opt for a bit of pie, mash and liquor; one of Jay's many fine qualities, he shares my love for what is commonly known as, 'food of the Gods'; a 2 and 2 completely covered in liquor sauce…. absolute top drawer! Half-way through our grub, and on one of the few occasions I've submitted to the whispers of the haloed angel on my right shoulder, over that of the devil on my left, I remembered I'd promised to make more of an effort and to watch my daily intake. So, with the conflicts of a steady conviction of enjoying my food, displaying the culinary skills of a teenager, and being elbow deep into one of my few remaining vices, I said to Jay, "Don't mention this to Gem, I'm supposed to be on a diet!" Now, by no fault of my partner in crime, but with the constant prying eyes, the availability and powers of mobile phones and unknowingly having your photo taken, before I got home, my trip to the pie n mash shop had been posted on social media by someone, so that was that blown! Luckily, she knows I can't defy either my God given birth right as a cockney or to bypass the unwritten law of an age-old East London tradition just in the name of a diet! Gem and I spend most of the year out in Spain now, going back to the UK mostly to visit family and friends…...and of course to keep aligned with said forementioned traditions.

You may know from reading Muscle or watching ROTF that my eldest Son, Matt, found me when he was an adult. I was so happy, to say the least, that he'd come back into my life, as were the rest of the family – we all welcomed him into our hearts, homes and with open arms like he'd never been away. When we met, Matt had never seen a photo of himself as a baby, and something I wanted to share with Matt, was something that I considered very personal, in fact it was the only thing I'd kept close to me of him for my whole adult life, much like the thoughts of him that I took wherever I was in the world. I gave him the photos from my wallet which I'd kept with me all those years and often looked at.

In 2009, I had a bar on the front on Southend seafront; Matt worked on the door with Jay, who even managed to talk Matt into training in the gym again, which was great. Even on the door, Matty kept away from the temptations of drink and drugs, for which I was both grateful and proud. Matt kept in touch with his other siblings and visited my parents, he had great banter with my dad, which was both heart-warming and lovely to see, but like some things in life these good times weren't set to last. I think coming back into the family, being welcomed by my other kids, my sister, parents, close friends, it was all a bit overwhelming for him after so many years away from us all. Matt found religion and became a Born-Again

Christian; he threw himself into it completely and wholeheartedly. People around us were surprised that this fiery gym-going bouncer could calmly recite a Bible verse as his reason not to become involved in violence anymore. Matt stepped away from the family and moved up North, where he lives with his wife. He will always be my Son and I wish him all the very best in life.

I acknowledge that in life, we all have choices and perhaps I could have got up one morning and made a conscientious decision to make a metaphorical U-turn, changed speed and trod a different path, but on the other side of that same coin, I didn't actually plan on taking the road to criminality, just one thing led to another and here I am today (not that I regret it, by the way). As many people reading this will know first-hand, it's very difficult to reach and remain at any decent level within the criminal fraternity, whilst maintaining friendships and a stable family life; that's not me making excuses, that's me setting out the facts and telling it like it is. I've come to terms with my failings as a spouse and shortfalls as a father and that's partly what this book is all about. When I've come to a decision and acted upon it, it's rare it's solely based on something as selfish as 'personal gain'. Whenever I've come out, 'on top', there's always people that have benefited from that decision, result and gain.... how and what type of business I am involved in, is a committed choice based on many elements and people's wellbeing has always been one of them. I've helped people in matters of business as equally as I have on a personal level, this is not a way of me looking for dispensation for any of my alleged or known crimes; simply because as much as I am willing to be accredited for the continued good I do for people, I am willing to be held accountable for the bad, as truth be known, there are very few angels in this world!

And as I've mentioned, I don't think I've ever been conventional in any sense of the word at anything, and parenting is at the forefront of my thoughts. Like any decent human-being would, I'd lay down my life without hesitation and in an instant, so they'd never experience either a seconds' worth of pain or suffering and that would be for any one of my children or grand-kids - and for all of my flaws, I hope that they each know that. There has been a level of criticism from people in the past and present, giving claim that even with my choices and the circles I move in, I could've very easily spent more time and involvement with my family; but to have done so, would've only put them in direct danger and couldn't have been any more selfish on my part. My lifestyle dictated that I had to keep my family at a safe distance from myself and my activities, because I could never live with anyone, even if there was a chance or possibility that would result in them being caught in the crossfire, should things turn bad.

With the work that I do, it doesn't allow me the luxury to dictate when and where I could become a target and everyone that works with and around me knows that. I'm not able to simply clock out and leave the office for the day, and as a result of that practice, then be able to demand that there is any less or reduced chance at an attempt on my wellbeing or life. My life isn't a Monday - Friday routine, and as much as it comes with certain privileges, it also employs a certain type of company and clientele; and it's a fact that world consists of bullets, blades and kidnappings, but they aren't the only consistent threat that you face either: The police know if you're the sort of villain that gets your kids to hold your cash or tells your missus where you're going and who with. It's also a common practice with both the police as with criminals, they'll target your closest family accordingly, because at the end of the day, the police have a job to do….and low-life criminals who without compromise, will indiscriminately target your family, and take what you've got. And that's why, if like me, you aren't that guy who puts money over blood, so they realise early on and there's less chance of them leveraging your loved ones if they aren't part of your 'daily routine' fancy.

I was working the door one night, when I got a call from an unknown number. The telephone tough guy said something to the effect of, "I'm outside the house where your missus and kids are sleeping and I'm gonna fuck them up, you cunt!" The chances were, it was just another bullshitter playing childish games with me because I'd beat him up or hadn't let him in the club, but I didn't take any chances, as if you've got my number, there's a good chance you've been around me or know me on a personal level. I jumped in the motor and drove round there, mostly at 2 and 3 times the speed limit all the way. With tools in hand, I was of the mindset that I was prepared to either end their life or give mine; anyone I find pointing so much as a finger, threatens, or emits any level of harm or malice towards my family, will without question come under fire. I checked all around their house, their street, then the next two streets. It turned out to be a hoax, clearly the voice on the end of the phone belonged to a spineless weasel and was the sort who was frustrated at being someone's prison cell bitch… anyone that can't face a man and threatens a woman, and their children is in the same category as a nonce and a grass. As my family read this book, I believe it will be the first time they become aware of the fact that this even happened! In all honesty, it wasn't the only time I'd done something like this either. It was quite common for me to take a detour to the kid's homes while they were all sound asleep in the early hours and check for suspicious people or vehicles, sometimes I'd test the windows and doors to make sure their Mum had locked up properly, then I'd slip off into the night and never tell a sole.

There's an unwritten, but known fact, that with a life and existence within crime; for however long that might be, where as much as you're able to live and revel in champagne VIP booths, own nice motors, homes and enjoy the benefits of a celebrity lifestyle, there's also a large part of it that consists of your thoughts and a consciousness of the dangers and threats towards those closest to you. For a better, but never guaranteed chance of a family's self- preservation and existence, it's very much a case of deciding one or the other…. a life in crime or a family…... and not both, as you'll never get to decide the fate and length of either your own or your family's life, safety or sanctuary.

I've always paid my way when it comes to my children, and I always made sure that they weren't in need of anything. Even at times when I didn't have much cash, they never went without and always had the essentials, then when I had a bit more, so did they, so in that regard at least, none of the kid's mum's can honestly say I shirked my responsibilities, even if they didn't necessarily approve of my means of income. Seeing what amazing parents Carley, Jamie and Jodie turned out to be, has made me realise that they would've preferred to have spent much more quality time with me than I gave them opportunity, which is one of my very few regrets in life. I'm very fortunate to have the close friendships that I have with all 3 of them now, although I will say, they have each given it to me straight, at one time or another regarding how things were when they were younger, and I respect them for that, plus it helped us to move on and become closer.

Whenever I think of or speak about Carley, Jamie and Jodie, I almost always refer to them as "the 3 girls," simply because they grew up as 3 very close sisters; they're not too far apart in age but also close in the sisterly sense as well, though as close as the 3 of them are, they are each very different, unique and interesting characters.

Carley, as a young woman, became almost like one of my best friends, at times it was like we were somehow connected in an almost spiritual way, we can almost sense, or know when there's something up with the other and of course, try to help. Perhaps unfortunately for her, or maybe worse still for her husband, Carley inherited my sense of humour, my temper and most of my mentality in general, I'd go as far as to say that, like me, she can be an aggravating fucker when she wants to be! Again, much like what I hear people say about myself, if you become close to her, you are lucky enough to have made yourself a fiercely loyal friend, for life. She recently started a campaign to help a single mother get cancer treatment in Mexico, but she didn't stop there, she flew to Mexico to help take care of the woman too, and for anyone whose low enough in thinking that my daughter went on a cheap holiday, you couldn't be more wrong! She paid for her own ticket, stayed at the treatment clinic the entire time, only consuming the very same diet as the patients and sleeping in a put-up bed for the duration of her stay. I know it was a tiring and emotional rollercoaster for her, but she was so intent on helping as much as possible that she forgot about herself.

With Matt not being about (through no fault or choice of his own), Carley was the eldest of my children that were around me. When she was old enough to be part of the rave scene, and me partying and doing the doors, it was inevitable that she would pick up a lot of her street wise from me. At one of the darkest times of my life, she also saved me a few times too, dragging me back from the wrong side of a bender and even taking my car keys off me on numerous occasions, so that I couldn't drive drunk...thinking about it, she may also have given me the odd alibi, when I'd had agg indoors too! Right up there with some of the best days of my life, was when I gave Carley away at her wedding; she married Nicky at a castle in Florence, Italy (not far from where they filmed the second Hannibal movie), with her beautiful sisters as brides' maids.

Jamie's late teens fell when I was at the worst stage in my adult life, I was the most narcissistic and self-centred version of myself - I'm truly sorry to her for what she saw and had to put up with. She probably witnessed more of my roid-rages, drug-fuelled bad behaviour and angry-at-the-world-outbursts than any other and certainly more than any child should have knowledge of, never mind see first-hand. I take full responsibility for the fact that, our relationship has never been an easy one. We've both had to really work hard at it and frankly, I'm lucky that Jamie has me in her life to the extent which she does; there was even a point in my life when I thought that she would never be able to forgive me and that I'd lost her. Thanks largely to her true strength of character, something I feel all 3 girls inherited from my dad, we actually came through the other side of all that adversity and toxicity, and we are in such a great place now.

I know and am happy that Carley was a big influence in Jamie's life. I remember I'd paid for Jamie to train in a whole load of beauty therapy treatments, so that she could peruse that for work, then she went to work in Carley's mum's card shop with Carley! Like most, Jamie's had her wild moments in life, but she never strayed far from a good path and as I've said repeatedly, she's an amazing mother who works hard for her family. Especially given the troubles we'd had over the years, I was particularly honoured to be asked to give Jamie away at her wedding, which was also a wonderful day; she married Rob at a beautiful manor house in Brentwood, surrounded by family and friends.

Jodie was born in October 1991 and within days of her birth, she became very ill with what turned out to be bronchitis, so she was admitted into the hospital and put into an incubator. Denny had to sleep at the hospital in a chair or a spare bed, whichever was available, and I was only allowed to be there with them at visiting times, which made the whole thing even harder because, as any new parent will know, all you want to do is be with your newborn 24/7, check their chest to make sure they're breathing, feed them when they become hungry, rock them to sleep and generally watch over them. Of course, we also had Jamie at home to care for too, so I split my time between them and luckily their grandmother, Thelma, was a huge help and support in looking after Jamie when we were at the hospital with Jodie.

One of the worst nights of my life was when we were informed that Jodie's health was touch and go; I paced the house, I went through every kind of emotion imaginable, from anger and rage to a crying, helpless mess. I laid on the bed that night holding Jodie's baby-grow tightly to my chest and although I've never been much of a religious man, I actually fucking prayed to God there and then for help, I mean, what the fuck else could I do? As a 20 stone steroid munching boxer, I felt as if I could do almost anything out on the streets, but I was literally helpless to save my baby girl from what she was fighting. By the time Jodie was over the worst of the illness and almost ready to leave the hospital, it was almost Christmas time, so I excitedly went out to the shops to buy everyone presents and get all the Christmas food in ready, it was set to be the best Christmas ever in that house, I'm telling ya! The idea of mum and baby being home for a magical family Christmas was short-lived, however, because Denny and Jodie both caught chickenpox! I cursed our luck as I threw all the Christmas food, item by item, into the bin!

Obviously, Jodie being so ill and us parents once being presented with the prospect that she may not make it through, made me even more overprotective of her for a long time after. Around 4 years old, Jamie may well have felt a knock-on effect from it all, possibly at times feeling a bit left out, of course, that was never our intension and I'm sorry if that was the case. I think also down to the events in her first months, Jodie became very clingy, especially to me! I used to call her monkey because she would literally cling to me like a monkey! If she slept in our bed, she had to be on my chest, or wrapped around my head; I never got a moment's sleep those nights! When I had to go out of the house, I literally had to sneak out of the back door, otherwise Jodie would be round my ankles like an anchor!

She might want to smack me for saying this, but I remember Jodie was a bit of a tomboy when she was much younger! The two of us have always gotten on really well, even to this day, our relationship and friendship has always come very naturally and easily for both of us. I'm so pleased that we have such a close and unbreakable bond and I look forward to someday giving her away on her wedding day (don't leave it too long Shane, I'm not getting any younger!) too.

There are many differences between raising boys and raising girls, but 1 very clear and prominent factor is that girls can be more sensitive than boys and I always had to be extra careful about what I said when I mentioned anyone of them, for example, if the 3 of them were there and I was leaving, I had to say "Bye, I love you all!" Because if I said, "I love you" to one before the other, outrage would surely ensue; cries of, "You love her more than me?" or "I'm always last with you" would be the beginning of a long and drawn-out argument that I hadn't intended to start…in fact, the harder I tried to be cautious, the more I used to put my foot in it!

As you'll come to realise, I don't have a favourite child, (most parents will agree that this is wrong, or simply not possible) rather, I have very unique relationships with each of my children. Any of my kids could have grown up to be very bad people or could've gone off the rails at any point and simply blamed me for it, which if it happens, is always especially troubling for parents of girls, but luckily all of my older children grew into decent, young adults and I'm confident the same will be true of Frankie and Alfie. I'm trying my best to be a more conventional granddad than I was a conventional father, and although it's extremely difficult to get everyone together in one place due to the size of my family, I really hope we'll all get together for a big holiday someday before I die!

Having spoken so much about the 3 girls, I really want to give a mention to their partners, because Nicky, Rob and Shane are all good men, and I couldn't have hoped for better lads to end up with my daughters. I think of them like sons' and our relationships are like that of friends, not such good friends that I want to hear about how I came to be a granddad mind you, but good friends nevertheless!

My other daughter, Madison, has just earned herself a place at a good university, which makes me proper proud! She studies hard and also holds down a job at the same time. She's growing up to be another strong Leach woman and I hope she achieves everything that she aims to.

When my second son Carl Antony was born; which is a combination of Carl an Tony and being symbolic of how many people used to refer to myself and Tony Tucker, I felt it was nice to be able to include a bit of my name in that of one of my Sons', without him having to explain to his friends why he has a West Indian name! Of course, Carl's middle name is in loving memory of TT, who had died just a few years before.

Though he may carry part of my name and some of my blood, Carl is entirely different to me when you consider my more publicly known traits. He was always sensitive as a little boy, something that matured into a desirable element of his personality as he got older. He's always cared deeply about people and animals and is extremely thoughtful in general; my Carl is a credit to his mum; she raised an exemplary young man! Studying hard at school, keeping his nut down and staying out of trouble seemingly paid off, so he must have inherited the majority of his genes from her side, else he would have been a right fucker at school! Similarly, Carl doesn't smoke, and he hardly drinks, in fact, the first time we ever had a proper booze together was my 60th birthday!

But the very fact that Carl isn't too much like me in these ways is the very same reason that I'm most proud of him. Thank fuck he didn't put me through any of the worries and stresses that I put my parents through, so thank you for that Carl and thank you for being the Son that you are to me. I will treasure any and every moment we have and will share, be it going to a game, having a beer or enjoying a simple pub lunch together.

One of the proudest days of my life was when I took my dad and Carl to watch West Ham play a match, 3 generations of our family stood together in Upton Park...words can't describe what I felt that day, it was very emotional for each of us. Dad was on his walking stick and even though he hadn't been to the ground in almost 20 years at that point, he had a good shout up and singsong, as did I!

Like many from similar backgrounds, a love for the beautiful game is something that Carl and I share, and I hope that we'll get the opportunity to fly out to Italy together someday soon, meet up with my pals there and have Carl properly introduced to Italian football, Ultras style! As children, my little sister and I always helped and looked out for each other, both in the home and when playing outside in the street. It wasn't just about playing the 'big brother' role and being 'protective' of a younger sister, it was in as much a supporting and nurturing way too. We had an honest and non-judgemental closeness, that today, as it did back then, would give most parents assurance that their efforts and parenting was a sign of what and how a healthy, happy and supportive family can be there for each other. It was also us contributing to each other's young lives, that I think was all the more normal back then; a time when brothers and sisters in the household were each other's first best friends. With mum and dad having to both work, I would stay in and look after my sister; but it never felt like a chore, or that I was being forced to do something that meant I was missing out on another Batman adventure. Even with me staying in to look after my sister in our parent's absence, brought a sense of pride and accomplishment to both our young lives. I remember when I would sit and teach her how to read and write, and something I'm sure she has tried to forget, but I remember vividly that when we were quite small, I used to make her wrestle with my mates to toughen her up! She hated that, but I thought that if I wasn't there one day and she got into trouble, she would have more chance of protecting herself! It's funny to think that even back then, in a time where children's lives was one of innocence and simplicity..........learning the ways of a world under the guidance of caring parents, living in modest housing, whose neighbourhood streets were filled with children playing ball-games and skipping-ropes, that I would be trying to educate my sister on ways to defend her from the yet unknown evils that would exist in both the world and my adult life.

Tracy always mothered me, she played the role with great patience and one that is a testament to her kind and thoughtful nature. She always made sure I ate, telling me to 'be careful' and don't get into any trouble......and that's been consistent, from childhood until this day, I would laugh and have to agree if someone suggested that's her way of getting back at me from all those wrestling lessons with my mates when we were kids, but she's always been there for me without compromise and without fail, each and every time. Whether it was down to me fucking things up with a woman, or pissed the kids off, when I've needed some advice from somebody who's not in my world, it has consistently been her I've gone to. Even my kids know that they can always go to their Aunt Tracy if they need something, she's just the sort of person that no matter what else she may have going on in her own life, there is no schedule, no right or wrong, or an inconvenient time or place, it's family!

Tracy has never been involved in or a part of, or anywhere close to what I do. She has her own house to keep, career, family and whilst she knows what I am, she has a 'normal' life, but has never really judged me on my 'career' or life choices, she was always the sister that never judged me on my actions, only to help fix the situation….and more so, me. I've always had a special bond with my sister anyway, but now that both of our parents are gone, she is the only person left who I've known for as far back as I can remember who knows and sees me for the person that I truly am, the same person who has been as loyal to me, and by equal measure is someone who has never let me down since our first shared steps in life together. My sister, probably without even realising it, has made a fucking huge contribution to the man I am today.

To me, it's amazing how someone, who is so far and dis-attached from my world, can still be able to help put back the pieces in my life when things go bad – each and every time and it's because of how authentic Tracy is with regard to my best interests and wellbeing, someone that's been that close to me, that she's been able to make such a difference in my life, without being in the thick of all the shit I've waded through over the years - that's some balancing act she's pulled off and as cliche as it may sound, there is nothing I could ever say, or do in showing my gratitude, or appreciation and I feel truly blessed to be have been given a sister like Tracy…..her willingness to help me, on each and every occasion, whether it's been down to life, love or loss, is a reflection of her only one true agenda and that has always been based on the bond we built as children…..and if I was to bet my life and soul on our relationship I know I'd beat the devil himself, as ours is one that's beyond any level of explanation - and there hasn't been a single second, minute, day or week in my life, that I've not thought or known that her support and being there for me is based on more than just a sister's love and care for her big brother – and for this, I'm eternally grateful.

Carley Leach – "Suddenly, the lights came on and the police were everywhere...they were searching for my dad…he had stabbed a man…"

Dad, who I comically refer to as gaggy, is the biggest hearted man I've ever come across, and I wanted to open with that fact, because it's such a defining characteristic that my dad is best known for, believe it or not! It's worth noting here that I've never actually called him Gaggy in the presence of his cronies; it was previously something that (until now) was reserved for banter between only the two of us. Dad would stop at nothing to protect his loved ones, he's just that way inclined and always has been, but nowadays, he also realises the value in spending time with both his kids and grandkids. When a few of us have taken our little ones to meet with dad altogether, I've often stepped back and observed him soaking it up, really appreciating having so many of his family members around him.

A consistent occurrence over the years has been for someone who doesn't know my dad to ask me, "So, come on Carley, what's your old man like?" and when I answer with something to the effect of "A right softie with such a big heart", their reaction is always one of complete confusion, because it conflicts with everything they've heard and the picture they've painted of my dad in their minds.

I have a childhood friend called Jodie (not to be confused with my sister of the same name), who's dad got sent down when we were only little. My dad looked out for her and treated her as if she were his own, without ever being asked to and in fact, I can't think of any of my friends that have gotten to know dad and don't love him to bits! Granted, some of the lads in my circle over the years have ended up with a bit of an awkward look about them as dad grabs them in a big man hug and gives them a kiss on the neck, but they tend to just style it out!

I feel that one thing we never went without as kids, was his ability and openness in fatherly love. I mostly attribute dad's great ability in how he demonstrated his love for us, to my granddad, being dad's dad. A rare gem of a man himself, my granddad had it hard being with my nan; she was one tough cookie who didn't have a clue how to give affection of any kind, although I will say, she did always have a beaming smile when us grandkids arrived to their house. Even at a young age, I picked up on how nan was, and towards dad in particular; she often said he was, "Such a fucker" and I don't feel like she ever really bonded with my dad.

How nan was, I believe, is the very reason that my dad has been with so many women. I've had time to ponder this on and off over the years and I've established a firm belief that if a boy experiences a lack of motherly love as he grows up, as a man he will likely have a desire, or even a need, to know that he is wanted by women and it would seem that if a boy is left longing for a mother figure, into adulthood he will continue to try to fill that void. Ultimately, what all of this deep and meaningful psychological stuff amounts to is, dad couldn't keep it in his pants!

That I'm aware of, I have 7 siblings, but I wouldn't be surprised if more cropped up at some point! My older brother, Matt, was adopted as a baby due to his mother's parents being strict Catholics, in an era when young or unmarried parents raising a child was taboo. When I was 18, Matt found us, which was a bit of a shock initially, but the most stand-out memory I have of that day is that it was like looking at a younger version of my dad standing on the doorstep. Matt was not only the spitting image of dad, but he has almost all the same mannerisms too, something that is pretty striking, given that he and dad hadn't seen each other since Matt was just a few months old! Once we were all reunited, Matt moved not far from my house in Essex and we spoke almost every day for a couple of years, but then one day, as quickly as he had appeared in our lives...he was gone again! He upped and moved away, and I haven't heard from him since, something we were all gutted about, dad especially, as he thought he had his eldest son back for good. I don't think Matt ever got over being adopted, but I really hope he's found solace.

When I was 3 years old, my mum kicked my dad out. I don't blame her at all, in fact, I'm pleased they didn't stay together, because if he had treated her the way I know he's treated other women in his life, he and I wouldn't have the friendship and bond that we do; my mum is a diamond and deserves better, something I've told dad and he's conceded. It was when dad started working the doors that things really changed...women were throwing themselves at him and he didn't have the will or strength to knock them back. He'd get home and rush to the shower to wash the scent of the women off of himself - my mum isn't stupid, she gave him chances, possibly for my sake, but she inevitably reached her limit.

Mum put up with a lot of dad's bullshit, stuff that I was too little to understand at the time, but as I look back now, I know they both truly loved each other, dad just couldn't help himself, he simply couldn't say no to a bit of skirt, and he broke mum's heart. I don't hold his mistakes and antics against him, it's just who he is, how he was made and raised, but I know he loved us both dearly.

After the break-up, dad used to pick me up and spend time with me, but there was one extremely memorable day when he took me to Denny's mum's house (the lovely Thelma), and on the sofa was a tiny baby. I went over and asked, "Daddy, who's this?" and he said, "This is your baby sister!" I stared at this tiny baby for what seemed like ages, I remember how much I wanted to hold her, so dad sat me down and showed me how...and that was how I met Jamie-lee for the first time!

Like most little girls, other than a sports car and a

unicorn, I had always wanted a baby sister and I felt this incredible happiness that I now had one, but there was also this over-powering sense of confusion, too. I was only 5 years old at this point and I had been dad's only child, now we were suddenly outside of the "traditional family set-up." Later that day, dad dropped me back home and, of course, whilst he was driving off down the road (probably at high speed), I was telling my mum all about the new baby that daddy had with his new woman...dad played a blinder there didn't he!

Mum was in shock at first, but her reaction wasn't so bad, until she tucked me into bed that night and I started sobbing; "I know why daddy's left...he has a new baby...he doesn't need me anymore..." I was just feeling confused, and also sad that my daddy wasn't living with me anymore. I didn't understand what that line might cause to happen next, but mother lion came out from within mum, and she went crazy at my dad. My mum's a real pussy cat, in fact her nick name is Mary Poppins, but fucking heck...he had pushed things too far this time!

Mum and dad are friends and they always have been, aside from dad's obvious (sizable) mistakes, they always had great love and respect for one another as people and as parents; once two people have a child together, there will always be an unbreakable bond between them. Mum could have slaughtered dad to me, made his name mud around our house and left me with a bitter taste, but she didn't do any of that, she is a much better and stronger woman than to go down that path. It's a common happening, mum slagging dad off to the kids because of the pain he caused her, but in the end, who are the biggest losers in that scenario? Nine times out of ten, it's the kids that end up messed up, so I'm thankful to my parents, mum in particular, for not putting me in the centre of that game in which no one comes out a winner.

There had been plenty of scary times growing up due to dad's line of work. I remember dad calling mum on the house phone one day and telling her not to answer it again if it rings and that we needed to hide in the house, stay away from the windows and wait for him to arrive. I also remember, even after they split, dad dropping big bags of cash off for mum to stash for him. £100,000 in used 50's seems like ten million quid in the mind of a small child, but I knew something was up and I never said a word to anyone about it.

Anything I hadn't understood as a baby or toddler, was soon to be made up for in my late teens! I knew about everything, all the women, the flings, the whole lot, as I'd become my dad's confidante in almost all matters, as dad and I grew to become best of friends. I know some may say that a parent shouldn't be a "friend" to their kids, but that was our reality; dad wasn't a conventional father, he didn't come to my sports day, he wasn't around to tuck me in at night, but we became close to each other in unconventional ways. Whatever dad was up to, I would always look out for him and cover for him, if need be, I'd be there to offer advice, or provide a shoulder to cry on when things went tits up.

Being Carlton Leach's daughter, I guess I grew up faster than most my age. To give an example, my 15th birthday party was held at Warehouse Club, where thugs, bouncers, gangsters, hardmen, faces, you name it, they were all walking over to wish me a happy birthday, then giving me cash, out of respect to dad of course. As I left one of London's top nightclubs with my school friends and realised that I'd racked up about a grand in birthday money, mostly from people I'd never seen before, I was feeling pretty damn good, and my friends couldn't believe it either!

Around the age of 15, and certainly by 16, I was no stranger to nightclubs at all, plus I'd seen and heard so much...stuff that most adults don't experience their entire lives, I was now so far from your average teen it was hard to believe my actual age and I fitted in with dad and his mates in any party setting, which meant I got to enjoy the very best of the 90s club scene from a prime position that many would have given a limb for!

Dad and I effortlessly bounced off of each other; we fed off of each other's energy and being a right pair of attention seekers, we didn't care who was watching as we danced, sometimes in routine, throwing imaginary balls across the dancefloor to each other and all sorts of crazy shit like that!

One night, my mate Jodie and I were going to Epping Country Club for a night out and we'd be joining dad and his lot as well. Jodie and I managed to get hold of a couple of jack jills, but it didn't take long for someone to notify my dad of this, and shortly after I started to come up, I was summoned to go and see my dad, escorted there by one of his goons. I quickly stopped thinking about peace, happiness and hugs, as I was completely bricking it, telling myself as I walked "Just act normal girl...just be normal..." "Alright dad" I said, as I tried to keep my feet still. "Yeah...you alright, you having a good time are ya?" he responded, suspiciously. I tried to convince him that I was fine and having a nice, normal evening, but there was no fooling dad with this stuff, he was on to me like a bloodhound. "Carley, what have you taken?" he asked me so sternly that any thought I'd have about lying was dead in the water, so I came clean about the pill and apologised, hoping that might be the end of it... "Who did you get it from?" I thought to myself, 'I'm not bloody telling him...the poor bloke will get a hiding' so this time I lied and said I found it in the toilets. He glared at me for what felt like ten minutes, then finally broke the silence with "Listen 'ere, don't you ever take anything from anyone we don't know! It's not safe... if you want stuff, you ask one of my lot about it." As Jodie and I walked off, we looked at each other and burst out laughing! Epping Country Club, usually referred to by its regulars simply as Country Club, was becoming known far and wide, but whether it was famous or infamous shall be left down to opinion and interpretation. We had so many amazing nights at that place, too many fond and funny memories to discuss here, but trust me when I say; that place could be as brutal as it could be magical!

One time I remember it being proper busy in there and we were having a wicked time, I was going for it on the dance floor when a big lump of a man approached me and explained that my dad had been taken out the back door because he needed to leave quickly, but I wasn't to panic as someone was already on their way to pick me up and ensure I got home safe. Suddenly, the lights came on and the police were everywhere...they were searching for my dad. I was informed of an incident in the men's toilets in which dad had stabbed a man, who now wasn't in a good way. I knew dad had it in him to be extremely violent, but I also knew that he was a fair man, too, so it's highly likely that the chap had deserved it. I knew the drill; keep your big gob shut Carley, head down and get out of there at the first opportunity, but the old bill had manned all the exits, they weren't letting anyone leave without being spoken to at the front door. There was panic and hysteria throughout the place, it literally took hours to empty the club one by one, but when it was my turn to give my name, there was only one thing for it...lie through my teeth and hope! The master plan worked, and we were scooped up in a car and whisked away in the midst of all the chaos.

When I was out, either with or around my dad and his lot, I felt very safe and protected, I was well looked after and looked out for, but I was aware of this looming potential for it to kick-off at any given moment; dad was always surrounded by a crowd of lunatics and roid-raiders and inevitably there would almost always be one twat with a chip on his shoulder or something to prove, an unfortunate part of that life that led dad to end up in more battles than he perhaps would have otherwise. So-called mates would, from time to time, want to see my dad fly off the handle just for drama's sake, I mean, how sad can your life be that you need to go out of your way to cause a dangerous situation, just because you're bored?

I went along to Sugar Hut one time with dad, he hadn't wanted to go that particular night, but he felt he needed to show his face and make a point due to a certain situation that had occurred. One of the snides, as I like to call them, you know the type; the fake friends, hanger-ons, users...well one of those fuckers was in dad's ear all night, winding him up, manufacturing a situation for their own gain. I knew it was going to go pete-tong, and I did my best to help dad see sense and just leave, but before I knew it, he went ape-shit! He knocked a couple of people out, he smashed tables and windows, no one wanted to go near him, he was screaming, daring anyone to try to stop him, but it was only ever going to end when he decided that enough was enough. Outside the gradually emptying venue, I went mental at the people who had caused all of that unnecessary shit...just more selfish arseholes who call themselves "brothers," what a load of bullshit that is, nine out of ten of those using that line are only around for the ride and to see what they can get off of the back of dad's name and reputation.

Many years later there was a similar turn out in Ibiza when dad and I happened to be out there at the same time...and it's lucky I was! A bunch of rich, pompous pricks were trying to drag my dad into their menial bullshit, whilst he was drunk and trying to have a good time. Dad was out of his tree and could barely compose himself, but certain people knew that if they said the right things, they could manipulate dad into doing their dirty work, which by the way, was pure egotistical nonsense anyway! I stepped in and told them all exactly what I thought of them, highlighting the fact that if this person really did consider my dad to be "like a brother" he wouldn't be attempting to take advantage of him and put him in a dangerous situation over their dick-measuring contest.

If I had a quid for every blood-sucking, two-faced Judas motherfucker that had ever said "Carlton's my brother" or similar analogy, I'd be rich...fuck me there has been so many of them, and I've told him this, but dad never wants to believe it and for some reason, he's always been so gullible in that regard. Having said that, dad does have a small group of certain friends, no more than five or six of them, who have been wrapped around him through it all and for all the right reasons as well, and those people are the only ones with the right to refer to my dad as their brother.

For those fortunate enough to have been around dad (and on his good side), will know that he's a great laugh, but he also loves a good wind-up...something I think he wishes I hadn't inherited from him! No story can explain that point better than the time dad had an important meeting in one of the clubs he looked after, and his dearest daughter spiked his drink just half an hour before his people arrived! I sat at a distance, watching as he started to sweat, his feet were going too...the people he was sat down with didn't know I was in the club, until dad jumped up and shouted over, "You fucking spiked me ain't ya!" He sat back down, shuffling about in his chair and says something like "It's ok, it's just my daughter, she thinks she's funny!" How I laughed...payback for all the times the king of practical jokes had gotten one up on me!

Looking back, I was a right cow at times, marching up to bouncers and demanding to be let in was commonplace for me, most were just trying to earn a living and probably didn't need me rocking up, telling them to get my dad on the phone! But honestly, I never meant anyone any harm, nor did I go looking for trouble, or to get my dad into shit either, but people on the club scene started to learn who my dad was, and on more than one occasion, that led to them looking to fight me...I don't know why girls do it, perhaps out of jealousy, I don't know for sure. One thing I do know, is that on the odd occasion trouble found me, I wasn't going to roll over, I was a live wire back then. One night, my mates had gone to the loo, and I was watching the drinks on my own, three birds saw their opportunity and came for me; one held my arms behind me whilst another started smashing me in the face repeatedly...as she came close to me to talk bollocks, I dropped the nut on her, just like dad had taught me to! You see, I didn't ever want to scrap, I wanted to have a good time, but if I ever had to fight to protect myself or my mates then I did, because I was raised in such a way that you looked after yourself and your own.

I also felt a protectiveness over dad, I mean, I know in my mind it should be the other way around, and dad has always protected me, but I really took it upon myself to look out for him. If we were clubbing or partying together, I was always on the look-out for someone who might cease an opportunity and make a move against dad, I guess you could simply say I watched his back! Many a time I was his alibi at home, so I'd be the one that dropped him off to strip clubs with his mates, but I couldn't sleep while he was out, so I'd wait up until closing time, then go to pick him up and take him back to my house so he could sleep it off and go home the next morning.

Me and boyfriends is a whole matter on its own, I mean, can you imagine being a teenage boy and having to come and meet my dad? Dad smelt their nerves from half a mile and always wound them up something chronic! If he was on the door or with his mates, they'd give any boy a right difficult time, then laugh their arses off about it. I took one boy to meet my dad once and dad was acting strange, he rolled back a rug and started pulling up the floorboards, then he pulled three guns out one by one, carefully placing each of them on the side next to him. Through gritted teeth, I said "Dad, what the fuck are you doing of?" Another time, that same boyfriend called my dad up and asked to meet with him, which dad agreed to straight away; "Meet me at the Half Way House tonight at 7, ok?" When he pulled in, dad was waiting for him with a bunch of his cronies, and when young Nick questioned this, dad explained he thought there was agg to sort out! But poor Nick had actually just gone to ask for his daughter's hand in marriage! Dad said to him, "Of course you can you silly cunt, I love you...I'm so glad you're gonna look after my daughter!" So, my boyfriend who sat and watched dad pull shooters out the floor and didn't seem too phased is now my husband (thank fuck dad didn't spook him)!

There were a couple of boys that didn't get round my dad, however. There was one in particular who was a bit older than me and one afternoon, dad handed me the kids name, address, car registration and phone number on a piece of paper and told me I'd better park the boy up within the hour, or he'd do it for me. I was angry and thought that I wanted to be with this person, but I realise now why I thought I wanted to be with him so badly: He was like my dad, and I was trying to fill a father shaped gap...yes, I had classic daddy issues and I know that now. Acknowledging such a problem is the first step in dealing with it and moving on with life. For the most part, I knew how to wrap my dad round my little finger, I was a cow for that, but I learnt from the best (didn't I daddy?) and I knew what I could get away with!

In terms of dad's choice of the fairer sex, many of the woman dad has dated over the years have been decent enough, but I haven't always liked or gotten along with all of the one's dad shacked up with. Some have been gold diggers or fame-hungry whores, but a couple of extremely strange ones had real issues with the friendship that dad and I maintain. One nut-job, who I shan't name, told dad that if he goes to my wedding, she'd leave him; can you imagine? Needless to say, dad gave me away on my big day and that loon is long gone, but there have been a couple of others since who have displayed signs of jealousy where mine and dad's closeness is concerned; perhaps they just don't get it, I mean, people are often frightened by what they can't understand, but it's not for me to have to try to explain to anyone how or why our relationship is what it is – I have my dad's back and he has mine, we do our best for each other, that's all there is to it...that's family!

I know there have been times when my sisters have been upset and struggled to understand why they didn't have the same type of friendship with dad as I did, but we've all done a lot of talking as we've grown up together as sisters and I've also explained my point of view to them, that I always longed for the idyllic family setting, living in a nice home altogether with mum, dad and siblings, much like what they appeared to me to have, but that wasn't the hand I was dealt. It's strange that my sisters were wanting to have a close friendship with dad like I did, but I was wanting to feel like daddy's daughter, not his best mate...I think we each realise nowadays that we all grew up in different environments, and that led to us all having differing types of relationships with our dad, but love and trust are two important consistencies throughout each.

Being my dad's daughter and effectively the eldest sibling, I've always felt this pressure to be consistently strong, to protect my sisters and Carl. It's stuck with me, the memory of each time one of them realised who and what dad was, I saw it hit them one by one like a ton of bricks. They'd sometimes look at me, wondering if I too had realised, but of course, I'd been living it and keeping it from them in order to protect them for as long as possible.

I was raised on films like Sopranos, The Godfather and Scarface. Joking aside, and (obviously) knowing there're fictional, there are morals, lessons and happenings in those films that actually reflected my dad's reality. Me being young, impressionable and the things I was exposed to, had an effect on how my mind worked and I was always thinking ahead and coming up with ideas and suggestions. There was a week in time when I knew there was something troubling dad and when he eventually explained that he had to go on a meet, but he wasn't sure if he could trust the nutcases he would be sitting down with, so I told him to tell me a bit more. Dad would be going into a restaurant in east London which was owned or controlled by the firm he was meeting, he knew he'd be searched on the way in; therefore, he wouldn't have a tool to protect himself once inside. I told him not to worry, I could fix this for him…I'd just go to the restaurant a few hours before, hide his gun in the gent's, pay my check and leave (and they say you can't learn anything from watching tv), but dad wouldn't have it, he said it was too dangerous, but I'd decided I was going to do it anyway. However, the day before the meet dad told me that he'd found a solution, meaning that my plan wasn't needed in the end. Our life has been like a film at times, and it's only later in life when you sit together at home and reflect that you realise how crazy it all sounds!

When it comes to dad's actual mates, the ones that aren't blood related to him anyway, I believe he's had very few genuine friends in his life, especially in correlation to the number of people he's known and helped. I witnessed first-hand that just from a couple of phone calls, he could summon a small military-type unit, armed to the teeth and ready to take on any kind of street battle. But out of the scores of men willing to fight for and alongside my dad, there was only a handful that wouldn't try to fuck him over for a couple of quid or would decline to make business deals behind his back. I could see that so many of them, smiling to his face, slapping him on the back, telling him what he wanted to hear, they were only there because dad and his name were useful to them at that time, for whatever reason. I've always been wary of people, I trust very few, and I wish dad had trusted fewer to be honest, because it was very frustrating at times to see him helping someone out that I knew…I just knew…that they'd disappear once they had what they wanted! I'm pleased that in the present, he's retained a few of the friends he had back in the day, the crew that always stuck by each other, and additionally, he's perhaps got three or four new-ish friends around him now that have the same old school morals and would stand-on if my dad needed them to, but that's it...the rest wouldn't pass a pressure test, mark my words.

When Tony died, I saw my dad plunge into a very dark place, and for a long time, everything changed. It's a story people have heard all too much about, so I won't go into details, but I pleaded with dad to get out and go straight; "Just get a normal job, Dad, please?" But his responses were always the same, his mind would never be changed, he was like one of the Italian mafioso, with a staunch belief that there is only one way out and that's to be 6 feet under. He just carried on, only ever going deeper and deeper in, the hurt and pain never left him, and more friends died, as is life, but others may as well have died, due to their terrible life choices and addictions. For example, the number of people who became untrustworthy and half the man they were previously thanks to a coke addiction is unbelievable, that shit really is the devil's dandruff.

As hard for me as it was to see the snakes and bloodsuckers crawling about around my dad over the years, I can take a positive thing from a negative and that is to say that it taught me to see people for who and what they are within a rather short time of meeting them. Another positivity via adversity is, I grew up longing to someday have "the perfect family life" due to how my childhood had been, but of course, there is no such thing as perfect. At times I obsessed about the house looking just right, the kids having to be exceptionally well presented and all manner of similar things. I had to realise that obsession is not a healthy thing and whilst doing your best is brilliant, we shouldn't be obsessively chasing perfection, although I have as close to perfect (for us) as can be through hard work and determination, both on my part and Nick's, to whom I'm grateful to for putting up with me and being my rock (cliché I know, but it's true).

I learnt many harsh life lessons as a kid and a young woman, down to who my dad was and what his life was like, but would I change him? Would I change myself or my past? No on both counts, because it all contributed to the person I am today, and I'm lucky enough to have been blessed with wonderful children and an astounding husband. My brothers, sisters, children, husband, mum, and dad…all of my family members have each played a vital role in me moving forward in life, changing, evolving, and I believe in small ways we've all helped each other. Life can be tough, there's no doubt about it. We all have to take one day at a time and do our best to be kind, love one another and treat others how we wish to be treated, I realise that we only get one shot at life, so we should all try to do what makes us happy. Being my dad's daughter has taught me to take whatever card you get dealt and make the best of it. I love you Gaggy x

Back in the day: Carley partying with Carlton & Gaffer.

Some things never change: Carley & Carlton partying in Ibiza.

Jamie-Lee Leach – " ….If I could wish for anything in the world for dad right now, it would be for him to have true happiness in a settled family home…."

I'm a firm believer that the past is where it is for a reason and for the most part, that's where it should stay. We say that our past is 'behind us' and I feel that there's a reason why it's often difficult, in the emotional sense, to take a 'hard look back' for most people. As is often the case for most, it's undeniable that my past has contributed to the woman that I am today and continues to help me remain driven, forward thinking and of a positive mindset. Dwelling on the past can be detrimental to our future, but it doesn't do any harm to look back on occasion and in that regard, I'm grateful of this opportunity to reflect on the relationship between my dad and me.

As a little kid, I thought of dad like a real-life Incredible Hulk who could and would, protect us from anyone and anything, nobody with ill intent was getting past our dad to get to us! That safety and security is priceless to any child, and I feel truly thankful for having that in my life, especially given that some people will never experience this feeling and may long for it until their dying day. Though he was a big, strong and tough kind of guy, dad also had a big heart. No matter what he was going through, our dad showed us unconditional love and the fact that he absolutely cherished us really shone through for all to see, which was reciprocated entirely by us girls; we adored him.

Even before my teens, I started to pick up on elements in my life surrounding my dad that didn't seem to compare to those of my friends. Dad's lifestyle meant that our lives and family set-up would always be a stark contrast to the lives of my friends; I remember thinking, 'I've not come across one other dad like ours!'

I'm not knocking my dad, we are what we are, but in all honesty, I found the situation with dad very difficult throughout my teenage years because I adored the bones of him and as I said, I knew he felt exactly the same towards me, but I craved normality so badly throughout those years. I'd analyse other kids with their parents, listen to friends' stories involving their nuclear family set-up, their day trips and get-togethers and I'd secretly feel desperate for just a little bit of that. As if being a teenager isn't confusing enough, I always found myself feeling immensely guilty for having those wishes of normality, because my dad was absolutely amazing in so many other ways and looking back now, isn't a parent's love the most important thing for a child? I think that yes, it is, although time spent together is so precious and a very close contender. As we as people grow into our own person and form individuality, we find the ability to question what normality actually is and, in the end, who decides or dictates what 'normal' looks like?

I consider us to have been very lucky as children because we didn't want for anything. First and foremost, we always had a nice home and food on the table, which I'm sad to say that all around the world, this is not the case for so many families. Dad and his friends showered us in gifts; everything from designer clothing to the latest gadgets. We regularly went on amazing holidays, trips out and meals in top restaurants, plus, we were lucky enough to meet certain people and go to places that most teenagers, or even adults, never get to. The VIP treatment and all the amazing things were lovely, but ultimately, they were exactly that, just things and deep down, all I craved was more of dad's time and attention.

It was a little upsetting at first, when mum and dad split up and it also meant that dad would be around less, but it actually provided some sense of relief because the peace and quiet that ensued was a welcome new factor in the house and I knew that together or apart, my mum and dad would continue to love us with every fibre of their being. Had there ever been an emergency, all it would have taken was a call and dad would have been there for us, probably with a small army if needed! It's no secret that my dad has always been 'one with the ladies', but that hasn't ever been an issue for me because I get along with virtually everyone and so long as dad's happy and the woman concerned is kind to me and my family, then everything's good!

I kept a lot of childhood hurt and pain pent up inside and carried it with me for many years. Around 6 years or so ago, dad and I had a real heart to heart conversation and all of what I had previously felt unable to say, came to the surface; I mean, I really let go! Not only did I feel liberated and free of all that I'd suppressed, but it put dad and I in the best place we've ever been in. Since that moment, there's hardly been a day go by that I haven't called him up for a chat about virtually nothing, in fact, I call him up almost every morning, put the phone on speaker and set the world to rights with him while I prepare the kids breakfasts. Moan, laugh, moan, laugh and laugh some more is the usual course of our routine calls and I love it, I look forward to it in fact. There is one problem, however, in that if I forget to call him, dad calls me to moan that I didn't call him! I guess you could say that we're now making up for lost time or laughs and chats that we previously missed out on.

Nowadays, dad will give us kids any spare minute he can find and perhaps he always wanted to, but certainly now, his lifestyle allows for it. It's so lovely for me to be a part of the relationship which we have worked together to build, not that things were ever bad between us, because they weren't, they were just...different! Dad became my 'go-to' for advice, guidance and reassurance, he will always take the time to offer a listening ear or a shoulder to cry on if I need it and I have no problem in saying that, as a 33-year-old mother of 2, I still need my dad in my life.

What we all went through together with Grandad was horrific, to see him the way he was towards the end was such a cruel thing for life to throw at anyone. It was painful enough to witness Grandad's deuteriation, but I also found it hard, knowing what it was doing to my dad. Most things in dad's world are within his control, but he was virtually helpless in this case, and I know that words can't really describe what Grandad meant to dad. We all pulled together through such a difficult time and us girls did everything we could to make Grandad happy and comfortable, both whilst he was sick and in his dying days; I hope that by us stepping up we were also able to ease some of dad's burden as well, because he had so much to deal with at that time. Grandad meant so much to us all, he was loved so deeply and is now missed by us all. I think Grandad's passing was a significant point in dad's life for many reasons, not least because he took stock and considered his own role as a father and as a grandfather. If I could wish for anything in the world for dad right now, it would be for him to have true happiness in a settled family home (not a nursing home, dad!). I think we'd all love to see our dad in that kind of environment, a place where all of his kids can visit with his grandkids, play games, have dinner together, watch silly films and laugh, just generally enjoy all that 'normal stuff' together!

The challenges we face in life, the obstacles we overcome and the difficulties which we endure, all contribute to the person that each of us are today and so we should embrace these victories, rather than waste our energy on regret. Dad and I are a prime example of what I'm saying, because if things had been, let's say, more 'normal' when I was growing up, maybe we wouldn't be as close or as strong as we are now. The value I place on time invested in another person is far greater than that I would give to material possessions and that is something which I derived from my childhood. I think that my dad feels immensely guilty that he wasn't a conventional father, but I want him to know that it doesn't matter, I want him to just let go of that guilt and continue as we are, because things are excellent between us now and for that I am extremely grateful. I wouldn't change my dad for the world, and I still adore him as I always have. I will love you always, Dad!

Jodie Leach – "Dad is definitely at his happiest when he has his children and grandchildren around him"

As a child and a teen, I didn't read the books or the articles, nor did I listen to rumours or hear say about my dad. I wasn't just ignorantly refusing to hear or see what was before me, more that I was worried to learn too much, because the thought of what my dad might have been involved in scared the life out of me! The more I picked up on over time, the more it would worry the heck out of me, so I made a deliberate effort not to know about the darker side of dad's life, plus it all had a sense of irrelevance to me anyway, because I only needed to be concerned with who my dad was to me, not so much who or what he was in the eyes of others. Now as a mother of 2 approaching 30, none of that has changed for me at all and whilst I'm happy to write this contribution to dad's memoirs, it's unlikely I'll read the book...in case it keeps me up at night! I'm content with how the relationship is between dad and I and I'm even happier that my kids have him as their grandad; what can be more important than that?

One thing I do know, firstly thanks to how well I know my dad and secondly as I've heard it on several occasions from reliable sources, is that no matter what my dad has gotten into, he has always maintained a high level of integrity. Dad is known within various circles to be fair, honest, loyal and reliable, which is something that I am extremely proud of him for, after all, you can't say the same for many people in dad's line of work! I have no doubt that if someone crossed dad or our family, that he is capable of doing bad things, but he's never been nasty without good reason.

Growing up, we didn't want for anything, we were so fortunate! We regularly spent weekends and school breaks at our caravan in Clacton and some years we'd get to go abroad twice, usually to Portugal. We always had great fun when we went away as a family and I knew that some of the kids our age had never left the county, never mind the country, so I've always been grateful for those experiences. If you know my dad, you'll know that he absolutely loves shopping. He often spoilt us anyway, but if we hadn't seen him for a week or 2, he'd take us on a shopping spree, and we'd go home with more stuff than we knew what to do with! But I had something that's more important than anything you can buy from any mall in the world and that is the love I have always felt from my parents.

I was a proper Daddy's Girl from a very young age and apparently, I used to cling to him like a monkey! I'm not even sure why to this day, but dad's nickname for me is Noddy, he still writes it in all my birthday cards! Dad was a proper softie who never told us off, but he did always demonstrate and tell us just how much he loved us. As a parent myself now, I know that the most important things a parent can do for their children is to ensure they're fed and that they feel safe and loved, which our dad unquestionably delivered on. There seems to be more and more broken families these days, which is truly sad for everyone involved and when my parents split it was no less upsetting for me, but thankfully, dad remained very much a part of all our lives. Sure, this Daddy's Girl would have liked him around a whole lot more, but we were still taken good care of and loved unconditionally by our dad, so I couldn't have asked more of him.

From as early as we learned about careers at school, I realised that my dad's work wasn't exactly the stereotypical Monday to Friday job with 9-5 hours, but at that point I didn't give it too much consideration, however, as I got older, I realized on a more conscious level that dad certainly didn't work in an office, at a factory or on a building site! I honestly didn't care what he actually did for a living though, because I had the love and attention which contributed to the childhood relationship with my father that I valued so much. After the books and films came out, more people started to ask about my dad and what he was like, but I don't think I gave them the exciting answers they were hoping for, because to me he was just my dad! Although dad was always willing to be honest with us about who or what he was career-wise, I'm pleased that I didn't take an interest in that other side of his life, because the relationship we have now is brilliant and of course, how things were in the past have contributed to that. I'm glad that dad and I are as close as we are, we speak on the phone almost every day and if he's abroad, he regularly video-calls so that he doesn't miss out on seeing the grandkids, both of whom would love to see him a lot more if they could; they adore dad like I always did! As he was with us as little kids, dad is extremely caring and affectionate towards my two children, which is probably why they cling to him in the exact same way I did decades before! We can all tell exactly how proud he is of all of his grandchildren and it's wonderful to see.

A few years ago, both of dad's parents died within 9 months of one another, meaning we'd all lost two of the dearest people to us in this world. My granddad, an amazing man who had always taken care of us all, suffered badly with dementia, which is such an awful thing to see take hold of a person. We all did our best to take care of granddad, as he once had for each of us at one time or other, which was difficult in itself, but even more difficult still, was for all of us to observe that life's roles had been reversed in such a cruel fashion. As I mentioned, a matter of months after granddad passed away, nan did too, and I hope that they are both reunited in a better place. I know that dad really struggled emotionally to deal with his dad's condition and death, but regardless of that, he just continued to be incredibly strong and so supportive of me and my sisters; he was always so concerned about us, how we were and how we were coping with the situation.

My dad knows, quite literally, hundreds of people from all over the UK and probably abroad as well, but whilst I obviously don't know many of them, I do realise that a lot of people over the years have been around my dad for the wrong reasons. I can't imagine living my entire life in such a way that I have to carefully consider every single friendship or relationship I have, what the reasons and motives are behind it and if it could turn out to be dangerous for me, but that's something dad has ended up having to live with. It's certainly not all bad on the friendship front, however, because he has got plenty of genuine people in his life and I can think of several who have 'uncle status' with us kids, those people who us girls could call even if dad wasn't around anymore, and they wouldn't hesitate to help us out. The best of it is, that those diamond people who we affectionately refer to as uncle, don't even need to be named or mentioned, they just know who they are and so do we.

Dad is definitely at his happiest when he has his children and grandchildren around him, that's for sure, but I understand why he needs to be in Spain for a lot of the year and I'm grateful for the effort he makes to keep in such close contact with us all when he's not in England. If one of us has so much as a sniffle, he still checks up on us multiple times per day and we know that if we needed him, he'd be there for us as quickly as humanly possible!

Dad, we all love you for who you are to us and nothing else matters.

Carl – "…. to me he's just my dad and an amazing one at that".

My dad has always been super important to me, as a kid I always looked up to him and got excited whenever I got to see him, and even as a man myself now, I still feel pleased once we have organised to get together. When I was younger, I never really understood what my dad was in terms of his career, nor the history of his life, I just had this sense and knowledge that he was a very popular guy. As I got a little older, the truth behind his life was revealed to me and a few things that had previously felt strange growing up, suddenly made more sense! But full credit to dad, because he was good at keeping his "activities" separate from our family life, until he believed the time was right, which is something I fully understand his reasons for.

There's no denying that the films, TV series', books and documentaries all make up a part of who he is, especially to the outside world, but to me he's just my dad and an amazing one at that. I understand that he's a busy man, so I've always cherished my time with him, much like I did with grandad, too.

Riding the rollercoaster that is being a West Ham fan with dad; celebrating the wins, being on the edge of your seat for playoff finals and even enduring the losses, has all been an amazing experience. For me, the pinnacle of this was going to Upton Park with dad and my late grandad, all sat together, 3 generations of men from our family, watching the team we each love playing at The Boleyn Ground, that's something I'm glad to say will be with me forever.

Even though I didn't follow in my dad's footsteps in terms of a career, I have learnt a lot from him, be it the serious and important aspects of life, such as generally being a moral man, or the significance of family, through to the arguably more trivial stuff that we sometimes inherit, like passion for football, or fashion styles. On the topic of fashion, I will note that whilst my old man is fairly trendy, I'll give him that, he does have some questionable clobber in his vast collection! It was in 2005 when we were driving through Spain, that dad introduced me to the music of Oasis, which I'd never heard until that point, but I loved that album and it's remained one of my favourites to date. What's extremely valuable to me, is that my dad is proud of me for the choices I've made and the path I chose to take in my life, and I want him to know of the huge part he played in steering me in the right direction.

As we have got older, due to various circumstances, we haven't seen each other as much as we'd both have liked, but this will be changing…imminently. Spending time with my dad means the world to me, and I can't describe how much I'm looking forward to sitting in a pub together to watch the football, or in the not-too-distant future, giving him a lift back to the retirement home (after all, you're getting old now dad)! But seriously, we have a big family, in which everyone has very different lives, ways and personalities, and it's always great to see them, but being with dad and the whole family again soon will be amazing.

I am who I am because of you, and I love you, dad.

Carlton with Carl.

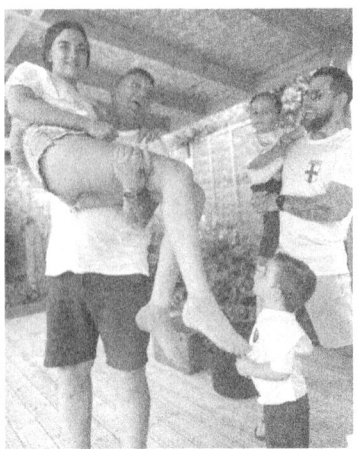

With Shane, Connie, James & Arthur.

With grandsons James & Arthur.

With Madison.

Henry, Carl, Matt, Carlton holding Callum & Norman, Carlton's dad.

Father's Day 2021

With grandson Callum.

With grandson William.

Family visiting me in Spain.

Recent get-togethers!

Carlton has his arm around Brooklyn,
Matt's eldest son.

10 RISE

The British "gangster" and organised crime film genre has been one that has always been of keen interest, and none more than by me, but not in a million years did I ever think there was a reason or justification in making a film about my life. Not to mention one that would gain enough traction allowing it to be internationally recognised and then gain a cult film status and following. Further testament to the original script and film, it's one that is still watched and found amongst many household DVD collections. What I think allowed Rise of the Footsoldier to stand out from other British cult-classics, such as Guy Ritchie's films, is both ROTFS parts 1 and 2, were not only (obviously) based on certain elements of organised crime and social topics, but also the raw, realism of what went on in my own personal life.

My natural progression and transition from hooligan, bouncer then, let's say enforcer, and depending on who had any level of involvement, also allowed my life to be (either less or more accurately) documented, but what many people don't know is how I ended up going from being embroiled in the underworld's muscle game, to actually having a best-selling book and movie about my life, especially without ruthlessly grassing a whole bunch of active people up; that has remained a popular route to book sales for several people. But the happenings behind this step, albeit simple ones, are something that I think my fans and followers of my story deserve to hear about.

I was contacted by Kate Kray to feature on Hard Bastards, and I figured why not, although at the time I didn't realise just how far reaching it would eventually become. Throughout the filming process, I got on well with Kate and when I heard that they were struggling to get more people to agree to be involved, I put forward, and helped her contact another 6 or 7 serious men that I thought might be up for it, most of whom ended up in the finished article. To me, Kate seemed to have a genuine intrigue and interest in the underworld and its inner workings, and I never stopped to think about this at the time, but possibly because she really liked my background, or in the spirit of returning a favour, her liking of my background or a blend of both, Kate organised for me to meet with John Blake of John Blake Publishing. I was a bit unsure at first, but she said she'd come with me, and we could just see what he had to say, no obligation.

John was what we call "a suit"……an upper-middle class guy who was well educated, nicely spoken and had financial stability in his life. The sort who works from the comfort of a nice office and probably hasn't ever gotten their hands too dirty! And don't get me wrong, good luck to the suits of this world and besides, John was a nice, decent guy, who always stuck to his word where I was concerned, unlike some! Kate and I were sat in John's office and he asked me a few questions that only someone with zero experience of real-life crime would ask, then when he mentioned guns, I found myself with my hand in my pocket, gripping my flick knife as I listened to what he had to say, "…but anyway Carlton, what's your weapon of choice out there on…" before he finished his sentence, I was across John's desk with my chiv to the side of his neck. The poor fella looked horrified for a few seconds, but Kate was absolutely rolling up with laughter! "I try to stick to blades where I can John!" I said as I folded the tool up, put it away and sat back down. The speed in which I'd opened the knife, made it over the desk and pressed it against his neck had even impressed me; I was rather chuffed with myself in fact! Realising it was just a practical joke (perhaps a twisted one, I don't know), John also started laughing his head off, he'd loved it and became so excited that he wanted to sign me up there and then! "We'll call your book The Knife Man, how about that Carlton? It will be great." I advised John that if I were to agree to a book deal, it wouldn't be all about a knife wielding nut case who stabs people every day, and eventually the name Muscle was decided upon.

Within weeks of his "knife-wielding encounter," John sent me down to Sandwich in Kent to work with his ghost writer, Mike Fielder, who had organised a cottage for me to stay in so that I could spend time with him, going over the stories, and within approximately 7 months of that, Muscle was on the shelves. Many years after working with Mike, I learned that he'd passed away due to cancer, so I agreed with the publishers to continue sending half of the royalties from Muscle to Mike's family…… and one thing that respectfully needs to be said, is anyone who ever earnt a tenner from my life story after that point in time, owes credit to Kate Kray and John Blake, both of whom clearly believed in me, so thank you both.

I could never have imagined in my wildest dreams, and I've had some crazy ones, that a book about me would sell so well…. even with the book sales increasing, I continued doing my thing and working security. It was whilst I was working the door at a restaurant in Ascot during the races with Sid, that Terry Turbo walked in and came over to speak with me. He mentioned that he'd heard about my book and would love to get a copy, so I got him one from my car, wrote it out to him and signed it, which he was pleased with. As we chatted, he told me that he'd just finished up on a film set, further explaining that he wanted to get into the film business properly and going on to say that perhaps I should make a film; I laughed it off in agreeance, but Terry seemed serious and said that he could make it happen. After I finished up work that night, I considered all the different avenues and possibilities, concluding with myself that, if this were to come to apparition, it could be a good opportunity for me to put a few good things out there about Tony and deservingly immortalise him and his memory in a good light.

A couple of weeks had passed since the Ascot races

and life was continuing, when Terry called me up with a film proposal, part of which was I would be paid £30,000 for the rights to my story. Thirty grand is a lot of money even now, but back then it was even more of a big deal. Perhaps I could have haggled for a little more, as the saying goes, 'never accept the first offer', but I'm not a greedy man and I figured that if I could earn that kind of money whilst people around me also benefited too, I'd be happy. As a prime example, with the film being made, I'd then help Terry get his wish of further acting work, not to mention certain people's roles in my life could be played out on-screen….in my mind, this was a win -win, as there would surely be plenty of opportunities off of the back of a film for a good few people to gain success.

Terry had organised some funding from investors to get the project started, as well as the Guilbey brothers to write the script…. things were looking really good, and the thought of my story being told, my chance at getting to set the record straight and helping a good few people out in the meantime, was sounding better and better after each day passed, plus there was no doubt "my friend" had everything under control. Then a phone call came from Terry asking me to attend a meeting with one of the owners from Carnaby (Andrew Loveday's dad), who's name I can't recall. The purpose of this meeting was basically for Loveday and Terry to re-negotiate on the current deal and get me to agree to a different one. Now I know many of you may well be screaming at the page right now and questioning why I didn't hire a lawyer and have everything checked over and their "move" was a massive "red flag," but I trusted my friend of many years, Terry Turbo, to be looking out for and considering my best interests as well as his own. So, I took him and the people he'd brought to the table at face value, and I agreed to be paid just 10k for my story, plus 5% of all profits in a royalties deal. Given how I'd lived my life up to this point, I tried to think in a sensible, selfless way about the situation; the long-term benefits for a lot of people, plus there's no denying a small trickle of steady income is a good idea in anyone's books, especially those with young children. With all of that in mind, and not wanting to hold anyone else back from earning a living, I signed the new deal, not realising at the time that it would only really benefit those that had put it together!

Non-fiction films are, more often than not, made about dead people, I don't know why, but it's true, isn't it? So, to stand on a film set, where people are recreating your life is, to say the least, very weird! I'd even go as far as to say that I found it very surreal and at times, overwhelming. I think I played about 4 cameo roles in the film, I got mates involved in various extras scenes: playing bouncers, hooligans, ravers and all sorts. I was on-set almost every day of filming; I wanted to be on hand to consult, making sure things were going to come across in the right way and even though the environment was new to me, I thoroughly enjoyed the experience.

Of course, events in films often do get "enhanced" or "dramatized" for theatrical purposes, and certain parts of the "plot" are often told in a way so as not to incriminate people that are still alive. Plus, I was keen for that film to be made in such a way that it was as close to the real thing as possible, after all, it was about my life and involved real people; things happened that affected the lives of actual human beings, not cartoon characters…....every happening and storyline had to be right and those involved had to be done justice. It's very easy for a no-mark (cheap import) who lived in Essex for a while, to sit in his favourite trucker cafe before going off to shovel gravel for the day saying, "Carlton made all that nonsense up about the Turks." I very much doubt he'd have the balls to say that to the family of my doorman who topped himself after they all got tortured! All that needs to be said about that gravel-shifting slob is, any level of criticism is easy to give, as it's one that risks little in terms of emotional or personal experience - I was actually affected by not only the loss but the taking of people's lives. I sought peace and a way to move on in life, unlike him, who only consistently seeks attention and a means of profiting from it all.

Once the film was finished, a private showing was arranged at a cinema in Soho for a select 20 or so people who were all close to and involved with the film; this was the point where the fun and madness of being on-set ended and the actual reality of what had been achieved really hit home for me! The scenario of me being lost for words is, more or less, rare as rocking-horse shit, but to watch those events from my life play out on a cinema screen left me speechless for the most part! Everyone that knows me will tell you that I'm bang into films myself and on a personal level, it has always been a hobby of mine, but to be a part of one was just next level!

Next up, Sky got in contact, wanting to film me and Anne going to the movie premier for the show Gangster's Wives, they even paid for us to stay in the ultra-luxurious Savoy Hotel so that they could film us getting ready in the lead up to the red-carpet event. Travelling to and arriving at the Odeon Leicester Square by stretch limo and featuring on a Sky TV series was an additional extra to the premier for me, but a massive, free advertising boost for the greedy and ungrateful film makers. We've all seen movie premiers on the news, but when I stepped out of the limo onto the red carpet where photographers were snapping away, lights were flashing and reporters were shouting, "Any comment Carlton," it almost felt as though I was in someone else's body - it was as much a strange as it was a surreal experience.

The premier's after party was held at Café de Paris, which was full of celebs, and everyone had a great time; all those involved in the making of the film were buzzing after finally watching it in its entirety. There were so many recognisable faces from TV and film that night, from Steve McFadden (Phil Mitchell in EastEnders) to Jeremy Kyle, but my personal favourite and by far the most memorable, was Barbara Windsor, may she rest in peace…we had a great chat that evening.

This book gives me a good platform to thank the most important people of all who were involved in the film's widespread success, not just in the UK and USA, but several other countries too, and those people are the fans; all the people who ever bought a copy of Muscle, went to the cinema to watch ROTF 1 or 2, maybe bought the DVD and have now bought this book, I thank you for your support and I for one know that it wouldn't be possible without you. My gratitude to the fans is one of the very reasons that anytime I've ever seen a copy of Muscle on the shelf in Waterstone's, I've found the manager, shown them my ID and signed all the copies in the store!

About 2 years after the release of ROTF1, complete strangers started to try to contact me, stating that they had never received a penny back from their investment into the film, and groups started to appear on social media where investors who'd had their fingers burned could share information…it bothered me because not only were these regular, trusting everyday working-class people, but people who felt they'd been taken advantage of…. the phrase, 'running off with an old lady's life savings' comes to mind. Things started to look pretty bleak in terms of anyone ever getting paid, myself included! It's always concerned me, how much my name is, of course, associated with that film, whilst at the same time, there are people out there who lost their savings through it, something which doesn't sit right with me at all, but I had no involvement in the business side of things, I was unwittingly being used as a springboard by several people.

Given that so many people, myself and Ricci included, had been short-changed from ROTF1, we decided to make a second instalment ourselves and name it 'Reign of the General', however, that project ended up on the wrong end of a court case and Carnaby finished up with the rights to complete and release the film, which you may now know as Rise of the Footsoldier 2. When I learnt that a 3rd instalment of ROTF was being made, I wondered where they were going to get another storyline from, so I posed the question to Andrew, who's written reply really was amazing to me; they were basing the plot on newspaper cuttings and hearsay! How can you make a film based on a man's autobiography, then start to release a string of fictional films under the very same name? In my opinion, it's a betrayal and an utter travesty, not only what they have done to the name 'ROTF', but also to the dead men who they are making up lies about (and as many have said, "Would they have dared to do so if they were still alive?"). From then on, no matter how much money I was offered to endorse the new fictional direction of these films, it simply wasn't going to happen with me, because as I said already, this is people's families, lives, reputations, memories and honour that we're trading in here, not just dollars and DVDs, and I have a higher moral standing than to be a part of something I believe to be morally wrong.

As I've also previously said on Twitter, these actions, in my opinion, are very deceptive and purposefully carried out in such a way as to allow fans of my true story, to believe that ROTF 3, 4 and so on are a continuation, or that I am in some way the source of information behind the storylines, but I would never be involved in such tracheary. So, if you take away one thing from reading this chapter, please try to remember that I'm not Carlton 'Rise of the Footsoldier' Leach anymore, because if there was anything more, I could do to distance myself from the association with that name, I'd do it in a heartbeat, due to what has been done using that name.

Largely thanks to the actors and film crew, ROTF 1 remains a British cult classic and whilst it is a great shame how certain parties have behaved for a quick quid and an attempt at being famous, a great amount of positivity has also come out of ROTF. For example, at my shows and via my personal twitter account, I've been able to help raise both money and awareness for charities and causes, but more about these things later. There have been many people I've considered to be celebrities that have wanted to speak to me; I was a guest at City Pavilion in Romford one evening, where Iron Mike Tyson was giving a talk; you can imagine my surprise when someone came to my table and asked if I would go out the back to meet Mike and have a chat, can't you! One of the greatest boxers of all time and a proper gentleman, he told me he'd seen the film and wanted to meet me, that was an honour and a pleasure.

My wish and hope was for my story to be captured and shown in ROTF 1, of course, that included the loss of my best friend Tony, but more so to include and show the main parts of who and what made me and my life as a whole; my childhood, involvement and days at West Ham and the muscle game. What the film is talked and referred to most is the Rettendon murders…...is it fair to ask that this event was the only part of my life that intrigued the film makers and one they could only understand and see as a marketable product?

There is no closing that would be befitting or give my total honest view on the whole series of ROTF's, but it's worth remembering there can only be the original story, and that's one that gives credibility to the title itself…... surely, 'Rise of the Footsoldier', would then have one included? As a man, I've always held my head high, I've never had to swerve or worry about bumping into someone. Having a film made about my life is truly humbling and a testament to how far I have come since my childhood and running amok as a teenager whilst supporting the claret and blue. There have been many chapters to my life and if I were to base them all over a 7-day week, the Rettendon murders took up one short lunch break of my life – and ROTF is just one of those chapters.

Ricci Harnett – "After all these years, the one thing that remains is our friendship."

In March 2019, I was dancing in a packed private room at a nightclub somewhere in Essex. The DJ dropped the track, Let Me Love You for Tonight by Kariya and the place went mental. I looked over to see Carlton Leach busting some moves with his beautiful daughters. We clocked each other and grinned like we'd been transported back to 1989. Gemma, Carlton's partner, had invited close friends and family to celebrate his birthday. I couldn't help thinking that him reaching the ripe old age of sixty despite living the kind of life he has, was some bloody achievement!

It had been a hell of a journey since the first time we met, all those years ago at Katz strip club in Basildon. I don't mind admitting that, back then, I was quietly shitting myself, having just read his book, Muscle. I was getting ready to play him in the upcoming film, Rise of the Footsoldier and the weight of responsibility had started to feel very heavy indeed. I'd been training hard for it but I was still probably at least two stone underweight and the dark, violent world that Carlton operated in seemed like another universe to me. He knew straight away that I was a bit out of my depth and maybe that's why, the next morning, he dragged me off his sofa and took me and my raging hangover with him on 'a bit of work'. 'In for a penny', as they say, and from that moment our friendship grew. I started to pack on as much weight as I could (legally), bench-pressing up to one hundred kilograms, my neck widening to the size of a tree trunk.

Before the film came out I'd been invited, along with Carlton, to a private viewing in a small screening room in Soho. I remember sitting next to him in that dark room, sweating, waiting for the film to start. I thought to myself, 'what if he hates it?' The film ended, the credits rolling to the song Heaven Knows, and we made our way out into the bright sunshine of central London. Carlton was uncharacteristically quiet. To be fair, it must have been fucking weird for him; it's not every day you see your life projected on a big screen, having to watch the harrowing moment when one of your good mates was brutally executed in a gangland killing. "Well done!," he said, quietly, still processing it. I think I said, "cheers," and we both stood there in silence in the hustle and bustle of the busy Soho street.

The film premiered in Leicester Square and had a limited release at the cinemas, but it was on DVD that it really blew up, doing huge numbers in the UK. I'm not sure why the British public went for it in the way they did, because it didn't have any massive stars in it and the story of the Rettendon Murders had already been told a few years before in a pretty good film called Essex Boys. The snobby film critics, who seem to enjoy sticking the boot into these kinds of films tried their best, but even they couldn't stop Rise of the Footsoldier being a runaway success - and judging by the amount of people who still stop me in the street, I'd say that it's definitely regarded as a cult British film.

I remember thinking at the time that it might change my life in some way. I'd been acting since the age of ten and had done alright in telly dramas and films like 28 Days Later, but this felt different because I was now a leading man, despite being a short arse and not having the looks of Tom Hardy. I thought maybe this would open a few doors for both me and Carlton and I guess it sort of did, but there was no first-class ticket to Hollywood - that's the acting game for you! The sad thing was that I'd fallen out with the production company who made the film, which was a shame because otherwise Rise of the Footsoldier Part II probably would have happened back in 2009.

I went back to being a jobbing actor and Carlton, along with his usual line of work, had started doing one-man shows up and down the country. Having been a stage actor, I knew how nerve-wracking it can be to go out in front of a live audience, but I was surprised just how well Carlton had taken to it. I suppose the bottle needed to battle it out on the terraces throughout the eighties had stood him in good stead.

He invited me to one show in some seaside town up north. Carlton, myself and West Ham Steve flew up together; it felt a bit like being on an awayday with the ICF! We were picked up at the airport by some hard-looking geezers and driven to a pretty rough-looking boozer on the seafront. It was a Saturday night - the town was heaving with pissed-up Hen and Stag parties - and by the time Carlton's show had started, the pub was packed with every local bare-knuckle fighter and his son. It went well though, and the night passed without any agg; that was until I stepped outside into the freezing cold for a fag and saw three old bill trying to pepper spray some lump on the ground, while these northern bridesmaids were screaming and swinging for anyone that moved. It was a bit lively, to say the least, and I was thankful to the hand that reached out and pulled me back into the relative sanctuary of the pub. I went to a few more shows after that, but eventually packed it in for my own health.

There were a couple of years where Carlton and I didn't see each other much, but he'd always pick up the phone if I called. I knew it niggled him that no one else involved in the first film had bothered to see how he was; it seems that everyone's your mate when they're making money but when it dries up, that's when you see who your real friends are. We'd spoken about the idea of doing a sequel because even though the first film was good, if you think about it, Carlton's character sort of disappears in the second half. You follow him working his way up from the terraces, to the clubs and deeper into the underworld, and then he's gone. It's almost like two separate films, with a bit of him smashing things up at the end. I was really interested in what had happened to Carlton after the murders; how the trauma had impacted not only him but his family, and how he struggled to carry on grafting in the underworld because people had turned their back on him, fearing he might be next.

Carlton and I both knew that if we were going to get the film off the ground, it was going to take a monumental effort. Because we weren't on good terms with the producers of the first film, we knew it was gonna cause fucking bedlam, but that was part of the challenge. I could write a book about the obstacles we faced making that film, but life's too short. Let's just say it was one of the most difficult things I've ever done. But in hindsight, we won more battles than we lost, such as bringing Coralie Rose back to play Denny and persuading Luke Mably to give up the sunshine of LA and come over to freezing Essex to deliver his cracking performance as Shawn. I'm proud of all of the actors and crew that went above and beyond to make Rise of the Footsoldier Part II the best film it could possibly be. The fact that it ended up featuring top tunes like Liquid's Sweet Harmony, Baby D's Let Me Be Your Fantasy and Josh Wink's Don't Laugh is another example of how Carlton and I stood firm amongst all the agg. I'm not saying the film's perfect, but we put our hearts and souls into it and it went on to win Best British Film at the National Film awards, voted for by the public, which meant a lot to us. We left it open at the end to tee up the trilogy but the producers decided to do the prequel instead. To be honest, I don't really recognise the franchise now but good luck to them.

After all these years, the one thing that remains is our friendship. I think back to Carlton's sixtieth birthday party and who had turned up that night to celebrate; real family and friends, good people that have shown loyalty to him throughout the years and it was an honour to be part of that.

Film makers & story tellers can try to pretend I wasn't there, but the proof exists. How many people have these?

With Ricci Harnett.

11 ULTRAS

To get an understanding of Italian football supporters; Ultras more specifically and their love for football, it'll help when reading anything that gives an insight to their world if you replace a few words and terms: Fanatical = passionate….extremist = supporter and the very word itself, Ultra = to live and die for your club, literally, but as well as their level of commitment and 'obsession' with the game, it's also important to understand Italians as a culture and how they view and appreciate life and absorb everything they come in contact with, but I'll get to that later. To say football is the epitome of local and popular passion - in everything they do and believe in, is an understatement. There're a few stories giving claim to the start or birthplace of the name Ultras (and the type of dedicated supporter), one of the most commonly accepted is said to have begun in Milan's Curva Sud with the Fossa Dei Leoni in 1968. On a side note, there's no disputing of the bitter, generation long rivalry between Fossa dei Leoni (AC Milan) and their arch-rivals Boys San (Inter Milan), as being one of the biggest. In the late 60s, a lot of other Ultra-groups were founded, as far north as the south, and their ideals and existence weren't reserved to just one or two of the main highly populated cities throughout the country. By the 1970's, there wasn't one Italian team in the three highest divisions (Serie A, B and C), who did not have an Ultra-group among their followers.

If you were to look up the word "Ultrà," it'll probably give you a standard, linear interpretation and tell you that it is the Italian term for "beyond the borders," and how this description dictates that Ultras are more than just normal fans on every level imaginable, but remember, with the Italians, there's a level of heritage and cultural identity that's always missed and their appreciation of the game easily supersedes that of a simple three-worded claim and attempt at encapsulating a sport held as close to their hearts as you can only begin to imagine. To be an Ultra you will have been born and bred with a belief that your sole purpose is to support and carry your team until the end. Ultras as a group were built and formed around a core of founders demanding that same level and desire to bond on a single belief. Typical traits include that of any anti-establishment philosophy, a bit of a rascal and revolutionist and someone that can't be told where to sit and on what level, or volume they're allowed to support their team. Your following was a result of where you were born geographically and also came from the local town Square centred of these same groups; a game steward has no chance of telling an Ultra of how little or in what capacity he's going to make his part of the world be known. A very high percentage were born of the working-class, so the cheapest tickets meant a real community bonding and following. Since its (Ultras) start, in many ways the usage and story about Ultras isn't solely about football, but a shared one incorporating Italian subculture inspired by it; both political and religious fundamentalism are the backbone of each Ultras group, some more than others. Like most sub-cultures in the UK, they identify with their upbringing that have influences within both local and domestic history.

For one reason or another, there's been a mutual respect and comradery with Italian football supporters and West Ham throughout the years, and non-stronger than with myself and different factions of Ultras throughout Italy. I'm sure there's some truth that with Paola Di Canio joining the West Ham squad back in 1999 and his commendable level of loyalty (and natural skill) helped any future friendship between Lazio and the Hammers, but as I found out through first-hand experience, the Italians and Ultras, is a bonding and friendship between different countries, clubs and myself that is one I've never seen or heard of anywhere else in the world and little did I know that in future years, Lazio would be my first stepping stone into Italy and Ultras as a whole.

My liking of Italian football and their level of passion (if that can be a strong enough word) was first realised back when channel 4 first started televising Italian football in the 90s. One team in particular I liked right off the bat, how they carried themselves and came across – S.S. Lazio, who to me, like a lot of Italian teams, were an embodiment of football and passion, but at the time there was something that bit extra I saw and felt about the team and the fans that I liked. They say first impressions count and thinking back to one of the first times I got to hear and see the Italian fans response, show of raw emotion and expression, the noise and involvement was on a level I'd typically only seen in English clubs during a big derby or play off....… except the Italians were like this every single game, week in week out. Of course, I had my own bias view that none were louder or more passionate than 8,000 - 10,000 West Ham loyal on an away game to Man-U, singing bubbles, drowning-out the feeble attempts of a singsong the cockney reds were putting out.

Not long after I was first exposed to Lazio and Italian football, I also got to hear the name Fabrizio Piscitelli, he was a very heavily respected face and main lad within Lazio Ultras. There was a documentary on both him and the accusations of country wide involvement in corruption, crime and the team organisation itself. Just the Ultras passion and influence rang home with me and West Ham … their team and the results they produce is something they take very personally, I think by many standards, they see the team as a reflection of who they are and what they believe in. So, when the Lazio team wasn't performing to a standard that was expected by the locals, Fabrizio headed 1500 fans to the training ground to express their issues and frustration with the trainer, manager and team, again, that's just the tip of the iceberg on what football is and means to them. That same passion, love, devotion…. involvement call it what you will, it's something that is born within you and part of your DNA. It can be compared to as the heart and soul of the team and club, you say fanatical - that's not even close. Imagine an English lad in the 70s and early 80s when that first seed was planted, disguised as a piece of leather and cleverly shaped as a ball…. the root and core of love for the game was born from there …. and Ultras, it's one carried on a monumental level until they reach the grave – devotion and commitment is the path for a true Ultra, there is no in-between.

It's been in the newspapers as much as on the tv in the past how politicians, business owners, club presidents, are as much fans of the teams as they were reachable and part of Ultras and their club involvement, they're all intertwined ……and their business dealings and strong ties eventually led to a government crackdown and the corruption that was said to exist. But (as with some firms in the UK having undertones in crime and the like), in Italy, it's again on a massive national level. The mafia originated in Italy, the (mafia's) very existence is one that is deep rooted in the country, all that goes on and with the strong numbers in Ultras, all I'll say is they might be different branches, but they're all part of the same tree – no football hooligan in the world can pull the respect and weight like an Ultra and I don't think it'll ever change.

My story and welcoming into the world of Ultras started with what must be at least 10, if not more, years ago, when Cass called to tell me he'd been contacted by a couple of Lazio's main lads. Alexandro, who was top man at the time had invited us out to Rome for Lazio vs Juventus home game and to meet Lazio Ultras main firm. Later, and after meeting up with the main firm, they'd said how they was trying to get hold of me, but it was near impossible; Cass had started to be a bit more 'public' with his projects and as a result was more reachable, I simply swerved social media at the time, that simply wasn't me. They said they'd heard of us and seen how we carried ourselves…… and let's be honest, it was no secret, and we were far from shy in openly telling the whole of the UK our willingness to fight for what we believed in. I'm not 100 percent, but I've always believed they saw a bit of themselves in what and how we demonstrated our side of things and they now wanted to share their world with us – it could be said, birds of a feather or great minds think alike.

Now, you don't even have to be aware of the level of extremism that exists within some factions (hence the word, 'Ultra'), but knowing how politics and political leanings are employed with Italian football supporters, beliefs and way of life, then visiting the home end, Cass not being your 'typical fan' within the community, was something that should've been on anyone's mind – BUT, as a testament to the respect and hospitality of Lazio Ultras, to see a parting of thousands of people when entering the curve and brought to the front (reserved exclusively for the top boys) was a sign of both respect and welcoming and that was appreciated – we were treated with the upmost of respect, nothing less. It was during this visit that I also discovered just how much of a following and support West Ham have; but I'll come back to that later. The radio station visit involved us being interviewed for a couple of hours, thankfully with an interpreter, and an endless number of supporters showing up. The whole trip was very impressionable, and I couldn't have been made to feel more welcome, so much that I was asked to come back and roll with the main firm.

Being allowed access to an Ultras group is on the same level as receiving an invitation to their home or a close family event, it's a place that is held sacred, and the curve is their home and their sanctuary – it's a reflection of their beliefs, ideals…... their very soul and existence ……. sounds extreme? You have to understand that an Ultra's life is more than just the game, it's what and who you support on every level, in not only your life, but those around you - family, friends and fellow Ultras – and nothing is done in half measures, even if there's an errand that needs sorting, someone within the same Ultras that you go to a match with, is probably going on that errand with you, it's not a matter of why are the same people you see at football involved in every aspect of your lives, it's why aren't they! Your neighbours, brother, brother-in-law, nephew, son... all part of the circle of people and who will undoubtably stand alongside with you in the curve. They are brothers in arms and like all passionate supporters, Ultras maintain a mindset where if there's an argument internally over a flag, banner, your right to defend the player, coach or manager will include a deep-rooted level of politics that will be infused and part of everything talked about ....and it's here an Ultras relationship can always be on edge.

It was by the next invitation and visit, that I noticed how serious and accommodating Ultras were at being hosts, as the same level of hospitality and welcoming seen on the first trip was equally as much, if not more on this one, nothing was an issue, and everyone couldn't do any more than they already were to make me feel welcomed. Once again, I was invited to their club house, reserved for Ultras top firm, where I did another radio interview, again all presented very professionally and supporting of what I'd been involved in. What impressed me was not just the support they showed for my book, Muscle but also Rise of the Footsoldier – simply because the 'Footsoldier...' film hadn't been released in Italy and yet it still gained a massive amount of support. What also impressed me was the volume of Ultras in the Curva Nord that were sporting West Ham scarves, caps and badges – I say this because anyone that follows, or is part of any Ultras will know and tell you of the loyalty and devotion solely to their own club, and then to take another team into their hearts, the value and support for an East London club and the way they openly showed it – that meant something and said a lot about the fans. Even before the closing of this visit, I was once again invited back and through each and every following visit, we built up a stronger friendship that ensured that I'd be invited back again.

It was on one particular visit and the last game of the season, Lazio's top man, Fabrizio Piscitelli; who I'd seen in a documentary back in the 90s and met prior (he was in prison when I visited some years before), had organised a massive street party. During the day was the Roma derby, and it was here, before and after the game we were walking the streets around The Stadio Olympico (Olympic Stadium) as all the roads had been blocked off by the local police which then gave his firm free range to come and go in the local city streets. The rumour was Roma fans were supposed to be turning up with a big firm and looking for a row, but in equal, if not more measure, this was Lazio Ultras manor, and no one was going to out-do them, especially now that their top boy was back – Fabrizio and Lazio Ultras were going to send a message and make it known that he was back and wasn't fucking about. Lazio Ultras presence is spread far and wide and even to other countries and within the Lazio ranks were some heavy-duty, high-ranking Neo-Nazis, who apparently maintained high placed positions within other extremist factions in their own countries and regions as they did here within Ultra's curve - needless to say, Roma's firm never turned up. To be in the thick of that level of passion, not so much the politics, reminded me of my early days with the ICF and walking the streets on a Saturday, pre and post a West Ham game, but I will add this, here they were very organised and made sure everyone knew their responsibility and place, constantly shouting and securing the lines – it was with military precision. The chants, the pulling of ranks into line, it was if they were rallying soldiers all together and into formations. It reminded me of the films I'd seen over the years of Roman legions and their generals leading them into battle, but instead of armour and spears, it was designer gear and Lazio chants.

Powerful stuff, and much like the infamous shouting out of, "ICF…. ICF…. ICF" back home, their several minute-long Lazio chants were like a surge of energy with each line and verse…….and with each song and chant, it was like someone was putting petrol on a fire, it infused a level of power that you felt through your body. It even got my chest inflated a few inches…. and made me feel like I was invincible… an un-fucking-believable feeling and like I said earlier, they take on everything they do with a high level of passion and invest a huge amount of dedication – It was raw emotion and love for the game, no one was interested in photos that would lead to false stories, it was about each and every person's cultural obligation in preserving and showing love for a flag, a banner and a group of people that celebrated as much as they felt the loss collectively, and as an Englishman looking in at this world, it didn't matter the language barrier, it wasn't about the differences in the spelling and soundings of words…..it was about a group of people and their involvement in a shared belief and goal. It was much like here as with a lot of other visits, I really understood their level of involvement and what they were doing and being in the thick of it with their top boy, Fabrizio was even better, I really enjoyed being around him, his passion and love for what he did was on a level you just had to admire. I got on really well with him and like I said a moment ago, each and every visit was something else and being in his company showed me just how much he truly loved, supported and respected a team, a belief and those around him.

The community's willingness and involvement showed and highlighted both his power and presence within Lazio Ultras and in a style of their own making, everything and everyone was part of what was going on, a real carnival atmosphere, the smells of the different foods, the sounds
coming from every direction and the energy from the people all around you, I mean, just imagine thousands of

people enjoying themselves and in on the street party. There were stalls that circled the whole way around the ground, a music stage for performances and even a London red double-decker bus driving up and down the street, completely wrapped in Lazio, West Ham and ICF flags, it really was just unimaginable. It was only after I was invited on stage and handed the mic, I realised I knew very little Italian, but what I did know was shouted out and they went fucking wild! Then, on top of all that to have thousands singing, "I'm forever blowing bubbles," just blew my mind. You can't begin to imagine the feeling and level of gratitude I have for these people and their willingness to accommodate me and share their love of the game and their culture. I was surrounded by the whole community, who was there openly sharing their world, which they made you feel was also now mine.

During the street party I noticed a large group of men standing by one of the roadblocks. Like I said earlier, everything had been blocked off by the local police and they'd used these big barriers in preventing vehicles in driving up and down the streets. It wasn't long after I noticed them looking in my direction and I was asked to come over and meet what I later learned was Inter-Milan Ultras. There was about 100 of their top boys that had massed near where I was standing. When I walked over, one particular member caught my eye, a black bloke standing amongst them. It was only as I got closer that I then heard the same black bloke greet me with an English accent, "You're Carlton Leach…. Rise of the foot soldier?" He then introduced himself as Ken. He explained he'd been living out here for a good few years and the Inter-Firm would like to meet me. I was introduced to some of the top boys – Franco, Moreno and a few of what are known as the "Old Boys," The Vikings and a few others, as much like West Ham, Ultras have different factions, whose members are of different generations and age groups and each generation has its own firm. It was during this conversation that I was invited to visit Milan on my next trip and to stay with Ken, who would take me to meet the whole Inter-firm. As much as Ultras can have extreme views, some if not most actually align and have the same beliefs; Lazio and Inter-Milan Ultras were of the same mind-set and are closely affiliated (basically cousins... best mates), same beliefs, politically, culturally and every sense of the way the same philosophy. In some respects, I guess you could say it's like there are 2 capitals in the country, Milan in the north and Rome south of them. Rome of course is known and listed as the capital of Italy, but Milan can be said to be the financial capital. There's an understanding and respect between Lazio and Inter Ultras and as it's said, "When either of the Ultras visit each other's city; they're not away fans, they're our guests."

Like all of my visits, whether I was in either a wine bar or a lovely restaurant, I was always in the best company and having the time of my life. And here I was, an east ender, born and raised from a humble working-class background, now in another country being wined and dined......they treated me like one of their own......family and like I said in the opening of this chapter, it's their approach and doing of things as a culture and a country that gives you an understanding of their involvement with football and what they embrace in their lives as a whole.....when you're meeting and spending time with friends and family in Italy, you truly start to get a sense of what and how they operate....having conversations, how they meet and discuss things isn't done on something as impersonal as a mobile phone; Italians do things on a very sociable level - they will meet up at a restaurant, they will take the time in sitting down to have wine, beer, food and talk one-on-one. Whether it's football, family or the people and the day they're involved in, it's all about tasting life through experience, not some falsity like a quick chat in passing by.

It was in the middle of all of this when I got a message from within the firm that someone wanted to talk to me outside. When I stepped outside the restaurant, there were two high ranking Lazio Ultras in a brand-new Porsche Panamera. No sooner than I jumped in, we shot off, hurtling down the road at neck-breaking speed. Not long into the journey, the brightly lit and full of energy populated streets soon turned into dimly lit, lifeless roads ……we then slowly pulled into what looked like a working-class area. Having a quick look around at my new surroundings, it looked no different than a massive council estate back home, but there wasn't a single soul or living thing anywhere, it was completely silent…... It was as if I'd landed on an uninhabited planet. It wasn't long after 1am, and here I am, sitting in a (easily) 150k motor with two very high-ranking Ultras, not a fucking clue where I was or what the plan is. I'm a very confident person and have been in situations and places a lot worse, but the fact remained I was not in Kansas anymore. No back up, no tool but knowing who I was amongst was enough assurance that if anything went side-ways we'd come out on top. I had another look outside the car windows, trying to get a look of what was around me, but it was near impossible, just grey, poorly lit buildings, endless silhouetted blocks and alleyways all around us, this was a far cry from the beautiful, warm lit, full of character, picture post-card type buildings and surroundings I was enjoying not long ago. We'd gone from hot to cold in a matter of minutes and here I was, in the middle of something. It didn't help that my understanding of the Italian language was at best only enough to say hello and thank you.

Even after a few minutes, still no cars passed…… and not a single person could be seen in any direction, until one of the lads muttered something and pointed in a direction where a shadowy figure appeared and was walking towards the car. Both lads were now smiling and seemed happy that who-ever this person was had now arrived. Throwing a package inside the car, the mystery character then disappeared as quickly as he appeared. Immediately they started to open it up and began offering the contents. I won't incriminate myself or those whose company I was in, but the illicit commodity now in my lap and literally under my nose would've got me a stretch only familiar to that of a major high profiled trafficker back home. Thoughts and ambitions to get back to the warmth and sanctuary of big buildings and Italian restaurants would've been more than an ambition for anyone, but, as they say, when in Rome.

One little story that's worth mentioning is how jealousy and politics can play a role even when you're in the perfect of settings. It was on a visit when Inter Milan were playing at home, and like countless times before I was in country by invitation. I'd made the effort in taking some people out to Italy so as to introduce them to Lazio Ultras… the introductions, insight and their very presence was only as a result of my doing. The same people I had taken, as I suspected, now felt it was necessary to try and discredit me and say things about me behind my back - this was seen as a level of disrespect by a lot of people, and none more than by my hosts – the downside for those that had something to say about me was it actually had the reverse affect, as their efforts, in an attempt in putting me below them only then made them look bad - this was all reaffirmed when I got a call from a high ranking Lazio Ultra bringing me up to speed. When people act that way, it always says more about them than it does about the person they're attempting to make lesser.

The feeling of success and wealth is typically only reserved for those that actually have it, but the feeling of respect and power was something I observed whenever I was in the company of these men. When you walk firm handed, with what must have been at least 10 high ranking Ultras into one of the busiest, largest, totally packed-out restaurants, I mean it was people wall to wall, then to have the owner personally come out to greet you, have a massive table magically appear and set-up where there was only floor space just seconds ago, tells you you're amongst top tier people. And if that wasn't enough, the owner would only allow both him and his son to wait on you – ensuring the service was nothing short of perfect and you would all return to his restaurant.

Over the years, the friendship between us all has gone from strength to strength, so the first opportunity I got I returned the same level of hospitality when myself and a pal, Dave D flew Fabrizio and some of Lazio's top boys over for the championship play-off when West Ham played Blackpool at Wembley. We put them up in hotels, made sure everyone ate and had a box at the game and really made the effort in making sure they knew their friendship was valued on the same level. Whatever side of the channel I met up with Fabrizio and his boys, it was always the best you could wish for…. a really good friend, whose visits and time spent with are those I'll always remember.

It wasn't long after that I took Ken up on his offer, and a return visit to Italy was on the cards, and no sooner had I just finished unpacking from my Rome visit, I was now packing away the basics for a trip back to Italy, more specifically, Milan! But this trip, I decided would be a bit different, as I wanted it to be more about Italy as a culture and not just football (it was out of season anyway) and the last thing I wanted was to take any West Ham 'political' baggage along for the (new) experience. So, I decided to take along one of my best mates, Lenny. One of the things I wanted to share with a close mate of 25 plus years, was how much the Italian culture and Ultras had made such a strong, and lasting impression on me. I'm a proud born and raised east London lad, West Ham is in my heart and soul…...my blood runs claret and blue, and it always will……. but there was something about Ultras, their love for the game and how they'd taken me into their hearts and lives, that gave me such a sense of pride in saying, "I'm a welcomed part of that!" …. in addition, I wanted to show how, what I called my new love affair with a country, and I wanted to share that with someone I called family; I guess the feeling was much like scoring the winning goal at the school football match, or winning a trophy as a kid, you'd want to run home and proudly tell your dad, or an older brother of what you'd experienced, discovered or achieved.

On the flight over, Lenny, who'd never been to Italy, and being this was a whole new experience, asked what obvious questions would be, "What if this is a set-up, I mean, you're Carlton Leach!" …." We don't speak any Italian, what if this goes sideways?" …... "How well do you know the bloke who we're staying with?" and on top of all that, Lenny isn't West Ham, he's a Tottenham fan (we all have one dark secret). Now, if I'm being honest, I could've really wound him up, making up stories about visiting Italy for the first time, that this …...or that could happen, but, as I assured Lenny, I knew in my heart, these were honest people, their intentions were coming from a good place and above all, I've been around and taken on board by the top people in Italy, if there was any thought or chance of being mugged-off, they wouldn't have allowed it. Plus, I've always been of that mindset, where I don't always 'plan things out', or over-think about a venue or building I'm entering; if I'd thought like that during any part of my life, I'd not seen half of what I have and missed out on some blinding experiences – I believe that you can't always rely on the light in a dark place.

We got settled in at Ken's place and was soon being introduced to a few of the main faces of Inters firm; a lot of the top-tier Ultras were away and spending time in their holiday homes scattered around the country, but the good thing about this visit was the time I spent there and the lads that I did get to meet, not only allowed me to relax and immerse myself in Italian culture and way of life, but also spend personal one-on-one time with them, plus, even out of season there was plenty of 'football talk'. Nino, Cesco, Franco, Moreno, Gerry to name but a few welcomed us from day one with open arms and much like when I was visiting Lazio Ultras, even before we'd left the company of our hosts and Milan, we were invited back ......and the next visit was to be an even bigger one.

The next visit couldn't have come soon enough, and it was nice to see there were some like-minded people, who enjoyed and identified with the passion displayed by the Italian fans, as during the flight, I was approached by some young Cardiff lads, who wanted to simply say hello, and ask if they could get a photo with me. I had to take my hat off to them, I mean, committing to a flight and traveling overseas to watch a game is commendable on many levels. So, fair play to Josh, Newt and their two mates, and as further credit to them, we've stayed in touch since.

When both Lenny and I got to Milan, it couldn't have gone any better, as straight away, we're amongst the top boys, once again including Franco, Gerry, Tony, Moreno, Nino, Cesco….and all of the top boys and entire Inter firm. The language barrier was a question from Lenny on a previous flight, but as he found out, when we arrived and started to get introduced and be around the main firm, friendship and passion for the game broke down a lot of barriers, plus a lot of people spoke English, so what blanks existed, were quickly filled in. So, here we are again, front and centre, and like I said earlier, this was a big one – It was the first game of the season, so everyone is buzzing with energy and all fired up and to top it all off, it's a derby game, meaning it's a full turn-out of ALL their firm – Inter were going to be out in serious numbers for this game and I mean from the top to the bottom; in layman terms the CEO's, managing directors, managers, supervisors, general staff – the WHOLE infrastructure was present and accounted for. Being invited to go at the front of any curve is beyond an honour and privilege; but to be referred to as, 'El-Capitan' and stood in a place that is only open to those that have spent decades in, giving nothing less than blood sweat and tears, going through what is called an apprenticeship and on top of that to be recognised amongst those natural born within those ranks is something else, plus the funny side of it, was again Lenny, who wasn't even 'football' in that respect, and being held at the front, to my side and as my number two at the curve become a personal joke between us. Leaving the game is bitter-sweet, I mean how can you want to walk away from that experience and not think how can that ever be beaten? But a few days partying, spending and enjoying time amongst Inter's top boys was much appreciated and one I have enjoyed many times since.

I quickly learned not to rush unpacking when I arrived back in the UK, as within a couple of weeks I was back amongst Inter and Lazio for a game between the two teams. Now Lazio Ultras would be in town, and news of this to anyone would then be forced to ask (at minimum), "What and how will this turn-out go, knowing of both my close relationship and friendship with both Ultra groups?" When Lazio Ultras did turn up, it was one massive meet; it was like your favourite cousins had come round for Sunday dinner or to celebrate a special occasion and like I said earlier, Lazio and Inter are very closely aligned in all aspects of football, culture and beliefs. They all met up in bars and restaurants on Inter's manor and every time you'd see one of Inter's firm, there would be Lazio's lads mingling amongst the crowd, interestingly enough, Inter-fans would often wear a Lazio cap or top when their cousins south of them were visiting their city and stadium as a sign of respect, and as a sign of how much I was welcomed in Rome, the Lazio Ultras were happy to see me with our shared family in Milan.

When news came of Inter-Milan playing Tottenham at home in the Europa cup, it was without question I was going to make sure my Inter family were taken care of, in-house and up front. When I was given the names of those visiting, I couldn't have been happier, Gerry, Franco, Moreno and his lovely misses Chiara and a few others, the news made it feel like Christmas had come early, and more importantly it was another chance for me to return the hospitality I'd received from them. One main hurdle existed though, that being Moreno was on a travel ban for away games, but not in a million years was I going to let something as trivial as a piece of paper and a judge come in between our brother from seeing our beloved team play, as when it comes to 'doing the right thing', I've always considered it an honour and I'll always commit and come through on anything when it comes to people I consider as family, each and every time – no question.

Gerry was traveling and staying with the main Inter-firm in London, but with Moreno bringing his misses, Chiara, there was no question that they, much like all of Inter's top boys, would receive the same level of hospitality they'd always extended to me. We had them picked up from the airport and we even stayed in the same hotel that we set them up in at Southend, I wanted to make sure everything was always taken care of; a phone call away wasn't personal enough for me, it was all about attention to detail, and things had to be done properly. Restaurants, places and faces, this was, like the many times before and after my way of showing my appreciation for how much I regarded them as family. When it came time to the game, like I've mentioned, Gerry was traveling with Inter-Ultras, but Morena couldn't simply stroll into the visitors end and be with the main firm, as sure as I'm sitting here, I know that the local authorities would have spotters out and looking for known people. But none the less, we made sure he was at the game…... and in style. So, a favour was called in and I had them in a box, allowing them to watch the whole game without threat or interruption from either the local plod or an ambitious

Tottenham fan, again we had to avoid any attention to his presence – plus, this was a family one. What a game that was, Lenny, me, and our guests loved it… a brilliant day with lovely people, and needless to say, they really enjoyed themselves throughout. But again, as a testament to a special friendship and level of respect and appreciation between both Inter-Ultras and myself, the next thing that happened, to this day is still one for the books. It was whilst we were all still in the box at Tottenham's ground that a familiar Italian face appeared and said that there were some people waiting outside and would really like to meet me…... and those people was the whole Inter-Milan team! Franco, one of the top lads had travelled with the team on their bus, and before leaving the grounds made the coach-driver pull around and park up, then sending someone up to get me and bring me to where the bus was parked, and they were waiting. The whole team…....not a supporter's group, or friends of the team, but THE whole Inter-Milan team…....! Imagine sitting at home and watching your favourite team on the telly, then to get a knock on the door, and when you answer it, there's the whole squad, who's popped around for a cup of tea, before they set off! Un-fucking-real…. These people have no limits to how far and what they are willing to do… that's beyond friendship… that's family! But, as much as I wanted to go and meet up with Franco and a team I'd come to love, and as ambitious as I am, I knew it'd be a bit of a mistake, as I'm not exactly one to turn away from any firm, but the thought of me bowling out through a stadium in the middle of White Hart Lane that's not long emptied and still thick with the local supporters wasn't exactly a bright idea; I've done some brave and equally questionable moves before, but this wasn't the time to see how long it would be before people clocked me. With a lump in my throat, and a sense of immense gratitude, I said I'd meet up with them on another visit.

On a later trip, like all of the previous visits to Milan,

Lenny was booked to come along, but had fallen really ill at the last minute, so he couldn't make it. So, here I am, going from having an extra set of eyes, to one that now meant I was simply more exposed, but with me, I've always enjoyed going into the unknown and this trip, being an away game meant venturing further out into the country, and that meant new and unfamiliar territory, thus further isolating me from what I'd grown accustomed to. All of this then makes it an unknown element…... but it's one I thrive in, and on - and as a result, I knew I'd be on cloud 9. But, knowing I was going to be picked up by one of the old guard, or old boys, Sandro and it was here I knew that I'd be with family and looked after. Exactly like with Lazio Ultras, everyone knew they had a moral responsibility, Sandro always made sure I got where I needed to, taken care of and it would only be him carrying that responsibility. Sandro was part of the old school, previous generations of Ultras, who still went to every game and was very much a part of what went on - it can't be emphasised enough with these lads, loyalty and respect is the backbone and seen throughout …. it didn't matter your age, standing or level in any part of Ultras structure, top or bottom, everyone played a part …. and played it well…. there's an unquestionable level of loyalty and respect throughout the ranks.

Arriving, and after spending several days with the lads and enjoying what was on par with any previous visit, I was given my ticket for the away game. Because of the government crackdown in previous years on extreme levels of violence and monitoring who's visiting the games, they'd introduced travel ID's, now initially, I hadn't thought this was going to be an issue, but after realising my ticket was in a name that didn't even closely resemble mine, I thought it might be a challenge getting into a stadium and I could run into a problem or two whilst visiting somewhere that was going to be a decent drive away from where I was staying, if not the best part of a thousand miles from home – but fuck it, I was with a firm that took care of their own! After the coach journey to Verona and arriving at their stadium, we all walked to the entrance of the ground. Now, like I said before, I'd noticed that the name on the ticket wasn't anything close to Carlton Leach, nor did it match that of the travel ID that I didn't have, but even if I tried using my driver's license as a substitute, it still didn't change the fact it didn't match the name that I couldn't even pronounce on the ticket, but it then further dawned on me what if I can't get in? I'd be stuck outside, and it could very easily kick-off, and I'd then get nicked and end-up in a prison cell …....that, and unable to string a single sentence together in Italian wouldn't be the best situation for me to end up in! So, I thought I best formulate some sort of plan to ensure that I got in. I looked and sized up each of the stewards that was checking tickets, one in particular looked like I'd be able to get past without too much issue, but, before my thought or plan could be put into action, a group of thousands formed around me and we all simply went in, en masse and in force. The old adage, "if your name isn't on the list, you're not coming in" didn't work and wasn't part of Inters MO, 10,000 Inter weren't letting one of their own stand outside simply because some governing body had set some rules, as here, the only rule was Inter, and when it came to decisions and who's coming in, that was a decision of their making…….and no one else's. Whether it was a home or away game, when Inter went to watch a game, they went in, and no one was going to tell them otherwise.

From then on, I started going to Milan regularly and each and every time, Franco and all the top people were always the best hosts and supporters during my stay. One group of people that I've failed to mention, are the Inters that run the pivot shops; they're the ones who set up and run merchandise stores for the group that then promote everything for Inter-Ultras and the games. They always go out of their way in ensuring that both myself and whoever

I'm traveling with are kitted out and taken care of – lovely, caring people.

Going to any of the games in the company of Ultras is something to be marveled at, and the invitation of Franco and the boys is right up there. At the grounds, the love for the game and team is nothing less than heart and soul……life and death. Much like football supporters in England in the 1960s through the early nighties; pure passion and club loyalty, openly displayed by entire generations and supported by the surrounding communities. The other most notable and commendable difference is Ultras never allowed their club history and devotion to be left behind, nor to be seen as some cheap yesteryear motto for what once was. They're always upping their game and the dedication shown week in week out, from one generation to the next is something that they'll never allow to be hijacked or duplicated by a single person or age bracket who feel they've got better ideas, or to dictate a selfish misguided view or interpretation of a club and its badge, for Ultras, back at the start, is the same as it is today, it is 'pane e salame' (straightforward). It's the club and the game ……and you behind them. The support given by an Ultra is that of the 12th man in the team and their hard-lined support is the voice of the same 12th man on the field. The curve behind the goal is an area and domain that is strictly Ultra-controlled. The rest of the stadium is assigned and has numbered seats and those away from the curve have to follow rules. To some, Ultras may be considered a minority or a sample of the team's support, but they maintain a level of support both vocally and openly that far outweighs any other fan base - fact! As it was once said, "They truly are a whole city all under one tent."

Going to a game with any Ultras support base and becoming more than just a guest is an unmatched (excuse the pun) experience and this is one that will, hopefully show just that. When you arrive at the San Siro stadium, where I was to watch my beloved Inter, you have to enter from the back, you're then led up what seems endless stairs until you reach the fourth upper tier of the stadium. When you finally reach the top of this skyscraper of a stadium, being able to look out at what was in front of you, with the sea of heads of fans, it's only then are you able to appreciate just how big the stadium really is; if there was any doubt by a visitor on the amount of people and the level of passion found within, the sound of 70,000 football-loving, passion-driven, life-long devoted fans will. Now add to that, the power and force emanated from 10,000 Ultras, all hell-bent in expressing both vocally and physically, their unquestionable level of commitment each side of the stadium, is one that is stronger and bigger than the stadium we were all standing in. The next leg of the journey would be to make your way down to the front of the curve; this is again nothing short of 10,000 fanatical hardened loyal fans. If you can imagine an immense amount of people, standing literally shoulder to shoulder, all packed into one unbreathable space, who's body count doesn't allow you to be able to tell one fan from another, you can get an idea of how many there was just standing in front of us. Anyone would've thought it would've taken an entire game to get through that amount of people, but as I'd witnessed on all my other visits to curves, no sooner as we started to move in the direction of the front of the curve, it was as if an invisible energy just effortlessly forced the en-masse of people to part and create a clear path straight to the front. With all of this going on, being led in by Franco, Tony and Gerry, the absolute top of the tree Ultras would be enough to leave any top boy from any firm speechless. When we got to what was a space at the front of that crowd, once again makes you realise where you are standing……in a spot that is only reserved for the top man…….and it was then, with this continued level of acknowledgement, respect and standing that I have in a circle of people, I knew I was no longer seen or looked upon as a guest, I've now become a person whose presence is seen as one of pure blood….and now family. I'm now standing in an established position to the right of what is nothing short of the head, the top dog and a person who instils a level of respect and a following that commands an army of over 10,000 like-minded Ultras, who are willing to fight and die for a single man's belief and a multi-generational club and banner's cause. This is the cream of the crop, and it's here that Italy, Milan and those soldiers around you that, not only support the club, but also you and everyone around you're with – the depth of that situation is one that can never be understood unless you become part of it.

Go to a game and see first-hand Ultras in action, you'll feel your bollocks tighten and the hairs on the back of your neck stand up…. and when they shout, "Oh, la vinciamo noi", being sung repeatedly ("We're going to win") it really is something else. The chants and songs don't last for a few minutes either… they can go on for 20-30 minutes, it's on the same level as an anthem, plus the banners that are seen at each, and every game is something I've never witnessed at an English match. Each and every game, these same banners are taken and displayed; each one tells an Ultra groups history and a story. Something I don't think would ever be seen or welcomed at an English football game as respectively this is an Italian (Ultra) tradition. 10,000 people will carry that banner over the tops of their heads and the crowd, displaying it so it can be seen by the entire stadium. There was another occasion that is without question one that is worth mentioning. It was when Lenny, me, Gemma, Gerry's (one of Inter's main faces) girlfriend Dina and her friends who were visiting from the US, were all flying over at the same time to watch a big game with Inter-Milan, in fact this game would exemplify without question the very meaning of the phrase, 'a big game', both metaphorically and literally. It had been announced by the governing bodies that after 100 years, it was time to pull down the stadium and build a new one. This news sent shock waves throughout the football community and the nation as a whole. It also made it a necessity for every red- blooded Italian that ever kicked, handled or been around a ball, supported a team, knew someone that had watched a game and everyone else in between to be at the stadium for what was said to be an historic event….this was to be the last game ever played at both AC and Inter Milan's home stadium.

San Siro is one of the largest in the whole of Europe, but more importantly the largest stadium in Italy, now add that fact to how much history, heritage, places of severe importance, and football means as a whole to both the Italian populace, Ultras and Italy, who was very much losing part of her past and cultural identity. Only then can you get an idea of why this was one of the most important games of a generation. AND add that it's a derby game – that meant for anyone that wanted to be at the game, this was on the same level as having Christmas, New Years, and all of your life-long birthdays rolled into one…the sheer necessity, importance and cultural value of the game was simply unmeasurable. People of all ages far and wide expressed how much they wanted and needed to go and were probably willing to sell a kidney to get tickets for the game, but the fact remained their chances were slim to none. It was reported that in excess of 85,000 tickets were needed for a stadium that could only accommodate a little over 70,000.

Arriving at Milan airport and being greeted like family had become part of a valued tradition and as always, my Ultra brothers had come through and in style, a brand-new Mercedes multi-passenger arrived and was ready to whisk us off to our pre-arranged hotel. It was also a nice to hear that two of the young Cardiff lads we'd met some years before; Josh and Newt, were also in town, and at the same hotel, but told me they needed 2 tickets for the game!!!

These tickets were rarer than rocking horse shit, and the only 2 hopes in the part of the equation was no hope and them having more chance of getting the Hope Diamond, but a quick chat with my Inter brothers and all sorted…I made this effort for the boys as one thing I've always respected and valued is loyal friends. So, the lads got their tickets, and we were ready for probably the biggest game the country had seen in many years. It was reported in one newspaper that the stadium had a record number turn up for the game, some reports suggest over 90,000 fans.

Much like before, when entering the stadium is an experience all in itself, the noise, the people, crowds are all part of the energy you'll soon experience when the teams are playing. No sooner had we arrived at the stadium, we're entering the curve, but the slight difference here was Gemma and the girls traveling with us! Women, wives, girlfriends, partners – none are allowed in the curve, that area is all 'business' and unless you've been invited and are part of a certain 'element' or 'football', it's strictly a no, bar one exception, but I'll come back to that in a moment. So, the ladies have now been led off to the numbered seats and away from the curve, but all the same, in excellent company with friends and family of the Ultras. What made it that much more special for me, was how Gemma enjoyed the game, as she said part of the memorable experience was when she helped with the huge banner, it being rolled out over both hers, and across thousands of heads and then seen throughout the stadium, plus the crowd involvement, the excitement, the feeling of being there…plus the banner and how she, "fucking loved it." Now, back to the part that will need explaining is the curve, 'business only' and girlfriends, wives etc. The only exception to that rule is when the top boy's misses is present. In this scenario, it would've been Moreno's other half, Chiara; she was as much Milan's twin sister, as she was Inter's mother.

As much as both AC and Inter Milan have their

(strong) rivalries and history, there has been an agreement between the firms and the 'level' of violence that is inflicted. This was as a result when some years back, both sides would always turn up firm handed and tooled up to the eyeballs. Deaths ensued and not long after, top boys from either side had a sit down, agreeing that no one should go to a match and never return home. It goes without question, at minimum, banter and fighting will always be part of the deal, but not lads ending up in the ground.

There is something special that can only be seen and heard from Ultras during a game and that's the level of patriotism and pride they have, and that of course is expressed by their chants and songs. The one game that still makes me laugh, was when I was front and centre in the Curve Nord (Curve Nord is Inter Milan when playing as home team, Curve Sud is AC Milan) and 10,000 AC Milan Ultras sang out in Italian, "We know you have a special guest amongst you (meaning me) but you are still shit" and on top of that, it was, and fuck knows how they did it, all choreographed with the lights on their phones, then held above their heads and spelt out... simply un-fucking real! It was explained to me when I first started to visit Italy, when you arrive, "Italy knows you are here" …... and that song, experience and visit showed that down to a tee.

There's been countless trips and visits and each and every time they've always outdone themselves. On one occasion, Gemma and I went out to Milan, and Inter had set us up in a beautiful apartment right in the centre of Milan. For the five days we were there, neither our arses or our feet hit the floor, we were wined, dined, taken to unimaginable places - nothing was an issue and no place or person wasn't more or less welcoming than the previous - the accommodating on their part is that what you'd imagine reserved for certain elements of society, but the one memory of that visit in particular that holds special meaning was when a surprise birthday party was thrown for me. When the world wide epidemic started to affect parts of Europe and restrictions where slowly being introduced and affect certain places, I was forced to miss a previous planned trip that would've meant I was there on my 60th birthday, but when I was there on this visit, taken out one evening, walked into a restaurant, seeing the entire place not only decked out in West Ham banners but, my hosts singing, "I'm forever blowing bubbles……" and, then have staff, other families and people visiting the restaurant singing, "Happy Birthday" to me in Italian is and was a part of my life that I hold as one of extreme value. I have to add that, with my Italian family, loyalty and friendship knows no boundaries and there are no words that'd be of any credit to that experience that Gemma and the people there that night that made it so special. There are a lot of people from the games and within Ultras that hold a special place in my life, but some will always be thought of as the brightest lit candles on a cake made of friendship, love and loyalty.

I feel a great sense of accomplishment when I think of my relationship with Italy. It all started with an invite, that led to a handshake then onto a friendship with Al, Fabrizio and the Lazio Ultras, shown then equally as much by both Inter and AC Milan. A country, much like England that has a proud, deep-rooted sense of history and as much love for the game. I will never allow a bad word or untruth be said about my Mediterranean brothers. Their welcoming and hospitality has never known any limits nor has their willingness to adopt me as one of their own.

The most difficult part of visiting Italy is and as I've experienced first-hand, that "Italy knows when you're here!" as each and every Ultras outfit already has pre knowledge of your plans and visit. So, you find a lot of the top boys reaching out and extending a level of hospitality that not only compliments Italians, their welcoming and accommodating nature but also as a representation of how much Ultras value friendship and loyalty. I found that I had to decide where I was going to hang my hat, or scarf so to speak. Lazio has and will always hold a special place in both my life, and I have an immense level of respect for them, but Inter-Milan had found a new son and are forever in my heart and are my soul. If I was asked to explain the relationship (process) of Lazio and Inter with me, it would be Lazio was my first serious relationship with Ultras, it will always be one that is respected and held as one of special value and meaning; much like your first girlfriend; the excitement and introduction to what a relationship was and should be. Inter was the next step in learning about what love and dedication was and is in a relationship; I became, I guess you could say engaged with and set for life with Inter. I would be willing to lay down in the road and stop traffic for Lazio Ultras; but I'd be willing to fall on any number of swords for Inter. That being said, even after aligning with Inter-Milan and Lazio as my cousins to her south, as I said earlier, they are one in the same, as each and every visit, both myself and who ever I'm traveling with are offered a level of friendship and hospitality from various firms, who by all accounts have different and opposite beliefs to that of Lazio and Inter, that being said, I can only ever be respectful and grateful to all.

As a sign of how firms can meet under 'one banner' and have a respect for a shared belief, there was one night I was invited out with AC Milan's top boys. Now, being I'm firmly aligned with Inter, and AC being their bitter enemies, in fact the two have the longest reigning rivalry, it then says a lot when both firms can meet and literally sit at the same table, so as to enjoy my company. AC have a massive West Ham fan base in their ranks, and if I'm correct, they actually have more West Ham fans than any other firm in the country. Massimo, their top man is a massive West Ham fan. Respect, and its true meaning, is a word that is honoured and understood by a lot of the top firms in Italy.

Over the years I've had valued experiences, on every visit, each and every time - the passion they have for their club is something that can only ever be felt, never put into words – I mean, how could you write about something, that would express and be a reflection of an emotion that then encapsulates what you are willing to commit your whole life to, and then have the same willingness to die for? …… you can't! - it's something that can only ever be felt and enjoyed - much like passion and faith – it can't be expressed in something as simple, cold an unemotional as the written word and then put into an inanimate object like a book - trying to do so would be an insult to Ultras and the level of passion they have for life, their club and the game of football.

With the support and friendship that Ultras have given me, is something I'll always value and hold high. The only way that same friendship can be (marginally) put into words is, once a door was opened just enough for me to see there was something in another room. On the next visit, that door was opened slightly more, exposing more light and evidence of something even bigger and brighter than the previous visit. The final opening of that door was a welcome and full introduction to a world, friendship and brotherhood that is typically only reserved for those born of that environment. When I've been asked and it's been commented why I felt that each faction or group treated me so well, and maybe it was an effort for them to out-do each other, I can say with my hand over my heart there's never been anything underhanded or an ulterior motive with their actions and I've always seen their welcoming and friendship as a way in complimenting not only themselves, but their country and beliefs. Ultras value friendship and loyalty, and to have that same level of loyalty and friendship returned makes them feel a level of accomplishment between like-minded people. Nothing, and I mean nothing was ever an issue…… simply a beautiful friendship and people.

For me, Italy and the people that I hold close to my heart, is a country, along with her soldiers who time after time have only ever increased both their loyalty and friendship with me. They have welcomed and made me feel as if they've adopted a son and for this, I hold sacred - my appreciation and respect for my Fratelli Italiani is unmeasurable.

Now compare that to the level of what we've been left with and today's game back home and the breed of hipsters and their half-brained, diluted philosophies. Sipping half a light-pint out of a plastic cup or a froth topped corporate brand Frappuccino and sporting half scarves, feeling displaced and offended that not everyone will align with their belief that a new corporate-managed, conglomerate mammoth of a stadium is the only way forward…... and much like the bastardisation of a club, the decimation of the beautiful game and the shadows these soulless shithouses cast over life-long loyal fans. It's the same fuckwits who also feel they should be the ones dictating what and how a club is run and supported. So many UK clubs have clowns running what was once a community based and supported football club and has now become a circus, and equally as damaging are the clueless clowns disguised as supporters paying for the cheap thrill and ride.

Moreno Inter Ultras — "…. to become his friend, nothing less than a privilege."

I met Carlton for the first time 12 years ago, in a hot Milanese summer at a weekly curva meeting. Not just anyone can turn up and be welcomed, but Carlton had arrived there through a mutual acquaintance. For me, as for many people who attend or have attended the Curva, he represents a kind of institution, a sort of idol. To meet him was an honour for me, to become his friend, nothing less than a privilege. Over the years, we have met several times, both in Milan and in London, and it is always a pleasure to spend time with Carlton. He loves Milan, his Inter family and during the "Derby della Madonnina" it's likely you could meet him in the Curva. There is a very good feeling between Milan and Carlton. I can say that I have met a legend and a man whose principles are based on family in the deepest sense of the word and on loyalty. I love you brother.

-Moreno, Curva Nord

With Gerry outside San Siro.

Dinner with friends in Milan.

CARLTON - The Final Say

With my friend Nino.

With my friend Moreno in Milan.

With my friend Franco.

When Newt & Josh joined me & Len at San Siro.

12 ¡ESPAÑA!

My first experience of Spain was a family holiday to Mallorca when I was 11 years old and for various reasons, I ended up visiting the Country on an increasingly more regular basis throughout my life and I've been fortunate enough to have my own place there for about 20 years now. When it comes to a holiday, or even retirement destination, millions of Brits each year choose between either Spain, or Portugal due to their close proximity to the UK, favourable climate, cost of living (for some, cost of drinking) and the willingness of locals to welcome and accept you.

To tackle a popular misconception, don't think for a second that it's a good idea for a British criminal to try to evade the British justice system by laying low in Spain; that whole concept is an absolute fucking myth and has been since the 80's, because for decades, upon receipt of a nicely worded letter from the UK, Spanish authorities will happily round-up anyone remotely of interest to an overseas government and hand them over as quickly as possible. Spain has long since made a stand that they don't want to harbour foreign criminals and to be fair, who can blame them? Believe me, like most countries, they have enough of their own criminals!

When I visit mainland Spain, it's about stepping away from the madness and not being a part of the rat-race for a while. I can still work when I'm plotted up in the sun for a month or two, but life in España just feels a lot less stressful for some reason! There's something intensely uplifting about rolling up your blinds each morning and being met by dazzling bright sunshine, no matter what season it is!

No matter your mood, troubles or problems, I defy anyone to take a walk along one of hundreds of Spain's Blue flag beaches for half an hour and not feel several times better in body and mind! Then there's the lesser-known coves and hopefully without sounding like a bit of a snob, there's nothing more relaxing, than being allowed an escape from the summer "all inclusive" crowds, just losing myself, in what the locals call the "calas," a series of coves, that are typically only known and visited by residents and people that have been here for generations. This is one of Spain's hidden treasures, that if I'm honest, I find hard sharing. Finding these coves, is much like having your very own private beach…or island – your own personal little getaway, better than any balcony or VIP suite, even with the best of views and it's rare that you'll see anyone for hours, or even the day when visiting these secluded spots. Don't get me wrong, there's nothing more that I appreciate than bumping into someone I stood next to at West Ham some 30 years before, or being stopped in one of the major cities or beaches by the same people that have supported me through my shows, the films and books I've been involved in over the years, as they will tell you how accommodating and approachable I am, but there's no denying, being able to literally escape and disappear in one of the few, unmapped areas of the country, and as much as this "escape" is an exclusive part of my life, is one that I don't ever need to, or feel, I have to be conscientious about in either my mood, or what's going on in my life, as there's no one around I have to answer to.

I really should take this opportunity to complement the job undertaken to keep the beaches and coastlines of Spain so pristine. I've observed on many an early morning, a team of people, plus a tractor, going to great lengths to ensure a sandy, litter free and welcoming playa is awaiting its public.

Now, for background, I'm a little bit of a "foodie!" and whilst I do come from humble beginnings, I can and do enjoy the £6 breakfast in the cafe with my mates, I can also sit at the table in any top restaurant in London to enjoy the food and discuss the menu, but I have to say that the seafood in Spain is truly exceptional, I'm talking top tier! Of course, it's extremely fresh, having been caught from the Med' a short time ago, but in general, they do know how to prepare and cook fish well in Spain and even the less expensive restaurants have on offer seafood dishes that would rival any fine city establishment the world over. I don't always realise until I'm back in Blighty, just how much I miss a good paella and try as you might to recreate the Spanish national dish, we Brits don't stand a chance at mastering it like a Spaniard!

You know already that I adore a proper cup of coffee and that's something that, like neighbouring Italy, Spain does very well; it's the "real deal," not that dog shit that is served in a branded paper cup, from someone calling themselves a silly pretentious name that they feel gives them an air of superiority, when in fact all they're doing is grinding from a mass produced, "corporate-machine," that's got less originality and authenticity than the crap they're palming us off with as organically grown and harvested coffee beans…no, no mocha-choca-whatever the fuck for me, thank you!

Still considering delights that your palette thanks you for, native fruits are in abundance throughout Spain and every day, without exception, I squeeze myself a glass of juice from oranges that probably came off of the tree the day before! You can literally walk-through streets and take a couple of oranges off of the tree yourself, or another common thing that takes place is neighbours or shop keepers handing you fruit as a little gift, I see elderly folk giving kids fruit or sweets all the time as they pass by and wish them a good day.

In the less touristic areas, which I tend to frequent, I'm far less likely to get myself into the kinds of trouble which are a stronger possibility when back in the UK. As I've gradually fitted and blended in with the local residents over the years, I've become much less of a target than I know I am in England and also in the obvious Spanish hotspots like Marbella, where I get recognised within minutes of my flip-flops hitting the pavement of Puerto Banús! This isn't to say that I never visit such places, because I do, but to retract from it all for a while, then delve in whenever I like, certainly does wonders for my thinking and my blood pressure.

Now, before any of you who are reading this, think that I've answered what you believe are the questions that you may have had, in terms of your retirement and buying of a second home, please know that as much as I've painted a picture of serenity and tranquillity, there's as many cons, as there are pros, and Spain has a good few, all be it subjective, but all the same, I sometimes find are quite frustrating traits that I still struggle with, and that's after more than 4 decades of coming here.

In my experience, pretty much anywhere outside of Madrid has absolutely shite internet, which to some may sound trivial, but considering how much we now use VOIP calling apps to chat and video-call, especially when we're away from our families for an extended length of time and when that call keeps 'reconnecting' or dropping out entirely, you can quickly find your device at risk of being thrown at the wall! A close second example of the frustrations of bad internet, is when you're utilising one of these (entirely legal) streaming services to watch the West Ham game, but the lagging and buffering just persists in interrupting your enjoyment.

The very concept of time, in Spain, can sometimes feel like an alternate reality; days can somehow roll into weeks, and those weeks into months, until you don't even know what day or month it actually is anymore, and if you aren't careful, every day can become like a mundane Sunday, because time isn't of particular importance to people in most of the Country, I've found. If you were to go to a local store in a rural, or even semi-rural area, and was expecting that store to open at a set and the published time, for example 9 am, then be prepared to be somewhat disappointed! An opening time of 9 am back home would typically mean the owner is inside, the till has change in it, the shelves are stacked with all what's needed, and the staff are ready to go as soon as the shop doors open (at 9 am). Instead, in Spain, that 9 am opening is actually 9 am -ish! Things like opening times for Spanish businesses are generally an approximation, and in order to keep calm about such things, you have to change your interpretation of what a 9 am opening time actually means! The posted time is a measure, or guideline... a sort of "suggestive time," as most of those that will be visiting the shop, are by and large locals and not in a rush. Relative to the subject of time, is the famous, or rather, infamous phrase 'mañana', meaning tomorrow and it's not until you've had to deal with lawyers or civil servants in Spain's government buildings that you come to fully understand why the Spanish are ridiculed the world over for their application of "mañana," because 9 times out of 10, tomorrow never comes and you are forced to simply admit defeat, or die waiting!

Not too long back, the A/C went in my place, and being it was almost 100 degrees in the shade, the trapped hot air in a building, is simply unbearable, so you actually need it to work. Anyway, no sooner than the coolness and necessity of my AC unit gave out, I was on the phone to a local air-con engineer asking for someone to come and take care of, what was a typical, common and easy fix. "Of course, señor! We will get to this most urgently, right away!" Now, I'm sure you'll agree with me, that hearing, "right away," and, "most urgently" would be enough for you to think this would be done in a timely manner? Wrong, and like the old adage, "It'll be fixed on Tuesday," and when Tuesday comes and goes, you enquire to the. non-existent repair man, only to be told, "But we didn't say you which Tuesday" ...you get the idea...

Spanish drains and shoddy plumbing can be the bane of your life if you're very unlucky with your property purchase, but fortunately, for the majority, it's just another slightly aggravating factor that, for the most part, you can ignore! An issue more specific to the Spanish Islands, certain places, especially near the sea, seem to suffer with an occasional waft of 'bad drainage smell', about which there is little you can do. In the western Europe of 2021, one does not expect to stumble across a bin in the men's room of a shopping mall, overflowing with dirty, shitty bog roll, simply because the cleaner is late doing the rounds and the drains can't cope with a few bits of wafer-thin paper! Seriously Spain, you're not a 3rd world Country, just make your pipes a few mm wider…please?

To anyone reading this who is able to work remotely, has a comfortable pension or other passive income, I would highly recommend giving the expat, overseas lifestyle a fair shot; your money will go a little further and the chances are, you may live better and for longer too! But for those who need to graft or hold down a job and maintain a steady income, it's much harder to pull off and I've been no exception, living almost half (or sometimes more) of the year abroad has been difficult at times. There have been occasions when my presence has been requested or even "necessary" back home and that in itself can be a real pain in the arse at short notice, because it's no longer "popping down the road" for a meet-up. I'm not immune to being skint for a bit either, and when you find yourself a bit short, it's much harder to get hold of a few quid when you're 1200 miles away, than it is when you're on home turf, but skint in the sunshine by the pool vs skint in the rain is a no-brainer isn't it!

But for all of her faults, Spain, for the best part, will always be this way. When I'm home, I have the luxury and benefit of being able to pop into a Tesco Superstore at 3 in the morning for a packet of Hob Nobs, a loaf of bread and a multi-gallon jug of milk, as much as I do in visiting one of the few surviving pie n mash shops in East London, but it's in the gems that are Italy and Spain, I can be welcomed and thought of, as much as a friendly Londoner, as I can be grateful for their warm and welcoming nature as a guest and part of their community. Like the UK, its positives and negatives are often one and the same, for example, you might complain that things are a bit slow in Spain, but at the same time, that pace of life is what helps things in general to feel more laid back and of course, you can get things done much faster in England, but whilst we're all steaming about everywhere at 100mph, remember, we're always complaining that we need a holiday!

Whether I spend more time or less in Spain in the future, I have eternal gratitude for the many years of great memories and I will die with a place in my heart for this amazing Mediterranean Country.

Talking business in the UK

Enjoying the views in Spain

13 THE MISSING MAN

When understanding why a level of success, or failure exists in the world of villainy, it's important, in fact essential for everyone to remember that it comes down to a few fundamental, basic rules, and one of those such rules is the people involved and the roles they play. It can't be said enough how trust and respect (of the code) is the core, backbone and very essence of what and how we operate successfully in organised crime, and no matter the time, place or generation, there is nothing that will ever supersede what is, and will always be, the old school ways. But try as they do, there will always be some who feel they can reinvent the wheel, but as much as they always fail, I demonstrate regularly with little, or no effort how backwards they are, and if something isn't broken, it doesn't need fixing.

But let's not over-simplify things or put the "horse before the cart," instead allow me to tell you on how the "missing man," easily highlighted a person's immorality, and by equal measure, a family's greed, and finally showed their contempt for the same people that protected and made them a lot of money. When it comes to any business deal or practice, the people you employ or allow to be around you, much like strong cogs in a machine, will, to a high degree, guarantee things will always work, but much like a machine, the cogs, their correct alignment and their longevity are only as good as the oiling, maintaining and the ability of the operator to keep it going; as only a skilled and knowledgeable captain can get a ship in and out of any harbor!

I'd long had suspicions, (but never concerns) that an Indian family who I'd given a great deal of personal attention and protection to, had been short-changing me on some work for a while, but what I didn't know, was how the liberty taking had stretched to such a point, and as a result of their carelessness and greed, a commodity, that if exposed, seen or witnessed and under any other circumstances, could've meant a lengthy stretch for one member of a crew and a few bods going missing from the other, but thankfully, our firm's guardian angel was looking over us on one such day, and the situation was managed respectively.

Now, when and if I'm approached for a price, whether acting in a minding, couriering or brokering capacity, different jobs demand a type and level of service, thus the job, involvement and attention to detail dictates a price; the difference in a Dr's and engineer's role, is as different as the very spelling of the words, as are their abilities and the results you'd expect from them – basically, you wouldn't send a boy to do a man's job and expect the same results for a different or lesser amount of pay! So when I'm told that a commodity, let's say in this example it's money, I have to make sure things are done properly, as it's my name being stamped on the service provided, plus the people involved have to be of a certain ability and capacity – this is essential, as I've said, if things go sideways and it's shown to be down to my negligence, my name is in question, my income would likely disappear, I myself would become a target, and not to mention the people I have wrapped around me, as I am responsible for their lives…in fact, many I don't view as simple employees and they're more than just like-minded, trusted people….. they're family!

It was whilst both Jay and I were enjoying the sun-filled days in Spain, having a few months to top-up our tans and enjoy what had been a good year for all of us, but like most parts of my day, I'm interrupted by calls from back home; I really must learn to simply turn that fucking phone off! After a few ignored rings, and the reminder from Jay that business we're in doesn't always work a 9 to 5, I answered the phone, and thankfully I did. It was one of the old firm, who for the sake of the story and lesson, we'll call Bill. Anything Bill had to say, was of value and importance and for him to be reaching out to me, was obviously a call I needed to take. "I need to see you, Carl…and I'm not talking on the phone…. you know I hate these things!" "Is anyone hurt, missing or is it something that can wait?" was my reply. "I'd rather talk to you in person, and I can be with you in a couple of hours, it's annoying me, and I need to sort this lot out, but I need your blessing." All the while, during the call, I could hear what sounded like a busy airport or train station in the background. I knew for someone as well-mannered and cordial as Bill emphasising "Need to speak with you in person" …...and "Need your blessing," whatever and whoever it was, this couldn't be good. "Of course, I'll have Jay book a flight and get you out here in a day or so, Bill" "No need, I'm at Heathrow now and the girl at the ticket counter has just booked my seat…. I'll see you in a couple of hours" then he hung up. Both Jay and I made a few discreet calls back home to see if the wheels had fallen off anything we had on the go, or as a sign of Bill's loyalty, he'd put someone in their place for trying to step out of line, or on my shoes in my absence – but no, in fact everything including a few extra bits of work and their returns, had ensured we could start looking at bigger premises and less hours in our work day…but that's another story.

Now, when weighing up a situation, I always….and I mean ALWAYS look at all of the pieces on the board, that includes names, how long they've been part of either sides firm, what was and how much is involved and of equal importance who lost, how much and who benefits or gains from the incident! Firstly, Bill…. Bill was a long-time member and part of my outfit, someone I'd known for many years in varying capacities …he was a good few years younger than me, but acted and walked with an air of confidence and superiority that suggested he'd been on this earth a lot longer than he had; maybe he just had a longer paper-round than all the other kids. He was very disciplined in everything he did, was always smartly dressed and never had a failure or excuse for any bit of work, and he'd been on jobs with not only me, but some of the most known in London. He was a pro, raised by the old guard and was unquestionably and immensely "proper"- he was a soldier through and through.

No sooner had Bill called telling us that his plane had just landed, both Jay and I were waiting in the arrivals area for him. As always, relaxed, and confident looking as ever, Bill came walking through the terminal, extending his hand, saying he was grateful I could discuss the issue with him straight away. "Luggage, Bill?" asked Jay. "No, sparky!" said Bill, while giving his trademark smile and wink. I'll admit, it was as fucking puzzling as the Times crossword, what situation would force a man to fly to another country at the drop of a hat, with no luggage, aside from a cabin sized "go-bag," just to have a conversation, but whatever it could be, a warm lit sunshine weekend was just ahead of us all and a few cold drinks around the pool would sort it. Bill was all business, he's just built that way, and with his unmeasurable amount of loyalty, no sooner had we walked into the villa, he took off his suit jacket, folded it neatly, placing it over a chair and began to explain how we'd been fucked over by the same Indian family and Maxi, and as he suspected, it's been since the start of the "new" deal, that we'd put together some 4 plus years ago. It was the best part of, if not close to 15 years, that I was approached by the same Indian family, looking to get some much-needed help, and my services urgently. In turn, I'd given them a lot of protection, ensuring they'd never lose as much as a pound note under my watch, which they never did – EVER! In fact, I'd go as far to make calls and my presence known when it wasn't always needed, some of which were during my own family's personal events, I simply considered them close and trusted friends, but I will add, that they never returned that same level of "hospitality" down to it being, "business" but that's fine…...as it always said more about me than it did about them.

As I'd suspected, and Bill witnessed, the family had foolishly lied….at no stage was it ever discussed, nor did they ever disclose, that they were sending multiple consignments of a different nature in the same crate. This was obviously their way of not only concealing the correct amount and type of money, but also something that we'd never have been involved in for any amount of money – remember, a certain type of commodity is a different type of carrier and price! I wasn't happy to say the least, they'd taken the piss for too long and I was tired of them thinking they could pay an apprentice's wages to a fully-fledged tradesman! I can't begin to tell you, that without me, the amount of people that would've absolutely rinsed them and taken them to the cleaners, even decent villains would've charged at least double what I was billing them, and not accepted anything but payment up front. So, from here on out…business would be business, it would be on my terms, a price of my saying and without either, debate or discussion!

Like I said, It'd been a suspicion of a few key-members of the upper tier chaps within what I do, that the same family had been short-changing me on this bit of work and the agreed price, but what made it that much more insulting, was not only their level of contempt towards me and the trust I'd extended to them, but the fact was, I'd bailed out and literally saved the life of one of their top earners. Now, the amount of money in any job is of the upmost importance, but to be stabbed in the back, wasn't solely what infuriated me, it was the turning around and seeing who'd placed that knife there. So, I decided on a plan on how to deal with them, making sure they paid the piper, and what should've been paid from the very beginning. Bill on the other hand, was a lot harder to convince on our suggested, some-what delayed attack. Bill wanted to fly back that same day, deal with them head-on and direct, as the disrespect and insult that had been shown to me, was by Bill's standards, a direct attack on the very institution that we all call the criminal fraternity, was a code he was willing to go to war for and their actions were simply unacceptable…..and as he so mildly put it, "You don't fucking do it, Carl….there's rules we all live by and no one gets a pass!" I honestly believe when they made Bill, it was with the sole intention of him being a benchmark, that we all should and are judged by. His mindset and track record is one that dictates, if he was given the choice, or option in changing direction or flipping, he'd rather give his life…he once said to me, "You take a man's integrity and morals away, it'd be like removing my arms and legs, and what life is that?" We all enjoyed, Bill somewhat reluctantly, a weekend of good food, drink, and better company. When Monday came around, and us seeing Bill off at the airport, and assuring him that no one would be getting a pass, I put into motion a plan to tax the family, put it on them that they'd been sussed and more importantly, they would not be taking the piss… and as Jay added in his usual sarcastic, but accurate way, "What are they going to do, go against you?….like fuck they will!"

As regular as clockwork, the family would have us oversee delivery of a large consignment, each and every week, but further adding to the headache and process, they would have our drivers do it in two runs, this was apparently their way of avoiding any "issues," but much like their attitude and deceitfulness, this I was also tired of. Anyone that works in a C.P or high-value target business, would never allow the client to dictate how the security and route is managed - it causes issues, promotes the chance of unnecessary complications and confusion, plus the insistence of double runs, and the way they constantly changed and added things when they felt it was needed, was never agreed to in the beginning. It cost me twice the manpower and time and needless to say, was again, just their way of saying they never trusted me…and this is after me handling business transactions for almost 15 years and without so much as a single coin or note being out of place, not to mention the amount of millions of pounds of goods and commodities. So when it came time to set up and confirm the details for the next run, we went along with it as we always did, but of course, and as we predicted, with their usual bullshit reminder of, "It is of the upmost importance you only have the very bestest of peoples on this and we have counted every note several times," further adding, "We have also looked at all the routes and there is no reason for delay, as traffic and weather are no issue either." One thing I fucking hate is being patronised, it was time to remind them, I'm the mechanic, and they're the oily rag, and like they say, every dog has its day! The set day and time was upon us, and as usual, we got notification that the money was picked up and on route.

The day couldn't have gotten any better, as we'd also gotten a nod from some-one we'd paid off inside their firm, letting us know the amount in transit was the exact same amount that Maxi had "lost," when he was sent to earn his first set of stripes….280K in used notes, was now both on route and on the table. I called my right-hand man up to check everything was in motion and as we realised just how well everything was going, we were in absolute fucking hysterics, we were literally beside ourselves with laughter..…. call it karma or coincidence…I call it happy fucking days!

It was later that evening, that my phone had a series of missed calls and what read, "urgent" text messages. I briefly looked over them, and as you can imagine, and to my surprise, the texts read that the courier hadn't shown up where he was supposed to be. I thought it must've been a (lot of) wrong messages and calls to the wrong number, so I went out for the evening with a clear conscience and not a care in the world. The next morning, or being more accurate around lunchtime, I returned to the villa and clumsily walked inside, only to find Jay sprawled out on the villa floor and motionless, but all the while donning the biggest grin and happiest expression I've ever seen on a person's face. He was still holding his phone in his hand when he finally decided to make an effort in slowly standing up, supporting the nearest wall and gracing the world with his fragile and somewhat unsteady body posture and presence. "Good night was it, mate?" I asked, to which he just fell to the floor and started rolling around in fits of laughter. When he finally got to slow down and find a space amongst the bursts of laughter, he explained that somehow, the courier hadn't come through and there was a lot of concern and panic with the now missing money. So, thinking this was "surely a mistake," I called the family, only to hear a panic-stricken, out of breath Maxi, telling me that there was a massive problem, as the money had gone missing! I, of course, calmly said I was as surprised to hear this as anyone, but it was only after him getting a tad too big for his boots, when he demanded an explanation from me, and wanted to know why I wasn't answering his calls or texts? Then, my tone and mindset changed, and that, as they say, was fucking it! "Listen here you little shit cunt, you're a fucking no one, you're someone I can make disappear within a second…an absolute waste of my time and if you ever speak to me again like that, I'll show you for the little slag that you are, do you understand me, you fucking cretin!" There was an instant string of apologies and excuses then given…rattling on about how it looks bad for him as this has to be fixed, or we'll all be in the shit. "I fucking won't," I reminded him…I'm not sure what else he was mumbling and crying about as, I simply placed the phone down on the countertop, walked over to the kettle and began making a nice cup of tea. It couldn't have been better timed, as after the kettle had finished boiling, I then picked up the phone only to hear the little maggot asking, "So what do you think the best thing is to do, mate?" I reminded him I wasn't his mate and I'd have to get back to him.

Now, on the scale of things and by my standards, in situations concerning the governing and management of extremely high amounts of used bank notes and who is on the piece of work, was quite important… and, if such an incident had occurred, both the money and the courier would need to be tracked down as soon as possible, but I don't need to remind anyone reading this, that I knew exactly where both the money and the courier were – in my possession and on my firm. Anyway, fuck him, I wanted to finish my nice cup of freshly made tea by the pool and last but not least, I needed to shower and get changed, as I'd heard that the new restaurant nearby is top notch and we'd made reservations.

I made a few courtesy calls, so as to show I'd made some sort of effort, as the family themselves had now reached out to me. When speaking to them, I said, "I was, of course concerned, as much as the money going missing, so had my courier." Again, the family expressed the importance and their true nature, when they pressed the issue saying, "People can be replaced, but money takes a long time to get," if they didn't have a stained soul before, they surely did now! When they asked if I could come by, they sounded as nervous as they did surprised, when I said with a great level of enthusiasm and conviction, "That's such a great idea, I'm on my way…see you within the hour!" The person I had next to me laughed and asked why I was going to make such an effort to see them, but as I explained, I'd taken my time in getting back to the U.K, and by their standards, I was avoiding the issue, but instead of continuing the so-so attitude, I'd now gone to treating it with a great level of interest…and that would confuse the fuck out of them…..like I said, everything was now on my terms and at my say so.

When we arrived at their H.Q offices, well, a

portacabin that was reminiscent of a bombed-out crack den, it couldn't be missed how it displayed all the charms of what should and was probably a condemned unit. When we made our way inside, using the makeshift, yet poorly disguised, milkcrates as steps, we were greeted with nothing more than limp handshakes and, "Please, my friends, please take a seat." Looking about the room, allowed me to come to a simple conclusion, that taking a seat in here, would only then force me to get an updated tetanus shot at the local hospital. I politely declined and said I was eager to put this issue to bed, all the while looking directly at little Maxi, who was looking lost for words and remaining very quiet, sitting on a chair in the far corner of the room, I guess he'd not been invited to sit at the table with the grown-ups. I listened to their complaints, concerns, and the overall issue of a "missing man," to which I replied, "I'm glad you've acknowledged that a human being was part of this equation, as without trusted people in this game, you have nothing, and we'd become no different than the people that I protect you from!" There was a short silence, which I was then happy to break, "And while we're on the subject of trust, my friend, the consignments haven't always been what they've supposed to be, but that aside just for one moment, what was agreed upon to be looked after, those amounts and what we've been moving for you, have been a lot more than what was contracted, agreed upon, and to add further insult, you failed to disclose to the very people that have always extended both their hand, as much as their trust and respect…so where and who does that fault lay with…you…your brother or Maxi?" And at the mention of his name, I looked directly once again, at the still, quiet, and cowering boy, who remained sat in the corner. "Plus," I added, "It goes without saying, that this isn't the first time a consignment has gone missing, by no fault of anyone, but exclusively under the watch and management of one of your firm, namely Maxi…. so, my question to

Maxi over there is, where is the money, my man and whose paying me, for both the job and compensation for a member of my firm…he had family, and this remains all on you!" A lot of stuttering and assurances of, "we'll sort this out," and "we'll all work together" was given, but as I said very firmly before leaving the office, "Yes, you will sort this out, and you will pay me what I'm owed going back four years." What unfolded just over the next week, was all I ever needed in terms of concrete evidence, on both the lying lowlife that Maxi is, and how little the family valued a service they'd gotten from me in over a decade.

It was within that same week, that a softly spoken, but at the same time, over enthusiastic Maxi was on the phone, telling me how they'd gained the services of someone who worked at Mi5, but also a private investigator, who'd not only been in the employ of two of the biggest and known crime families in London, but also crime syndicates around the world. Another call was from what sounded like he was in a fast-moving car, whose occupants were in their teens, loud incoherent music and, "We're tailing him, we're on him, brother, we're going to get him, and you'll see me go to work on his arse," if anything, Maxi was good entertainment and was all I needed for a good afternoon laugh…. but not a single word he said could be taken seriously, and all I thought was, 'Jesus wept, Maxi-Montana was back…. look out world'. He sounded like a kid who'd seen a naked woman and gotten his first erection, bought his first Stone Island jumper and seen his very first gangster film.

The very next day, and unbeknown to me, Maxi was now a first class, world leading expert on finding missing people's items, as his message read, "I've found his burner phone," and, "I know this is his!" Not long soon after, he left a voicemail explaining, he'd found it in a large bin near a block of flats, and "We've finally tracked him down" …...plus, wait for it, he'd also found the missing-man's wife, who apparently worked in a family-owned jeweler's shop in Hatton Garden. When I heard all of this groundbreaking "evidence," I just had to tell someone, and who better than the king of sarcasm – Jay! Jay was just beside himself, I'm sure he'd pissed himself, or at minimum broken a rib, due to his level of laughing. When he did finally get the ability in composing himself, he said, "You have to keep fucking with them, this is too good to pass up." I agreed, as there was nothing better than watching them chase a person of my making and imagination…....and their top man, Maxi who was at the helm of the investigation, was just too much of a level of entertainment ….and like the old saying goes, "Give someone a long enough rope and they'll do the damage all themselves." So, the next opportunity and request for an update and to, "keep us in the loop," we agreed to a time and a place to meet with the family and the private investigator, who had apparently, with the joint efforts of Maxi-Clouseau, had found the missing man and his location.

We pulled up at the address given, which was an all too familiar location; one of their many lots - a portacabin and what seemed to be an endless supply of mindless minions, who always appeared to be just milling and floating about, serving no real purpose in life and with no direction or objective. Walking towards the office, I was greeted, called and welcomed inside one of the glass-mirrored offices, that on every occasion before I was always forced to wait outside, whatever the weather. Stepping inside, I was initially surprised by a somewhat improved, all be it standard set up - a solid floor and no mould on the walls, but then thinking of the excessive wealth and success they'd gained, you'd think they'd at least put some carpet down and a few pictures on the walls. It was also then that I reminded myself, that the invitation, location and where I was standing, was once again a reflection of how little they respected, or valued my support and the unparalleled service they'd been given for so long – as previous meetings that were to measure the consistent, large amounts of money I'd ensured were made and protected for the family, I was made to wait outside, or if I was invited to some form of "shelter" and "accommodation," I was sat in a portacabin with a leaking roof and an unstable floor. Yet here, they were willing to over accommodate, in terms of a presentable, clean, and stable meeting place for a total stranger, such as this "leading P.I." Their opinion and view of me, was as clear as day - a slap in the face of what we do, and their actions was one of disdain and disrespect, not only to me, but also to proper people and villains, the likes of which they saw as beneath them………I'd had enough and was going to flop on them once and for all!

Maxi, of course was doing a job befitting his natural ability, due diligence and was guarding, what appeared to be salmon sandwiches and bottles of Perrier water and no sooner than we walked in, we were approached and treated, once again with limp handshakes and false smiles. Taking note of who else was around, I assumed was their "P.I," by his involvement of the spreading out on the table of large black and white photos, but by his looks, had missed a good few steps on the ladder of "recovery." It was nothing less than cringe-worthy, to hear Clive; the P. I's analysis, of what had happened to both, the missing lump of cash and our missing-man. What was supposed to be evidence, was nothing short of theories, ill-educated guesswork and random out of focus photos, showing nothing more than the backs of people's heads, some random high street, a very non-descript warehouse and different parts of London. I'd honestly would have been embarrassed to have admitted to anyone, that I'd paid for the "services" and "work" that had been shown and then put in front of me.

After hearing the "expert's" view and insight, watching the incessant nodding of their heads in agreeance of the findings, I could no longer control myself and I had to put it on them, letting them know how fucking stupid they were. My first aim and target were the two heads of the family, who I reminded, that after almost 15 years of (grossly underpaid) service and (exploited and misused) loyalty, they were, and had been duped on this run, by no one else than ME! I went on to explain, that the person they were looking for, and apparently tracked, found and was ready to pounce on, was in fact a person of my own imagination……and didn't even exist. And before they had chance to make comment, I brought to their attention how their contempt and greed will now cost them dearly. The years of them lying about the size, types, and nature of the consignments, was done with such a level of arrogance, ignorance, and disrespect, it not only jepardised the safety of the people involved, but also my name and that would not be tolerated by the likes of them. It was then, I added that the missing 280k was a tax, a sort of back pay, and was only just the tip of the iceberg in terms of what I was owed, and before they could make any effort in defending their actions with, "But this was the first time"….and all that bollocks, I reminded them there was equally, if not more credible evidence this wasn't! And as much as I couldn't prove there was a lot more in past shipments, they couldn't prove otherwise either, because the only people that had been caught out and proven to be lying, was themselves.

Next, I took aim at Maxi-Montana, reminding him, not only of his countless fuck-ups and school boy errors, but his ability, standing and wellbeing was only as a result of me, and me alone – how on many occasions, that I'd vouched for him to proper money and connected people, that would of, on any other day had him over a barrel, and not only taken him for every penny he had in front of him, but also what he owned. And finally, their P.I, whose only comment, was somewhat of a compliment, when I said that I had to take my hat off to him for squeezing the parasites who'd hired him out of at least 10k, and what I know is the amount he'd asked for in fees.

I'd really pissed on all of their cornflakes, and at first, I thought they were all going to burst into tears, they just stood there, totally motionless, but, after looking at each other with the saddest puppy-dog looking eyes, and after a few ums and ars, and what must've been the most embarrassing, and uncomfortable few minutes of their spineless lives, one of the only things softly muttered by one of the family, was once again, a sign of their true colours, and a testament, to what matters more than any amount of integrity or moral standing in their world - "So…..you had the money?" I was for once, simply lost for words, they didn't even try and deny, defend, or justify, that they'd been caught out lying, or even make an attempt at giving reason for their underhanded and scamming ways against me. They'd not yet considered the fact that they'd now crossed me and was going to be in the big-bad world unprotected, but again with "THE MONEY!" My parting comment was what sealed the deal, and under my terms, and that was, "If you want to ever do business with me again, you'll pay the back pay, plus anyone you approach, will from here on out know of your excessive greed and willingness to rip them off, and also, everyone, including villains, whether old school, or otherwise, will now see you as a target – as you, gentleman, are now in open territory and fair game."

As of writing this, I've no doubt, Maxi-Montana has been given a lot less opportunity and promise of a fruitful career and existence, the family, will now have to tip toe through their business deals, as the money they move and the commodity they're involved in, is for the best part, unprotected and up for grabs…literally, and as for me and my crew, well, we are a lot better off as a result of what was nothing more than dead-weight.

14 MAGALUF

Magaluf, or Shaga-luf, has been described as an Oasis by a few, but a poor man's Ibiza by many others…. the Blackpool of Spain. One business associate I have, has a son, who insists on going to what my associate calls, "The armpit of the Mediterranean……a place vacationed by pissed up brits, in football shirts and vest tops." Some laughable reports will tell of a time, when Magaluf, or Shaga-luf was once, "a jewel of the Mediterranean," but there's no denying it is commonly seen as a cess pool of brightly coloured straw hats, with "Kiss me Quick" across them and t-shirts that read, "There's a party in my pants."

Another pal shared his own experience, when he observed a pair of teenage kids treated to seeing their dad and his new girlfriend, shamelessly embarrass themselves in the resort's clubhouse, when giving their best drunken rendition of, Right said Fred's, "I'm too sexy for my shirt" on stage…. and on the same trip, meeting a character at a local bar called, "Big Dave," from the north east of England, and got to hear his endless tale of "cracking it," after he'd sold his fleet of kebab vans and share of his girlfriend's nail salon, but one of the funniest experiences I'd heard about, is when a honeymoon couple booked an all-inclusive holiday, that promised them sipping champagne from crystal cut glasses, but instead they found themselves guzzling a warm piss-tasting substance, from a shared plastic cup. And as many will attest, Magaluf, and some of the surrounding Brit "hot-spots," have gained a bit of an unsavoury reputation, who, as a result of some of my fellow country men's efforts, their own omission and behaviour, have catapulted the perception of a civilised Britain and her populace, back 100 years, in terms of our advancements in manners, and our ability in being able to control ourselves, whilst drinking unscrupulous amounts of local wine and beer.

But for me, it doesn't matter where I lay my head, hang my hat, or what side of the road I'm driving on, I've found there's always a chance of a bit of business and a few quid to be earned, if you have an eye and nose for it, plus the ability to work, get along with and be around most people that you meet on any given day.

It was whilst I was in Ibiza, that I got chatting with some lads, who said they had a bit of business in Magaluf, opening a new bar and something else to do with a ticket agency. Their pitch and sale was, "an exclusive opportunity," and, "there's money in this," which at first I thought, 'if a deal is too good to be true, it usually is', but the offer was on the table, or bar, and a little part of me thought, 'Nothing ventured, nothing gained'. One thing I use as a measure of people when they're discussing business, is to not only observe how and where they discuss things, but also how they conduct themselves when there's alcohol involved; because not in a million years would I sit and discuss any type of serious business with complete strangers, who were as open and comfortable about discussing plans with me, who they've just met, that involved financial transactions, contracts and agreements, because if they are that open in that setting, what and how easy would they be to corrupt, or talk to someone else who could then apply a little bit of pressure and encouragement to see what the score is? It's not being paranoid; it's simply not having your pants pulled down because of someone else's carelessness. And the fact remained, my gut feeling was, and proved to be, this would turn out to be nothing more than a complimentary piss-up, but in fairness, they seemed like (and in the end proved to be) decent people who carried themselves well on both occasions that I'd ran into them in Ibiza.

So, when they invited me out to Magaluf anytime I liked through the summer, offering to put us up in a €750,000 penthouse apartment, I took Kian's number and said I'd be in touch. I remember thinking, 'why did this feel like this was one of those, "once in a lifetime deals, but you've got to sign up now, as there's only a limited number of seats?" Anyway, we enjoyed the rest of our time in Ibiza, but much like each and every time I'm at the will and command of my island mistress, otherwise known as the White Isle, I'm somewhat able, all be it reluctantly, to break from her warm and welcoming grasp and board a plane back home. Once I was back on the Spanish mainland and away from the calming-madness of Ibiza, I took stock of my mighty island and what was going on around me. All was quiet on the western front, the TV had little to offer, and we still needed to unpack. So, within what must have been a record amount of time, and a few minutes of thought, I decided 'fuck it, why not!', things are on the go-slow here, and I have a business angle of my own in mind – So, after I got off the phone to Kian and shouted, "Pack the cases again, Gem, we're off to Magaluf next week," I called the chaps and told them to hold the fort a little longer. Many of my mates think I'm borderline insane going off like that to meet up with people that I don't really know, but you only live once, plus, I get a good take on people and for every time I've taken a bit of a chance and been ok, I've swerved 10 similar situations because my senses warned me off, so this can't be all bad, right?

This was around the time that my good old friend Jazz was just about to launch his new vodka brand and he'd made me a nice proposal to become involved with the business, which in itself would have been a pleasure, but if I needed to work around music, vodka and hot countries to put some deals together, then who was I to decline? I'd see what the lads in Magaluf had going on and sus-out if there were any deals to be done with Jazz's new line while I was there.

We landed in Magaluf and there was already a car waiting outside to take us to our accommodation, which upon arrival to, I gave a thorough security inspection before cases were unpacked and we got comfortable. We met up with Kian, his missus, Allan and their pals for a meal, after which things went from 0 to 60 in the blink of an eye, and as experienced many times before, we soon found ourselves "slightly intoxicated" in a club! The whole of the week there would follow a similar pattern, as the saying goes, "Eat, sleep, rave, repeat!" I was so well looked after out there, to the point where I couldn't get a round in, even if I tried, they just wouldn't let me. Granted, my original suspicions about Magaluf being like a poor-man's Ibiza, with absolutely no class to it at all, where all entirely confirmed, but I was in really good company and experiencing something that I never would have, if I hadn't come to know these people in Ibiza. I can be around the richest or the poorest, the best or the worst that society has to offer, so long as no one is fucking with me, I'm pretty comfortable in most situations, so it was a simple case of…party on and get stuck in!

We spent most of our nights in a venue aptly named Alex's Bar, where the owner knew Kian and the lads well and recognised me; he proper looked after us, each and every time we walked through the door and realising that perhaps we were best kept away from certain punters, we had our own section, which never ran dry.

One night, we were at a bar on the main strip and there was a bit of a commotion not far from us, and something which must've come from my days of doing the door, I took a casual interest in what the fuss was about, when one of our group came beside me to explain; there was a midget stripper unhandcuffing himself from a young "lady," as other females were swarming around him, then as a gap appeared in the crowd, I realised he was showing them all of his manhood, which was almost as big as the rest of him – talk about a "third-arm!" The guys in our group excitedly explained that this fella's drinks and kebabs are paid for through the whole season, entirely by drunken women and that he shags more girls than most fellas could possibly dream of on their holiday! I leant back on the bar, took a look around me and felt like I was in a twilight zone episode; every hen party and stag-do that had ever graced Southend's club scene…personified! It was then, that I questioned myself further, and 'what the fuck I was doing', as here I am at 56 years of age, pissed up on the main strip in Magaluf? Just taking into account of what was going on around me, and the people, who were in their 20s and 30s, all without a care in the world, or any inhibitions and what must have been freshly divorced men in the 40's and 50's trying to re-live their youths! Later on in that particular evening, I went into the toilets, and something instantly seemed off to me; there was no fucker to be seen! Before I even considered doing what I'd came to do, I paused instinctively to think, perhaps I was in the wrong toilets, or I was being set up! I heard strange animalistic noises coming from one of the cubicles…now feeling a bit paranoid and noticing that the door wasn't completely shut or even locked, I pushed it open with my foot, half expecting to find a man dying of an asthma attack or had done too much gear and his world and mental state was crashing down around him, but what I found was far worse. The midget with the enormous cock was just finishing up from smashing some slag in against the wall! "Ah, sorry about that!" I joked as I hurriedly headed towards the nearest urinal, once again thinking 'where the fuck did I bring us!'

Late into our night we were at Alex's Bar, the group we were with really were a right fucking laugh and even Alex had left his post to join us several times through the night! As is often the case, due to an argument made a thousand times worse by some drunken and, let's say, overly outspoken females, a fight broke out on the dance floor, which then quickly became a mass brawl! People were grabbing their belongings, guys were grabbing their girls and all heading for the door, rapido. I carried on drinking my Goose and casually observing, until the brawl spread from the dance floor over to near us, so I straightened up and readied myself, just in case. Bouncers were running in trying to put a stop to the fighting, which seemed to be effectively "fanning the flames!" Also pouring petrol on were the gob-shite girls, who Gemma cleverly managed to talk into stepping into the ladies' room for a moment, then she wedged the door shut to keep them at bay for a while; genius, I thought! There was a clear winning side emerging in the events that were unfolding before my slightly drunken eyes; a crew of African guys, absolutely massive lumps, were knocking down most of who came their way. Somehow, a couple of the lads in our group became entangled in this tear-up, I guess because they live and work there throughout the season and know a lot of people, especially the venue owners and security, but as hard as I'd tried to stay out of this mess, I too was drawn in when I saw one of our group about to be knocked into next week! The biggest guy of the African crew ran at this lad and was about to seriously fuck up his face, but as he came closer to me, I chinned him with a quick left and went to continue hitting him, being as he was about twice my size, young and athletically built. I figured I'd better try to end this one fast, or I'd be laid out with the other bodies on the floor, snoring! Anyway, as luck would have it, and to my disbelief, he went straight down! "Fuck me, thanks Carlton, I thought he was gonna kill me!" came a cheery voice over the sound of the music. The biggest of the troublemakers was out of the game, for the moment at least, but then I realised I now had his mates stood before me in a half-circle, deciding in their minds what their next move should be. This time I was surely fucked, and backing down isn't an option, so there was only one thing for it: "Come on then you fucking cunts, let's go!!!" With that, and to my astonishment, they backed down, and thank fuck they did because they would've weighed me right in! With that, we went outside to get some air and take stock, just as the mobile security patrol ran in through the doors to help finish the saga that had now emptied out the entire venue. I started noticing people talking, taking photos and videos all around, a few distant mentions of my name in lowered tones were enough for me to call it a night, because as Kian was now saying, the Guardia Civil wouldn't be far away now! Alex knew what could unfold and he ushered me and Gemma round the side and into a taxi…and we were gone!

On a more positive note, however, I was really surprised how many of the old east end and West Ham lot are living and holidaying on that island, I ran into scores of them throughout the trip, which was lovely. I was also greeted by several people who remembered me from the rave and club scenes and even got asked along with a top group from Middlesboro to watch a World Cup game that was being aired at a roof top VIP bar. Being as it was only round the corner, and in the spirit of checking out new places, we went along. By the end of the day, we were invited to their wedding which was later in the week! They were a real good bunch, and we had a great time that afternoon.

I'd had a tip on a good tattooist in the town, and I'd been wanting to get some cover-up work done for a while, so partly to get the ink done and partly to get away from this bunch of insane party animals for a few hours, I booked the work in. Gemma had a bit of work done by another artist in the shop at the same time, so we were both laying on opposite beds, looking and feeling half dead, discussing how Kian, Allan and the rest of them really needed to slow down a bit! I remember approaching the 3.5-hour mark and the tattoo machine (artists hate it when you call it a tattoo gun) started to feel like a hammer and chisel against my ribcage! Hungry, hanging and feeling aggravated, I decided to get the last half hour done when I was back in England, as I just couldn't put up with it anymore, so I paid the man and fucked off out of there sharpish!

Believe it or not, in amongst all the madness, I had managed to get several venues, including a 5* hotel, on the hook for Jazz's vodka. I'd exchanged cards with several big business owners who were interested in making the switch to the new product and I'd even pulled Jazz himself in on a meeting via a video link. Sadly, as you know by this point in my book, the deals would never come to apparition as Jazz passed away later that year.

I should explain that I purposefully went just days before the official summer opening parties and having initially booked 7 nights, believing that would be enough to take a look around, party and explore possible business opportunities. We'd extended our stay by a further 5 nights already and having partied that away, the guys were on at us to stay for "just one more week" to "just do a few opening parties," but it was high time I started going to bed at 10pm again, as opposed to 10am!

During the plane journey home from Magaluf, even though I was a bit worse for wear, I did a bit of thinking and it hit me, the stark difference between how the Magaluf lads had treated me compared to how one dog in particular had and, "This club is yours as much as it is mine Carlton, you know that my brother," being virtually forgotten about for 3 days and handed a table bill before the sun had even gone down. I guess some people have short memories when it comes to the help they'd received getting to where they are, not to mention all the times they've had their arses saved, thanks to the name of another. The world has more than its fair share of people who have given their "unquestionable loyalty" and promises of shared wealth once "they'd got paid."

It was 12 days of our lives that Gem and I had been robbed of and would not get back, but nevertheless, it was another one of my spur of the moment moves that hadn't turned out too bad; I'd made contacts for the vodka, had some interesting experiences, great laughs and the hospitality shown to me by Kian and Allan had been second to none!

15 STARK RAVING MAD

When the first acid house raves really started to kick off, it unquestionably took the whole of the UK by storm….and what clubland history would respectively preserve, honour and later show, were these raves were not only the biggest, but the most iconic that the UK has ever seen - the year was 1988.

The organisers were people on a mission; their mindset was one they believed was as purposeful as it was to be a (necessary) life changing event for those attending. The promotion, ticket sales, meeting points and (of course) not letting the authorities get wind of what was going down, all took military like precision to pull off. It was also a process that would, for a time, allow the success and later iconic status, that many raves earned…... and this was achieved long before the existence of the internet, or any mainstream advertising (there simply wasn't either a budget or need for a Johnny loudmouth to fuck things up).

After a few phone calls, having the right minds behind the idea, a few clued-up people would literally scope out, plan, and execute a break-in to host a venue. Sometimes it was a chance spotting of a field, other times it would be the scoping out of a warehouse, but whatever the decided and agreed upon location, one of the most consistent parts of the equation was, the event was typically only accessible via a yet unpaved and easy to miss dirt road on a remote piece of farming land, or an industrial site that hadn't seen a crowd of measurable size in many years. This proven and effective well thought out logistical process, would draw in after each event, even more over enthusiastic, pill-munching teens and twenty something ravers regularly, all looking to get out of their heads and off this planet.

Even now and after 3 decades, a marriage (or two), kids, a house and a career, you'll hear people talk about the lasting impact the events had on them.….it was always more than just about turning up and being part of what you'd read in the Monday papers... it was them being completely off their tits; watching dragons fly over their heads and being in the middle of a collection of people, all on one wave of borderline hedonistic behaviour. You felt as if your soul and very existence were not only being fed, but dependent on and by the pulsating beats and a light display that created an energy you felt was as exclusive to you as the hallucinations you were experiencing – everything was beyond either explanation or reasoning, but this is what was created by those that put the events on. This was a time when promoters were into the scene as much as those attending the events themselves – they knew what they were doing...a handful of people, that would look to out-do their own efforts from their previous all-weekender.

Through working at ABC, I knew John Smith and the lads who founded Genesis; that was one of the original and undoubtably best illegal raves around. Without sounding arrogant, it was a no brainer why and when they asked me to organise the security for all their events; we knew what we were doing and how to make sure there was no issues on any level. The team behind Genesis became like a little family right from the off. The actual logistics could be tricky, but again, having a tight-knit outfit who knew it was more than just looking the part, ensured that the event went on without so much as a hiccup, and allowed all involved parties to see things through successfully.

I put together a crew of 12 or 13 lads, around half of them were people I knew from West Ham's terraces, the others were reputable lumps who one of the crew could vouch for, and all of which would stand their ground. Almost overnight, we'd gone from being suited 'n' booted bouncers in dickie bows, working until 2am, only taking home about 60 notes a shift and often smelling like the inside of a brewery, to turning out in our terrace attire, a fraction of any trouble; if any at all and even though we were working until sunrise, leaving with 500 quid in our hands, there was always a sense of 'that was fucking worth it!'. In hindsight, we didn't realise what we were actually a part of, the short opportunity we would have to enjoy it, and that people would be desperately trying to replicate those nights for forever more!

The promoters had their own underground network which they used to advertise an event at a secret location - everything from cleverly distributed and placed leaflets, to pirate radio, even public phone boxes and pagers were utilised to get the word out. Then the ticket holders would be told to gather in a certain spot and wait for further instructions, then right at the last minute, they'd be given the location of the rave and make their way there in droves. I remember one record shop in particular, called Record Village in Walthamstow, was one location that you could get details from, if your face fitted!

Even I didn't find out where it was going to be held until the morning of the event, then as soon as that phone call came in, I'd let the lads know and we'd make our way to the previously unknown location to hang about while the equipment got set up. Then as night fell, hundreds of cars would suddenly appear......it was if they'd came out of nowhere and from every direction....and as they got closer, you'd notice they'd all switch off their headlights. You couldn't but help notice the occupant's facial expressions as they passed by – all with the same grinning faces, looks of eagerness and exhibiting high levels of excitement. These were people that all wanted to simply get out of the same cars that transported them throughout a mundane working week and experience a sense of freedom...... visiting or revisiting that better place, which was born of their own minds, with a little assistance from Ebenezer. And credit to every one of them, as this part was done with little, or no supervision at all. Hundreds of cars would effortlessly fill the venue parking lot that was no more than a neighbouring field or adjacent flat lot;

literally hundreds of cars parked all within an hour.

Ferry Lane, between Walthamstow and Tottenham, is a place that springs to mind, as there were several massive warehouses there and we used the old cart warehouse along there one time. One of the most memorable raves I ever worked must be the one in a tyre factory under Bow Flyover. Not wanting the filth to see my car if we'd been raided that night, so I parked at The Astairs club in Whitechapel (where we also ran the security) and jumped in with one of my lads to get to the industrial estate. In general, it was a great rave with good DJ's, a great sound system and the right chemical enhancement to keep everyone dancing until sunrise. I recall the smoke machine doing overtime that night, and the heat in the place became almost unbearable for the last few hours, what with those old types of roofs, metal shutters and almost a thousand people out of their trees dancing away; I was that thirsty, it was one of those scenarios where you felt like you could stick a straw in a reservoir and empty it out. But, luckily for me, being security, I didn't have to wade through a floor filled with empty plastic water bottles, cartons of used Ribena or queue at the makeshift bar like the punters for a bottle of water!

When all was said and done and the time came to "do the off," I walked outside to be greeted by a new day…...the air seemed so clean and fresh to me; I was putting the sensation down to the Jack Jill's, but honestly, it felt lovely to be outside in the cool morning air, so much so that I decided to walk back to my motor. It was around 8am by now, so all the "normal" people were starting to go about their usual daily lives; walking, driving, or cycling from A to B, dog walkers and joggers were out in abundance, too.

I noticed a few people looking at me oddly as I passed them on the opposite side of the road, then a few cars slowed right down to stare at me, which I thought was weird; I knew I wasn't covered in blood as there hadn't been any aggro that night, but I looked down at my shirt and jeans to check anyway…nothing! I was completely up and together, so I thought 'Don't know what the fuck everyone's problem is today!'. The looks and stares continued throughout my journey, one woman put her arms around her two kids, pulling them in closely to her as they stopped and stared at me, I had become like some sort of walking freak-show. I felt as if I'd stepped out of the rave into a different place in time. I was now just a few minutes from the car, so I got my keys out at the ready; the 20 minute or so walk had started to feel like an hour and I just wanted to get away from there and work out what had just happened! Up ahead, an old couple with their fresh loaf and morning paper were scurrying across the street to avoid me as though I was a mugger. I put the key in the door to unlock the car wondering why I, a Londoner born and bred, was being treated like a lepper as I strolled through my own manor, but as my arse hit the seat and my eyes met the rear-view, all became abundantly clear in an instant! My face had been turned completely black, I looked like a fucking chimney sweep who hadn't seen the tin bath for a month. Long before air-con or heated screens (were common place), you kept a cloth or a 'Magic Sponge' to clear your misty screen, so I grabbed whatever I could and started trying to rub this muck off of me, but it was useless…….decades of brake dust and rubber from the old tire factory had been liberated from the walls and roof of the building by body-heat, moisture and disco smoke, and settled on the unwitting faces of almost a thousand illegal ravers! I managed to get the majority of the stuff off of my eyelids, but when I blinked, I looked like a black and white minstrel driving along. It was blatantly obvious, I needed to get off the road quickly, so I went round to Deny's house and jumped in the shower…she was laughing her head off at me; "Look at the state of ya, what on earth have you been doing you silly fucker?" I must have stood in that shower, repeatedly washing myself for almost an hour, the black dirt just kept running off of my face, neck and hair!

When I was a young man, I rarely drunk alcohol, maybe a pint here and there, but I wasn't a big drinker or drug taker. I was more into contact sports, working out and keeping fit. We've all heard those dramatic stories of life changing events that instantly open a person's eyes to God, perhaps a near-death experience, a trauma or alike. They see a bright light, hear a calling, or have a feeling come over them like a wave, then BOSH: Their whole world changes in a split second and they see life in a different light. Well, all of that is comparable to when I took my first pill and danced all night, even though I was actually working the doors in Stratford! It was as if I found another world, a better place hidden within our own world, a place that only the enlightened knew how to find. I could now see incredible beauty where I once only saw ugliness, light, and happiness where there was once only darkness. I'm reluctant to make a direct comparison to religion, but that really is the kind of impact it had on my life. As the Ecstasy flowed around your body with an intense warmth, so too did the tunes, you became one with the music, you heard every single note and felt each vibration as if it were originating from within your very own heart, in the moment, you could almost fall in love with the very voice of a vocalist on a track! It was all about love. We brought thousands upon thousands of people together into a scenario that would usually see several fights a night and a couple of stabbings per month, yet there was virtually zero risk of violence or aggression at all, it was like going to another planet for 10 plus hours.

The night my mate Musky gave me that first E, there was a group inside from Poplar and another lot arrived that were all from Stratford, I knew they didn't mix and there had been issues with these two groups in the past, so I thought I'd need to be on high alert as trouble would be imminent, but no! The first time I walked through, they were all hugging each other and dancing about, I couldn't believe my eyes...but there you go, a key difference between E and coke is right there. Musky had warned me to only take half of this pill. Heeding his warning, I gave the other half to Dave and shortly after dropping them, we had 2 other bouncers swap with us for the front door and we went down into the club. As I said, all the sensations around me were heightened, it felt great, but then I clocked this strobe light doing its thing to the beat of the track and I became fixated on it. Dave came next to me and yelled "What the fuck are you doing Carlton, everyone's staring at us, let's go!" I replied, "I can't Dave...I can't fucking move!" I honestly couldn't move my body to walk, nor could I stop staring into this blinding strobe light! Dave grabbed my arm to help me, but somehow, we both stacked into a heap on the dancefloor, Dave jumped up, I managed to stand but still couldn't walk away from the strobe; "Carl, hold my hand, fuck sake let's go!" Dave was 6'4" and I was about 17 stone, so when he took me by the hand and led me through the crowd, you can just imagine what the punters were thinking of these two big bouncers floating across the dancefloor hand in hand, can't you? My antics didn't end there either, because all the guys on the door were laughing. I went upstairs, thinking I might find some sanctuary for a moment, but next thing I'd laid the factory lockers down on the floor and started dancing on them. Hearing the noise, the lads all came up to see what was going on: "Come and dance on the stage with me you lot...come on...it's the bollocks up 'ere!" Everyone around me was almost crying with laughter, but I just carried on dancing on these lockers that I'd made into my very own stage...madness!

Once I had a taste for E's, and bear in mind I was getting paid to go and work as well, I couldn't wait for the next rave to come around! As well as the team working security, I used to have loads of my mates come as well. I think I just wanted them to share in the experience, I could not believe what a great time I would have, so I wanted them to come along and witness the sensations for themselves, and to be honest, that was the only way to truly understand the illegal rave scene; being there! The number of people I helped through their first E was unbelievable, I still speak to several mates who have almost identical stories about their first E with me, that's why it had to be such an epic scene in the first film.

One time, we were in a huge warehouse, it had 2 floors and the promoters had kitted the place out with DJ equipment that would have rivalled the best licensed clubs of the time......with speakers, smoke, strobes, and lasers that seemed to be battering the walls. There was a group of punters that I'd seen at other raves, and we got chatting, they'd clearly had their smarties and were on a good vibe, so I told them to come upstairs with me so I could show them something. Once at the top of the stairs, they all stood in a line in front of me...waiting...I told them to turn around and look down over the railing, which they all did, it was an incredible sight that I'd introduced them to; 3-4,000+ revellers having the time of their lives, not 1 unhappy face, not a pair of still feet or arms in sight. They turned to me like I was a Messiah or something, hugging and thanking me for what I'd shown them...insane when I look back on it!

By 1990, I wasn't double dropping pills, sometimes I was taking 8 or 10 in a night! But there was one occasion when we were working security at Raindance (another famous party and always an excellent night) and the place was absolutely banging with about 8,000 people packed in, and it was here I took 12 of these pills called New Yorkers. Years later, one of the promoters took part in a documentary, which I believe is on YouTube to this day; he told a story from that night of how he was walking through thousands of ravers in search of his head of security, and there he was, this big mean looking lump, in a tight vest, dancing about and hugging everyone around!

The football terraces that had been my preferred playground for so long were starting to change, the pitch battles were easing off, the Old Bill were starting to get a grip on things and simultaneously, the rave scene was kicking-off big style. I was soon to discover that decades of generational hatred between two parts of London, not to mention one of the biggest rivalries in terrace and hooligan history was quickly fading away and a new type of weekend energy was being introduced.

So, I was getting paid good money to enjoy myself, and a reflection of how things had changed (for the better?) was the Bank Holidays at the Town and Tavern. This was run exclusively by one of Millwall's top boys, Jacko, along with his brother. The place would be full of Millwall's firm, no West Ham boys would really go there, until I walked in in my denim dungarees and Reebok boots (not the velcro ones!) with a few of my pals to have a good time. So, there we were, a handful of West Ham getting out of our boxes with Millwall's top boys, sweating our nuts off, looking like hill billies, dancing and hugging each other; tell me something other than Ecstasy that could have made that possible back in the day?

Many people of a certain age would have heard of the M25 Raves, and we provided security for scores of those. The location was ideal as it was so easily accessible for ravers and easy to disperse in different directions when the sun came up! I remember seeing some of the newspaper headlines of the time, depicting farmer's fields left looking like aliens had landed and left crop circles, but it was thousands of ravers who had descended upon that spot to have a good time and out of the way of the rest of the world. One morning, I woke up feeling the warmth of the sun on my face, but then I jumped up due to the feeling of sliding down; I looked behind me and saw cars pelting past me...I'd woken up on the bank down the side of an M25 crash barrier near the Gatwick Airport turning! We must not have realised that the field we took over that night was so close to the UK's biggest motorway! We'd had a marquee there and everything that night, I don't know how we didn't all get nicked for that one.

New laws and bigger budgets were giving the police more capability to shut us down; it was a battle we were going to lose – you can't fight the biggest and most well-funded gang in the world, can you! On one occasion I arrived with a few of my security lads to watch over as the promoters entered the warehouse to get set up, but shortly after, and very conveniently timed, four van loads of gavvers pounced on us out of nowhere. Thanks to that, I got nicked with a bag of some of the best E's I'd ever had down my sock. The illegal rave scene was never going to last forever, but I wish we'd have gotten a few more years out of it to be honest! The Old Bill started to catch up with us, whereas in the beginning they were always 2 steps behind. I really believe that they must have been paying some snitches on the inside of the movement to get locations.

Once the underground rave scene started to be hit hard by the law, we started to work the nightclubs instead, and I took up the spot as head doorman of Paradise club, the first 24-hour rave venue…with a license! From there I took over the security at Ministry of Sound, which had only been open for about 6 months at that point, and no matter what kind of venue you put in that location, running the security there is always going to be a major juggling act, because it's on such a naughty manner, especially if you're a known ICF member. Standing on the front door in SE1 was risky, but I didn't give a fuck, I actually took the responsibility of the safety of all those thousands of people quite seriously……and that's where the juggling act came in; faces and families from each corner of London and beyond would turn up to the Ministry, and rather than be a cunt and try to stamp authority left, right and centre, I struck deals of mutual respect with most of the proper people that would come through. For example, there were some little firms that were outright banned from most clubs, but I'd speak with them, let them jump the queue, but in return I required their best behaviour in the venue and any issues with other firms should be dealt with away from the club – if it's one thing I learned and took away from the illegal rave scene….and necking countless bags of E's, it's easier to be a businessman than unnecessarily be a hooligan with a baseball bat – like they say, "you catch more flies with honey than you do with vinegar!"

I remember on more than one occasion, I took a night off to go on a date, and much like when I was having a night off enjoying a VIP area or quiet corner of the club, I'd still keep a radio with me in case of emergencies (see…I told you I cared about the other doormen and the safety of the punters!). Several times a night I'd hear people going ape shit at the front door or pleading with the other bouncers; "Just get Carlton up here, he knows us!" or "Get Carlton, he'll sort this shit out!"

Now this happened on the regular, but one time in particular, it was late in the night and the club was virtually full to capacity, we were turning scores of people away at the door, but this firm I knew turned up outside with some young ladies in tow and when they found out the situation, one of them pulled out a massive wedge and held it out to me. I was earning well anyway, so I ushered him over to one of my guys, gave them the nod of approval and they were in; turned out there was £1,500 in that bung. So, all the doormen went home double happy that night, with a little extra top-up on their wages and a free lesson courtesy of Carlton's school of economics.

Around 90/91, Fitzroy and Linval introduced me to this guy who was always bouncing about all over the place; one of those fellas who was 100 miles an hour, but a likeable character; his name is Marvin Herbet. Marvin got himself barred from Ministry by a club manager, but I was able to get him back in, provided he'd stay on his best behaviour. Dave Dunn turned up one night to see me, he had a guy in tow who apparently wanted me to give him some work on the door, but things were busy on the front door as usual, so I let them through into the club and said I'd catch up with them later.

During the night, a shout came over the radio that a man had been stabbed, so I rushed in with a couple of other lads to see "what-was-what". We were expecting to find absolute carnage, so it was a surprise when there was no one about with a stab wound, but we were quickly told that the injured party had fled (it transpired that he'd fallen to his knees crying and crawled out through a fire escape). The problem we did have on our hands though, was that my doormen had collared Marvin and when they told him he had to leave, he went berserk and was fighting with the lot of them! Leaning on the rule of mutual respect, I tried to speak to him, but he was too far gone, both in terms of temper and gear. So, between us, we managed to drag the big fucker from the tunnel to the main entrance. The others were holding onto him, especially as he had a tool in one hand, honestly…he was truly relentless, I had one more try at telling him to calm down and speak to me, but he got the other hand free and plunged it into his pocket…I was not going to wait for a knife or a shooter to come out, especially not with this fella, plus, enough was enough and although I hadn't wanted it to come to blows between us, I had a responsibility. I grabbed my tool, shoved one of the other doormen out of my way and smashed Marvin in the head with it. Now unconscious, they carried him outside; he was in a pretty bad way, but he's a tough bastard. I paid someone 40 notes to drive him to the nearest hospital and spent the next few hours and days feeling pretty gutted that he'd put me in that kind of position. We'd all wondered what had happened, who'd been stabbed and then disappeared, and it didn't take long to learn that Bernard had made himself busy in the club, got involved as though he was one of my doormen and came proper unstuck, because Marvin saw him for what he was, didn't respect him and chivved him! I guess he shouldn't have stuck his nose in…

For a long while after that incident, even after I'd left Ministry, rumours would circulate that Marvin was going to turn up that night to shoot me in revenge. People on their way to shoot me was something I was starting to get used to hearing about on a weekly basis, and many of these people were credible threats, I have been shot at and analysing just my time running nightclub doors, I put a stop to many other plots against me too. Marvin didn't try to come for me, I'm sure that if he had it would've been a war, but perhaps he realised that with his actions against me and my doormen that night, he was in the wrong. I also got to hear from several sources, including a later conversation with Marvin (you see, much like me, some people can be reasonable!) that during the brawl at the Ministry and during my fit of rage, there was someone that felt the wrath of two men hell bent at killing each other and got caught in the crossfire, so to speak, resulting in them getting knocked out! So, if you're that person and you're reading this, my heart felt apologies go out to you and I hope your next visit to the club was a lot less eventful.

Years passed and I was walking through Marbella with Lee Knight; we were lining up a talk show out there with me, Freddy Foreman and Jason Marriner. A blacked-out BMW passed us, screeched to a halt and this voice shouted "Oi, Carlton!" I thought "Yep, here we go!" Marvin leant out of the motor and asked how I'd been, and we agreed we needed to meet up, just us two, to discuss past events, which we did.

The next time I was in that area, I was on a bit of work for a certain Irish football chairman and Marvin and I got together a couple of times with some other pals for the odd meal and nights out. I got a call saying that Marvin had been shot and it wasn't looking too good for him. So I went to the hospital, but due to the nature of the situation, the Guardia Civil wouldn't let anyone in, but by some miracle, Marvin eventually got discharged and came to meet us, hobbling along on crutches! He been shot 4 or 5 times, lost an eye and a bollock, but he was still in decent spirits, all things considered! He didn't know at the time, but I looked at him sitting there all patched up, talking and laughing and I thought back to that younger version of him, relentlessly steaming around town, doing his thing and not giving a flying fuck…I thought 'Fucking hell, this bloke must have more lives than a cat'.

Back to present day, it's admirable how he's turned his life around and is trying to do good in the world. He's one of those people who can be described as 'like Marmite, love him or hate him', but I still say he's a loveable rogue! The story about Marvin is one prime example of meeting a person through 'clubland' and forming, what is now looking like, a lifelong friendship.

I look back on my days on the doors as climbing the ladder, of course, that ladder was headed straight for serious criminality, but it was a steep learning curve, an opportunity to earn your stripes and make connections, some of which, like Marvin who I just mentioned, would last for decades. That kind of level of mutual respect and shared experience is something I have with many people and a lot of it stemmed from my time on the doors. I was no push over and I was far from a mug and no matter who or what wanted to test or challenge me, I never backed down and that stood me in good stead for the future.

Sid – "…. he makes the people around him, rather than them making him."

For Carlton's sake, let's just say that he's 'a few years' older than me, or even better, that I'm a few years younger than him! But on a more serious note, he took me in when I was 14 and whilst I'm sure I would have survived somehow if he hadn't, I'm extremely pleased and grateful that he did, because my life would certainly have turned out very differently without Carlton's influence. Unlike so many immoral people he and I have encountered through the course of business and life over the years, I always have and always will repay Carlton with the most valuable currency in our game – loyalty.

I can attest to the fact that Carlton, from a very young age, has always been very streetwise, one of the most switched-on people I've ever come across in fact, and that's one of the reasons why he's made it to the top of several of his chosen fields, for example, you don't become one of London's most feared and respected bouncers, without being pretty sharp. Of course, being 'handy' and extremely violent goes a long way too, but Carlton possesses the ability to step back, analyze all possible moves available to him and choose his timing carefully, which is one of the many things he's tried to teach me how to do over the years and I could not have wished for a better mentor.

When I was 17, Carlton got me a job on the door with him and he always kept me close, taking me under his wing, and that was for my benefit, not his, but he never once asked me for anything, not 1 favour or attempt at using me for his own personal gain. In '88 when the illegal rave scene was really taking off, I used to be involved in organising the raves for extra cash, as well as working the security with Carlton and his men. Although it was great fun casing warehouses, staying a step ahead of the Old Bill by keep changing pager numbers and fitting out a warehouse with a sound system in a few hours, working and earning my stripes on the door was where it was at for me.

You may have read the story in Muscle, of when Trigger tried to murder Carlton on the boat, so given my closeness to Carlton, you can only imagine what I felt when London's rumour-mill started to turn and "Someone shot at Carlton" became, in Chinese whisper style, "Someone shot Carlton". I was working at Club UK in Wandsworth that night and when I heard shots had been fired on The Barge, I raced through London to make sure he was alive. I don't know how I kept control of myself or my car, until I'd found out that Carlton wasn't dead, but I remember it hitting me like a ton of bricks, just how much he meant to me, even back then.

Carlton had an army of doormen and heavy-duty muscle about him in London long before he ever moved to Essex, a fact which I think a lot of people choose to forget, because it suits their own agenda to pigeon-hole him that way, but he is his own man who's always gone in his own direction, regardless of what's going on around him; a leader, not a follower, he makes the people around him, rather than them making him.

Carlton had his own unique ways of working the door back in the day, the most prominent being that on an average shift, us lads wouldn't see him all night, until he came out towards closing time to pay us, but even on the coldest of winter nights, he was always sweating like he'd run a marathon. One night, I went into the warehouse thinking 'Where the fuck is Carlton?' And when I eventually found him, dancing away in a dark corner, he talked me into trying a pill, about which I was reluctant, but I trusted the boss and gave it a go; remember that scene in Rise of the Footsoldier with the E? – well, that wasn't about me, it was based on a man called Ice, but that was my exact experience as well, down to a T, except the fact that we finished up filthy-bloody-dirty at the end of it all, thanks to the state of the warehouse we'd broken into! There was never a dull moment on the door with Carlton, that's for sure.

Given Carlton's levels of humility and generosity, both in terms of cash and opportunity, and as a man who respects the criminal hierarchy and chain of command so much, I cannot believe how many people I've witnessed trying to back-door him over the years, usually where a little bit of extra cash is on the table in the short term. I've lost count of how many times I've picked up a tool and told Carlton to "leave it to me", but he's rarely allowed me to follow it through and says, "there's more than 1 way to skin a cat, Sid!" I guess if everyone who ever made an attempt at passing Carlton over got served up, we'd probably be banged up by now, and for a poxy couple of quid at that! Instead, for those who simply can't be taught the rules, Carlton's usual approach is to close twice as many doors in their face as he could've opened for them in life, so to those of you reading his book now, wondering why he didn't call you with that new number; surprise! -he knows exactly what you did and what you're about and you came off worse.

There are many people out there that will refer to Carlton as their brother, cousin or as family, because they want to be associated with him, what he stands for and all the benefits that can come with that metaphor actually being true, but 9 out of 10 of them are full of shit and have no real basis for their claim. These chancers are almost always the ones that cause the grief within our circles and their phones are usually out of range when they're required to repay a favour or put a situation right.

Carlton's parents (may they rest in peace) knew me well, so well in fact, that they'd not only tell me off on occasion, but if I'd done something wrong, even as a young man, they'd clip me round the ear and set me straight. If they were both still here today, they could still do the same and receive nothing but an apology from me, because they were very good people, who I respected immensely. I have too many stories to tell involving Carlton's folks, but when I was training at Talbot's Gym in Leytonstone, Norman drove over about 4 times a week for almost 2 years to train with me, which was as much an honour as it was a pleasure for me.

Carlton was the best man at my wedding, there simply was no other choice, and he was there at the hospital within hours of my children being born, both of whom don't just call him uncle, they only know him as an uncle. There are things that Carlton has done for me, which I can't discuss in detail, that the average person probably wouldn't even do for their own flesh and blood, he's treated me like a real brother since I was a boy and as far as we're both concerned, I am his brother. We share a kind of unexplainable, emotional connection, which can best be understood by my telling of what happened at his film premier: On the set of the film, I'd found certain things difficult to watch, as they were just too 'close to home', but when I sat in that cinema and saw certain things playing out again before my eyes, I had to get out of there, I had reached a point where I couldn't take anymore re-living, so I headed for the gents to be on my own and gather my thoughts. Carlton was sat with the film people, and he couldn't have seen me slip out the door in the dark, but as I looked up at the mirror after splashing my face with cold water, Carlton walked through the door. He hugged me, looked at me and said, "I know bruv". I didn't need to ask why he had also slipped away from the crowds, I already understood.

For anyone who's been introduced to me by Carlton, you will know me as his foster brother, the title by which he refers to me, a term which isn't an empty one and something he doesn't say lightly. From me, that love and respect is reciprocal, and he is a member of my family.

Carlton has connections throughout the UK and internationally; it's actually quite something to see him go to work on the phone fixing a problem or putting a deal together! But as I've witnessed over time, he didn't go looking for these connections, he doesn't go out of his way to pal people up, they come to him and introduce themselves, leave their number or business card and tell him to call, should he ever need anything. My honest belief is that Carlton could have been even further up the ladder within the international criminal underworld, had he chosen to, but he recognises the true meaning behind 'Heavy is the head that wears the crown!

Congratulations on all of your achievements Carlton, thank you for all that you've ever done for me, and never forget that I'll always be right here should you need me; I love you brother.

16 THERE FOR YOUR OWN

Quite often, I've been seen as some sort of iconic figure, or a "legend," and in addition to the complements I've received for assisting and helping others (that are very humbling and appreciated), in my mind, none of my actions that would be considered courageous, or seen as an act of bravery could come even close to what I'd call the REAL and genuine heroes of our society, as there're some people that I'll always hold as a measure in terms of their bravery and selfless behaviour - Her Majesty's Armed Forces.

I was raised in an era and a time, much like teachers, those within the NHS and other parts of the public sector, the British armed forces were highly respected, not just domestically but also globally. This group of men and women were something special and were by any standard, regarded as some of society's best – they existed on a platform they built and was one that society had a great deal of admiration for. If you were to look around the world and see the special and elite forces that are considered the most proficient at what they do, there's a healthy number whose history and background are mirrored on that of the British military – an institution who openly display a recognisable level of discipline, respect, and a uniformed presence. In fact, so much that it once made boys still in their mid-teens lie about their age so they could don a uniform, proudly do their bit for King and country, and serve in World War 1.

"Never in the field of human conflict was so much owed by so many to so few," was part of a speech given by Sir Winston Churchill, and a line that truly gives credit to those that were willing to give their lives to protect, not only their own families but those of the country's populace they'd never met. That alone is one of the most selfless acts a human being can give; especially when you consider how many of the armed forces who are now homeless, struggling with PTSD and not only fighting, but trying to manage other mental health issues that are ignored by the same people and government they were willing to protect.

The Somme being a prime example. The sacrifice and willingness of men that gave their last breath of air in July 1916, promoted a lot of commemorative speeches. One of the most commonly known was, "We owe them a massive debt, the least we can do is remember them…." I then have to ask, how far from the powers-that-be (and many others) deaf ears has that message fallen short of? It makes my blood boil to see how many men and women have been treated so disrespectfully and discarded after they finished their service. How many people, in both elected and un-elected positions, were part of the decision process that sent these brave men and women to war, have ever served, or understood what it's like to have experienced a life on and after being on the front lines? Even the lowest skilled of mechanics cares enough for his tools to put them away after the job is done.

You could very well jokingly comment, "How could those within certain levels of government have any idea – after all, their wants and needs are brought in and served to them on a silver platter…" as much as everything else, I understand wholly that our serving men and women accept a daily serving of life or death, with a side order of living and working in some of the most unforgivable conditions imaginable, on a regular basis. Some might argue that the soldiers signed up for service and by their own doing accepted the risk – and I'd agree…...but they didn't sign up to be a forgotten member of society after they'd given their all either. It pains me to say this, but I doubt there exists, any solid proof that these same men and women, who never left their post or let us down, are truly respected by politicians for their service, and I also believe many are seen (by some elements of our governing bodies) as nothing more than cannon fodder.

Take a long hard look at what is expected of a British

soldier…. perfection and success, both on and off the battlefield, and nothing truer is said when they exemplify the values and standards I hold personally in my life. When a British soldier is willing to give their very soul for both Queen and country, how can that be faulted over anything else? Think about what that serving individual has committed to and ask yourself, how much of your own life would you be willing to sacrifice for a complete stranger? Some people struggle with a minimal amount of morality in giving up their seat when an elderly person, or an expectant mother is standing in front of them on a bus or on the tube.

A soldier is willing to fight and die for a country and flag that represents hundreds of years of tradition – and much like the many colours of the Union Jack, there are many cultures and races found within our borders…..when a soldier selflessly puts their life on the line, they epitomise the best qualities of a human being – they don't ask who they are defending when they enter a battle or conflict ….they have no interest in what team you support, or what religion you practice….only that they will be carried off the battlefield if they should fall and if they do make it home, that they are remembered for giving more than most will ever be willing to give. They commit to a service and in return are paid pennies……and all for a job and a level of responsibility that they carry with an immense amount of pride.

I never served, there's been times I've often wondered what and who I would now be if I did, but the past is just that, so when I was given the opportunity in paying my respects and contributing to these true heroes, I happily did. Shortly after the release of Muscle in 2001, and as I've said earlier, I started to get letters via John Blake Publishers from a broad range of people; some of those letters were from those serving overseas and to say it was a compliment, would be selling the experience and their efforts short. I tried to reply to most, but the letters I always found time to reply to were from the men and women deployed and posted overseas. I'm not sure if I've ever shared this thought with anyone; if not, those reading this will be the first, but I was a bigger fan of them, than they were of me – it was and remains truly humbling to be given that much support....

With the renewed war efforts and continuing overseas conflict, the letters continued, but also now with the ease and comfort that modern technology has brought us all, as it was also a time when I found how much the world had moved forward in terms of advancements and simplicity (once I'd gotten over the first few technical hurdles) – the internet! This was something relatively new to me, but the (obvious) benefit allowed a much larger audience to reach out and in return, me being able to reply.

The new-age conveniences of email, messengers, DM's and alike, provided a welcomed avenue for those who supported me through buying Muscle and those who'd now watched ROTFS, including members of the military's UK based family. Mums, dads, and wives asking if I'd be willing to send messages, videos and autographed items out to those on the front lines – what heartless self-centred person wouldn't! One night, I had Ben Whiteside of 1st Battalion Royal Welsh in my bar in Southend when he was on R&R; it was nothing short of an honour to be in the company of a member of the British armed forces.... and it goes without saying, I made sure he had a good night! During his visit, I happily took down his contact details and sent him and his mate's messages while they were in Afghanistan; something they all said they greatly appreciated receiving and I only hope that this small gesture helped to boost morale, even just a little bit.

One show I was asked to put on and should've been a night of laughs and lifelong memories was when I was approached to do a show that was to be hosted on the military base itself, but as soon as the request was sent up the chain of command and the top brass got to see my name on the permission slip, it was an instant denial. Those that had asked me to appear were obviously disappointed, but I don't think anyone could've felt more let down than me. From what I've been told, traditionally, the usual form of entertainment meeting approval, wasn't exactly on par with a night that all the lads would've related to and enjoyed, the types of entertainment brought in, was nothing more than muppets and puppets – who would've known that Rod and Emu were still of interest, and a less threat than good old Carlton Leach – shame really!

My first ever show was held in a venue called The Sky Bar in Basildon, where one of the partners was a pal of mine called Mick Norcross. Anyone that knew Mick will testify to his countless acts of kindness and being one of the most welcoming people they'd ever met, but like a lot of good people, he is no longer with us. Mick tragically took his own life, shortly after putting out a mysterious tweet, leaving behind not only a lot of good memories, but also a family. I don't know the details, but imagine what kind of place, mentally and emotionally, a man must be in to decide that there is no other way...RIP, Micky. That night, Mark Noble was coming along with me to the show, at the time was no older than 17 or 18! We met just around the corner at the Holiday Inn to make our way there together, and in addition, and as I found out, a lot of people turned up to support me, including a lot of faces, villains, footballers, East Londoners, and people that had known me for a very long time. So many in fact, it was said to be about 2 and a half thousand people; I couldn't walk three feet without being pulled in for either a handshake, hug, or photo. What made this show that more memorable (other than it being my first), was the overwhelming amount of what I can only describe to you as, heightened anxiousness. I'd never felt anything quite like it before, and all I could think about was fucking off to an empty room somewhere to be alone for 5 minutes. It's madness when you think about it, as anyone else that's faced even half of what I've dealt with in life; the violence, dangers, and pressures, would've never wanted to see a human being or be able to deal with even a mediocre lifestyle again, perhaps not even face the everyday world, and yet, here I was poised to go on stage and still wondering if I'll be able to string a sentence together. Was it good old fashioned stage fright, the lack of experience…? fuck knows, but I couldn't give any excuse or throw the towel in, I had to deal with it. So, I decided to simply put one foot in front of the other and I found myself walking out to a huge amount of support and what (thankfully) turned out to be the start of a lot of good nights…. plus, I like to think I've come a long way since that first night! I started to travel up and down the Country for these shows, some small and intimate, some filling an entire theatre, like the time myself, Howard 'Mr Nice' Marks, Jason Marriner and Dave Courtney collaborated in Swansea.

The next time I was to do a show at Sky Bar, it was under fairly different circumstances. We heard an awful story of a schoolboy from Basildon who has down-syndrome, who was attacked whilst walking his dog through the local park. The poor lad was terrified and hadn't left his house for weeks, so we decided to try to help a little. The good people of Sky Bar laid on the venue free of charge, Wendy and I organized a whole load of film memorabilia to sign and raffle off and we invited the boy, along with his family, to come for a great night out. I managed to get him up on stage with me, I presented him with a book, DVD and signed t-shirt, all of which he was chuffed to bits with! He was a pupil at a specialised school, so we donated the money raised that night to the centre, but the most important achievement that night was helping to build his confidence back up a little after those cowards beat him up for no reason at all.

There are some drawbacks to having a reputation and a past like mine, but I figured if I could promote the film, earn a living and also raise a few quid for charity by advertising where I'm going to be and turning up as promised, then sign me up. These events were a new concept to me, and thinking back, one of my first thoughts was, 'How the fuck am I going to pull this off?' I'd envisioned something along the lines of me being expected to dress up like Des O'Connor or Bruce Forsyth, tapping across a stage, and trying to sing one of the classics. This wouldn't have been good for anyone, not to mention the poor people in the audience, but thankfully as I found out, it was more of a Q and A and just a case of presenting myself for people to come and meet. Again, as I've said, it's nothing short of humbling to have people make an effort and give support for what I've done. It was also during the shows, that I thought it would be the perfect opportunity to raise some awareness and support for some charitable causes; one being Help for Heroes. The saying "I'd give the shirt off my own back" is one that very few are actually challenged to prove willingness, but with the cause being one I found close to my heart, I literally found myself giving the shirt off my own back at one event. It was during one of the first events that the promotors were auctioning off some of my merchandise, when someone shouted out from the crowd, "How much for the shirt you're wearing, Carlton?" to which I replied, "How much you got?" .... at this point, there was no stopping me and without a second thought of where I was going to get another shirt from, I took the shirt off and signed it for the new owner. That person's single act of kindness and all those that came out that night raised a healthy amount of money, not to mention one event that both myself and a lot of people would remember well. A photo of me (shirtless) signing that shirt, can easily be found with a quick online search, and I bet people must find it sometimes and wonder 'what on earth is he doing?

As much as I've taken great pride and made efforts to be involved in supporting the British military, another cause that, as much as it pains me to be involved in (due to the suffering and pain you're exposed to), is one that I do with a heart-felt conviction - Children's charities. No kid should be forced to suffer at any age, as cancer, (amongst other diseases) don't discriminate a child's age, colour or standing in the world. No parent should be forced to see their child suffer the painful horrors of treatment, just so their child has a shot at what should be their born given right – a childhood and a chance at life. If you were to do a web search on how many illnesses and disabilities children are born with, you'd have to question where the justification and reasoning comes from! What infuriates me even further is how the British government appear to show little or any involvement in helping some of these poor young souls improve their chances at a life they justifiably deserve. Especially when you consider how much money is sent overseas…. what happened to charity begins at home?

Obviously, there are millions of worthy causes out there but, unfortunately, I'm not able to help as many as I'd like to, especially financially, and I realise it's a drop in the ocean, but as an example of my involvement and something I take to heart, a guy called Wal approached us and asked if I'd be interested in hosting a boat party on the River Thames, which I gave some thought to, spoke to a couple of mates about and eventually decided that it wasn't a bad idea, plus we could take the opportunity to raise some money for a good cause while we were at it! It was whilst we were advertising tickets for the event, which included a charity auction, that an artist by the name of Davey Brown got in touch and offered to paint a portrait of me on canvas and donate it to the auction, a kind offer which we accepted, having looked at some of his old school and casuals' paintings! Davey did a cracking job, the painting looked exactly like me, but he didn't stop there; he took the train all the way down to London from Newcastle, with his son, to deliver the artwork, ensuring it didn't get damaged. My mates made a fuss of Davey's lad, showed him around the boat a bunged him a couple of tenners, but as hard as we tried to get Davey on board for the party, he politely declined and went off into town to show his son some tourist attractions. The man was more than welcome to join us that night and he wouldn't have needed to buy so much as a drink, but he didn't come for that, he travelled down purely to deliver a painting for a charitable cause and show his son the Capital, that's selfless. I wish Davey all the very best with his work and in case you were wondering, the portrait raised around £400 that night! I Can't always give money, but one thing I can always give is my time, especially now I've become a lot more accustomed and proficient at using Twitter! So, if a tweet or a link can be shared and it raises so much a tenner, then it's worth it. It's also about general awareness sometimes, too; the reach of social media can be extremely far and if enough people do their part, it's amazing what can be achieved.

Isla Caton is a girl close to a lot of people's hearts – especially West Ham supporters and those living in Essex. Much like any parents, all the Caton's wanted was to have a family, experience the joys and happiness that comes with raising children and build a lifetime of memories. Instead, this little angel's parents were told the heartbreaking news that their daughter Isla, who was just 2 years of age, had neuroblastoma cancer in early 2017. To this day, Isla continues to receive treatment; and even though her life so far has been one of pain and suffering she never complains and welcomes each day with a smile…. it's nothing short of heartbreaking to see such a lovely little girl with such love for life go through so much, just to get a taste of what millions of other children have without a fraction of what Isla experiences every day of her life… and most of her required treatment is being funded privately through various fund-raisers and supports; as heart-warming and faith restoring as it is to observe the level of public support, my personal view is, why is it necessary for fellow citizens to wade in, and where are our government in all of this?

Much like so many days, I was browsing over the internet and reading through the news, when a photo of this smiley girl in big boxing gloves, accompanied by some text, caught my eye. It was the story of a young girl called Emily Shutt. Like any decent human, and being a parent myself, it hit me …. I instantly felt sadness and felt I should at least invest a bit of time reading up on her story. I followed a few links and discovered that she was a real fighter, who was undergoing treatment for her illness. I sent a tweet wishing a speedy recovery and hoped that all would be well. Shortly after, I received a message back from the admin who was running the social media account thanking me for the message, to which I felt morally obligated to reply. I helped where I could, retweets and reaching out to a few people, hoping some assistance could be sent her way. One day, a post on Twitter went up, letting supporters know that the now 7-year-old was going into hospital to undergo a necessary stage of the treatment, and there would be an update letting everyone know as soon as she was out of surgery and in recovery. I once again sent a direct message asking for an update and to let me know how it all went. It wasn't long after that I went to the twitter account expecting to see a photo or a message giving good news and thanks of support, only to read the heartbreaking news that things hadn't gone well….and she didn't make it! I had to read it again, as this was meant to be "part of the process", but it was as I'd read it the first time; an innocent 7-year-old girl was taken from her family, in turn leaving an unfillable void in a parent's lives and a little girl who'd never experience the joys of a deserved childhood. I never had the honour of meeting little Emily, nor her family and core supporters, but through the personal updates and chats, I felt close to the situation and was truly gutted when I read the tragic news that night. Always smiling no matter what lay ahead, Emily was another fine example of a true fighter and a real hero.

What a parent values the most, shouldn't cost them the ultimate price – the life of a child.

17 FRIENDS

I imagine, as I write this, that some of the people mentioned will come as a surprise to many, perhaps some are from unexpected walks of life, or not the kinds of people you thought you'd find in my book, but my life is made up of people from varying backgrounds, with jobs, careers, families and businesses - what some from a crime background may class as 'normal people'. For instance, Mark the Sprayer is a good friend of mine, always willing to help me out, be it with my cars or just to sit in his kitchen and have a chat, another is Tony Fawkes who's company supply all the (non-Umbro) West Ham clobber; at least twice a year he sends me a parcel of merchandise and at Christmas, when we were in lockdown over in Spain, he wrapped Christmas puddings and Mince Pies up with the clothes because he knew we couldn't get into town to get the usual trimmings…so thoughtful! Brian up in Scotland, a prime example of a Rangers Hammer, Shawn, Kieran and Kayleigh, Raz and Anita…I could speak of so many that have touched my life in some way, but there are just too many people, whom I know and have met, to mention them all in my book, though that's not an insult or to their detriment, more that I wanted to demonstrate that just because I took a certain path in life, doesn't mean that I don't know or socialise with persons who didn't take that same path, plus, there are certain people who I felt, for my own reasons, deserved a mention in a book about my life. To those of you who have welcomed me into your towns, cities, even your homes throughout the Country and over the years, I am truly grateful for your support, kindness and hospitality; thank you and I hope to run into you again someday!

Jay: I've had a level of trust with for what (in a comical way) could be best represented and measured in dog years; as the value and worth he has and means to me on every level would appear to contradict both the years he's actually been at my side and around me – the trips "around the block" and ventures we've shared could never fit into any amount of text, nor would they display the appreciation I have for him in any conversation. To try and attempt that, would be selling him short, but to compliment and bring an understanding to the importance and depth he brings to the table, not only as the son, brother, or family member that anyone would be blessed to have, but also within their ranks and beside them, is near impossible, but I'll try and give a few words on who Jay is.

It's a relationship that was initiated by a mutual friendship back from when he was in his teens. It started as an introduction through who some know as Crusher, and it's since that introduction that I've never been let down. Jay is a man, who for as young as he is, carries himself better than a lot of people twice his age. A sense of traditional and conservative values in his mannerism are what allows him to hold his head high - promoting who and what he stands for, without having to speak a word or tell anyone of his beliefs, direction, or agenda. He's a person who I regularly have the pleasure in sharing a table, meal, and a conversation with. Each and every time, it's one that's not just a reflection of a valued friend…. but someone who I've trusted the best interests and life of my own blood.

In a crowd of any size and on any level, Jay is someone who's never folded or walked away – even when he's willingly worked amongst people on a "higher pay scale" …. he's a man who can loyally operate and get results whatever the situation requires. He doesn't have to change his mask, stance, or personality just to fit in or get things done. What and how he is, is that of what he's presented to me since the very beginning – some might say he's "an old head on young shoulders." When he's dealt with business matters, they're handled the same approach every time, and that is with the upmost respect – the job is done and completed 100 percent. My honest opinion is things are done this way as a sign of his insight and understanding of both his unwavering professionalism and promise of his willingness to see things through without fault or failure. The main difference with Jay and a lot of people I've seen working in the same capacity is, he can control a situation where others (fail) at controlling people. His mindset is one of never overstepping boundaries; only looking out for my best interests.

Like I've already said, his loyalty and comradery mean he's there until the end – he oozes confidence, maintains dignity, and has an unmeasurable amount of reserved humbleness... these are the basics of what makes the backbone that fuels Jay's loyalty and trust – there's never a question on his level of reliance and dependability – it's something that's simply who and what he is and stands for; anything less wouldn't be him. His dedication to the "cause" is a standard, without sway or faulter in his approach or M.O, in not only what, but how he represents me; there's never a question or concern on any business transaction – whether it's a pound note or a bag of stones, much like Jay, what was started with will be there at the end.

West Ham Steve: Stevie Guy is actually something of a pre-cursor to hearing about a few of my other mates, because I've met several good people through him over the years. When I meet people for the first time through the course of business, or life in general, I have to be very careful and cautious, but if I'm introduced to a real friend of Steve's, I can let my guard down a little bit and skip past a few initial filter layers, because Steve knows my situation and I know that Steve has a proven judge of character; he can pick out the chancers and the mugs from 50 ft away. Of course, we've met and introduced each other to scores of people over the years, but for a very select few, Steve has given them the nod with me, a sign that 'this one's got a bit more about him', so I know I can extend that extra trust to the new member of the circle. Steve knows the value of this ability, too, and that's why, I'm sure, he's only used it about 3 or 4 times in all the years we've been friends.

I knew Steve from the terraces, a regular and sociable face on the scene, his nickname says everything you need to know about him and his club. When the meets and the fighting trailed off and everyone started to go about other ways of letting off steam and chasing whatever they were chasing at football, we didn't see much of each other for a while, but when we finally got it back together, we picked up where we left off and had some amazing times together. Steve reminds me a lot of Alf Garnet for his laugh and how bloody opinionated he is, something I've told him many times and to which he grumbles something…then laughs like Alf Garnet!

Steve has pissed off and fucked with a lot of people over the years, but he's always been fiercely loyal to me, and that's a fact. He'd do anything to help me out, sometimes even without me asking him, for example, I recently returned to the UK and was stuck in home quarantine, with that government call centre calling me daily to check I was home, I mentioned to Steve how frustrating it was becoming and that the first thing I'm going to do when I get out is go for pie n mash. The next morning Steve calls me and asks if I'm going to be home; "Of course I fucking am…I'm not allowed out am I!" I told him, to which he replied, "Ok brother" and hung up. About 3 hours later I had pie n mash at my door, with a fresh seafood platter and drinks, it was like a mirage. Of course, Steve was stood 2 meters away when I opened the door, he didn't join me for the feast and no rules broken… for any floors Steve that anyone may point out in Steve, he has all the best qualities of a true friend, and I wouldn't change him even if I could.

Jason Allday: Jase and I were introduced around 2008 when West Ham Steve asked me if I'd help with and contribute to the book Jase was writing in memory of his late brother. As emotionally difficult as it was for Jase to put that book together in the circumstances, his drive and determination were impressive, and I enjoyed being involved with the project. I knew after 2 meetups that we'd stay in contact for years to come and that's exactly what happened; anytime Jase is heading back from the States we arrange a get together for a proper catch up, which is always a real pleasure. From a modest background, yet self-educated, having solid links to many respected people, yet being so genuinely humble, Jason is the definition of his own favourite phrase: "One of Your Own." Jason and I have written this book together so far, and I realise how much I've leant on him now that I'm writing this bit on my own, purely because he refuses to have any part in it, in fact, he asked me not to write about him at all, and that right there is a quality that sets a man apart from the crowd; he doesn't want to share in any fame or limelight, he's genuinely happy to help me out and be a part of something by doing what he loves to do – writing! Given our connection and backgrounds, for me, money couldn't buy a better person to have worked with on my book. Thank you, Jase, for your time and effort, I know you've gone the extra mile on this for me.

Mad Jack: There was a regular customer at the Ministry of Sound throughout 1990 whilst I was running security there, he always wore expensive silk shirts and had big hair. I came to know him a little bit, initially because, as I said before, I did my best to take care of the punters there and this fella realised that fact where others didn't take a blind bit of notice. One day, we chatted at the bar and this guy gave me a $100 bill…I remember asking if it was real, thinking it was a bit of a practical joke, after all, what was this guy doing with US dollars in a South London nightclub? That night I asked him "What was your name again mate?" to which he replied, "I'm Jack". Whenever I talked to Jack, he'd come out with mad facts related to a topic we were discussing, for example, if you said, "Fuck me, it's as hot as the sun itself in here tonight!" He'd respond instantly with; "Actually mate, the sun is ten thousand degrees on its surface and twenty-seven million degrees at its core." He was baffling, but also, he was always prepared to back the regular doormen up if there was any trouble, I remember one time in particular, he must have seen me charge through the tunnel to a shout at the main door, when I looked round Jack was standing there casually, he gave me a wink and a nod that I interpreted as "I'm here if you need me, but I'll still be here if you don't."

From our encounters at Ministry, I nicknamed him 'Mad Jack' and it stuck; all the doormen knew him as Mad Jack too and when I left there for the next endeavor, Mad Jack and I always kept in touch, and he'd pop to see me at other venues from time to time. Knowing how I operated, Mad Jack got me in over at Shades to do the security there and he worked with us on the doors; he was one of the most solid doormen I've had the pleasure of working with.

There was a period of time when I couldn't reach Mad Jack by phone, he wasn't at home and nobody had seen him, so whilst I was a little bit concerned, I figured it probably wasn't out of character for a guy named 'Mad Jack' to just go away and get his head down for a week or two, so I thought little more of it. Around the same time, Denny comes into the lounge one day and says "Carlton, you've got a VO here from a Paul Harris." "Paul Harris? I don't know any fucking Paul Harris, stick it in the bin or a drawer!" Weeks passed and I just kept thinking, who's this Paul Harris, what's he after, who's he connected with…then the phone rung one afternoon, I happened to answer it and it was Mad Jack on the line: "Carlton, I sent you a VO, why ain't you bothered to come n see me?" I paused and thought, "He hasn't sent me a VO?" Then it hit me… "Hang on a fucking minute, your name ain't Paul Harris, is it?" When he confirmed that it was, I couldn't believe it, we'd known each other all these years, drunk together, ate together, gone back-to-back on the doors together, and I hadn't even known his real name! I visited Jack inside, stuck some money on his account and gave him some decent trainers for the gym.

I got offered a bit of graft over in France, a protection job at a cash & carry, but I had other things going on back home, so I said I'd send one of my top men, loyal, trustworthy, and tough. Mad Jack went and took care of what needed to be done across the channel, but they liked having him around so much that they gave him a job! He worked as one of their top people for years and every time he'd pop back to Blighty, he'd turn up at my house (usually unannounced) with a boot full of fags and booze, almost every Christmas I was sorted for alcohol and the reason he always did this? Because he never forgot the things I did for him. I didn't visit him in nick or get him a job for anything in return, I did what I did because Jack was my mate and I was sure he was there for me if I needed him, but he'd always insist on a token of appreciation here and there and for that level of respect and loyalty, Mad Jack will always have a place in my heart, right next to Paul Harris. The definition of a diamond geezer…and I still call him Mad Jack to this day!

Sid: As I look back now, I'm so glad I took Sid under my wing when I did, for 2 reasons; the first is that Sid's uncompromisable loyalty and genuine friendship is worth more than gold and the second reason is that, had he ended up misplacing his loyalty in the wrong people, he could easily have been serving life by now. Sid has wanted to put a number of people down for me over the years, and a more selfish person would've allowed him to do it and said, "tar very much", but I preferred other methods of dealing with things and at 6'4" with dreadlocks and the shoulder span of an American fridge-freezer, Sid was rather easily identifiable in most situations! On the doors, Sid could have done some serious damage to people, but he always opted to talking people down or tricking them into thinking they'd got their way (when they actually hadn't), rather than smashing people up when it was avoidable. One time when we were working in Ascot, this bunch of arseholes turned up, completely pissed and acting like fools, so Sid stopped them and explained that they were a bit too drunk and to try the venue down the road, but they turned proper lemon; "We don't give a shit about you, the bigger they are…the harder they fall! We're coming in so move!" Sid smirked and replied; "It's not me you should be worried about, it's him over there that's gonna ruin your night!" He gestured towards me, who they hadn't noticed until that point due to the fact that Sid's frame blocked the entire doorway anyway. Their entire attitudes changed in an instant, I was casually leaning on a post, as they started to consider my height and build etc., but this huge, mean looking lump telling them that the short guy over there is a bigger problem than he, must have messed with their minds too much and they turned away without hardly another word! To me, Sid is my foster-brother, that's literally what I consider him and whilst he has fucked up on a few occasions, I'd never let anything happen to him or his family, he's off limits.

There are 3 people still around me who were part of the core firm back in the day, Sid being one, plus Little Matty and Kev "Shoulders." So, including myself, I call us the original 4! I can't talk about a lot of the stuff we've done together…I am under no illusion that Sid's contribution to this book will contain some banter, so I'll finish up by explaining that Sid and I used to joke and both refer to each other as "slippery" (one of us might say, "Hello slippery, how are you?" and the other would respond with "I'm ok, thanks slippery.") I started referring to him as Slippery Sid and before long it stuck, other doormen would hear that and start calling him Sid, but his real name is actually Randolph! - Sorry Slippery Sid, but the lids off of that one now brother!

Fearless: Gary served as a Royal Marine and I have to say that I've never come across anyone else quite like him, he's an enigma, that's for sure! Our chance meeting had its own randomness about it, being at a caravan park in Clacton, but the shit we've seen and done together since that day has, at times, been crazy and he's taught me a thing or two along the journey.

In the muscle game, Fearless is the kind of person we'd describe as 'a 1-man army', but something of a nomad, he'll never be tied down to any one place or stay on any certain path for very long, not since he left the military, anyway. If he'd have wanted or needed it, I'd have had him on my firm every day of the week, but I would never have asked that of him, instead I prefer to see him and Jo going wherever in the world their mood takes them, because that's when he's happiest and that's what he deserves. With that said, however, I know I'll always have Fearless in my corner and that was well and truly proven the time he dropped everything, got on a plane, and flew all the way across Europe, because he'd heard there had been some trouble and he wanted to be there to back me up. Great Britain was lucky to have the man as a soldier, I'm equally as lucky to have him as my friend.

There are many people who have enriched my life, several of whom I'm not able to go into detail about, and there are of course others whereby I can't even mention their names at all.

Paul Ferris, a name many of you will know of throughout the UK, but especially in Scotland; a name that's synonymous not just with organised crime, but also with deep respect, pure integrity, and intelligence. Whenever I was fortunate enough to be in the company of the late Wilf Pine, he always spoke to me about Paul, as Paul was someone who Wilf held in high regard, and there are few better references in the underworld than that! You may be surprised to learn that Paul and I have yet to meet one another, though we've spoken several times and plan to get together in the future (I'm sure once we've left the location, we'll share some photo's online!). If you want to learn more about one of the most legendary faces of Glasgow, I recommend grabbing a copy of Paul's book.

Dave Walker I met around 7 years or so ago, when I was approached to be on his podcast, SDCC, all about West Ham and its fans. Dave knows his stuff when it comes to the Hammers, both past and present, and he really brought the worst of my humour out, I mean, all the terrible jokes and lines were pouring out continuously as we chatted! We kept in touch from that day forward, particularly on match days, but the friendship between Dave and I is a prime example of two people who are mates, simply because they get along; Dave isn't in the underworld and is likely never to need a favour or want to use my name in a deal, he's a family man who loves our club and wants to get along in life. Dave and his dad came out for my dad's funeral, both wearing their claret n blue, and even though they didn't know my dad, they'd turned out as a sign of respect to him and me, which I really appreciated. I'm sad to say that Dave's dad is experiencing some ill health at this moment, and I'd like to wish him well and send my best regards to him, Dave and all their family at this difficult time. Dave, you know where I am if you need anything!

Not to confuse matters, but I have another Dave for us! I was introduced to Dave QPR via West Ham Steve, an interesting concept, I know, but as I've said before, we're all mostly mates away from the grounds nowadays and Dave's "2nd team" is The Hammers. Dave's been to a few of my shows around the country, we've been in each other's company on several occasions, including my 60th birthday party and we've always gotten on really well, we tend to talk football and the politics of football for hours, plus he shares my love and interest for Italian football, too. Dave never expects anything from me, he doesn't ask me to call up his cousin's sister's brother's uncle to wish him luck on his wedding day, he's never pulled me into aggravation, we're just pals who have a great time when we get together. All my best to Dave and his lovely missus Sophie.

Steve Ash and Drew from Bournemouth are two people I'm pleased to know, and I'm grateful to Wilf Pine for introducing us back in the day. Bournemouth, for me, is one place in particular where I am welcomed, taken great care of and always leave having had an excellent time, thanks to a great group of fellas down there who run security, do things the right way and keep in contact with me throughout the year.

Crazy Steve needs little by way of description! I was in a… "situation…" out in Spain about 14 or 15 years ago and needed to get some lads to join me over there pronto. Of course, Sid was one of my first calls and he was straight on the case. Crazy Steve had walked out of the prison gates about two days previous, but when Sid told him the scenario, he was on the next flight he could get, and great back-up he made too! The best bit of this was, at the time, I'd never met the guy before! But anyone willing to do that, especially as he'd not long had one holiday, is someone I'll always have time for.

Tuffy, from Slough, always comes to mind when I think about those who have always been available for me, even if we don't speak to each other for 6 months, or even a year, we can still always reach out to one another. We worked security at a few raves together back in 88 and 89 but lost touch, then ran into each other again years later and have been mates ever since.

Con, a man with his own reputation, born to an Irish family and raised in north London; I won't say too much more, but you know who you are mate! I know you've got my back and vice versa. Getting together and keeping contact in fits and starts, I only wish we'd have spent more time together.

Andrew Pritchard is a name some of you may know;

he was a rave promoter that properly knew his stuff, he's got a book out himself, and he's also had a bit of misfortune in getting banged up a couple of times. It was through our involvements in Genesis that we originally met and remained friends ever since. I've actually sat round his house on several occasions, with the two of us discussing script ideas, because we both believe that a movie about those Genesis days would be amazing!

Paul, AKA Pitbull, is one in my circle who has always been there for me and had my back, another ready to go to work if need be friend, and as much as his size, menacing look may give some a level of apprehension, once he knows you, his devilish grin and dry sense of humor will charm anyone that's in his company.

Terry Mac, his lovely wife Tracey and their family are personal friends whom I hold in high regard. Down to earth, accommodating lovely people.... they're West Ham family whose door is always open to me and likewise.

Wendy helped me in any way she could after the release of ROTF, booking shows all over the country and organising everything from posters to logistics. I was pleased to be at hers and Ian's wedding a matter of months ago, and I wish them every happiness, but sadly that was also to be the last time we were all back together with Shawn.

CARLTON - The Final Say

With Crazy Steve

With QPR Dave

With West Ham Steve

Mad Jack

With my sister, Tracy.

Still hitting the gym.

Printed in Great Britain
by Amazon